PENGUIN BOOKS

OUT TO LUNCH

Paul Levy was born in Lexington, Kentucky, and is Food and Wine Editor of the *Observer*. Educated at the universities of Chicago, London, Harvard and Oxford, Paul Levy, Ph.D., and Fellow of the Royal Society of Literature, describes himself as a lapsed academic. He has won every British prize for food journalism at least twice and recently became the first food and wine writer to be commended as a specialist writer in the British Press Awards. His articles have appeared in *A La Carte*, *Punch* and the *Wall Street Journal*, and he wrote, with Ann Barr, the best-selling *Official Foodie Handbook*. He is the author of *Moore: G. E. Moore and the Cambridge Apostles* and co-literary executor of Lytton Strachey.

Paul Levy lives in Oxfordshire ·with his wife and two daughters.

PAUL LEVY
Out to Lunch

With an Introduction by Ann Barr

PENGUIN BOOKS

PENGUIN BOOKS

Published by the Penguin Group
27 Wrights Lane, London w8 5tz, England
Viking Penguin Inc., 40 West 23rd Street, New York, New York 10010, USA
Penguin Books Australia Ltd, Ringwood, Victoria, Australia
Penguin Books Canada Ltd, 2801 John Street, Markham, Ontario, Canada l3r 1b4
Penguin Books (NZ) Ltd, 182–190 Wairau Road, Auckland 10, New Zealand

Penguin Books Ltd, Registered Offices: Harmondsworth, Middlesex, England

First published by Chatto & Windus Ltd 1986
Published in Penguin Books 1988

Copyright © Paul Levy, 1980, 1981, 1982, 1983, 1984, 1985, 1986
Introduction copyright © Ann Barr, 1986
Photographs by Gered Mankowitz
All rights reserved

Reproduced, printed and bound in Great Britain by
Hazell Watson & Viney Limited
Member of BPCC plc
Aylesbury Bucks

*To the Wednesday Club
and to Jane Grigson*

Contents

Contents

ACKNOWLEDGEMENTS

My thanks to *Punch, A La Carte, The Wall Street Journal, Harpers &
Queen, The New York Times, Quest, Connoisseur, Departures, The
Literary Review, Homes & Gardens, The Observer* and any other
newspaper or magazine in which some or all of the pieces here first
appeared. It is very likely that the editors who commissioned them will
not recognise these essays. That is because, knowing the craft of journalism almost always involves cutting for very good – but not literary –
reasons, I have hoarded the originals of most of my pieces; and it is in their
virgin versions they appear here for the first time. Others I have rewritten
extensively, finding that I no longer agree with my earlier opinions. For
one reason or another, usually the 'spike' all journalists dread, several of
these pieces have never been published before.

I am grateful to Gered Mankowitz for his flattering photographs, to
Angela Mason for her puns, and to Dasha Shenkman for doing so much
more than an agent ought to do to put this book together.

Introduction

Paul Levy bestrides his narrow world like a rhinoceros. He is always thundering to attack some misjudgement by Michelin, crooked wine practice or sloppy government regulation. He is the best of the few food and wine writers who realise their subject has become mass market. A responsible food and wine critic now studies big business, additives and the world situation, as well as his or her palate. (Most still see their duty as detecting a good wine list or salt in the butter.) It takes great energy and a thickish skin to patrol food and wine in the 1980s. Which is why you can liken the man who does it (he pronounces it Lee-vee) to a rhinoceros.

Paul Levy came to food writing by mistake, in 1977. He had intended to be a don, and had been to four universities, Chicago, London, Harvard and Oxford. He was born in Lexington, Kentucky, in 1941. He is small and fair, with pale blue eyes, his head covered with little pinkish curls like a lamb's. In the last eight years he has added roundness and a beard and lost a few curls.

He considers himself lucky to have gone to school in America, because he did classics *and* chemistry, and has enough science to cope with wine and food adulteration scandals and nutrition.

In 1977, he was living outside Oxford (he has never lived more than ten miles from a major university, but he insists on a vegetable garden), near the end of his ten-year struggle with his book (and Harvard Ph.D.) on the philosopher G. E. Moore. He was making extensive use of the Strachey family papers. When it came time to arrange the disposition of the Lytton Strachey estate, he was the only person who knew where everything was. So he became joint executor, with Michael Holroyd. This led to two Strachey books: *Lytton Strachey: The Really Interesting Question* and, with Michael Holroyd, *The Shorter Strachey*.

One of Paul's English friends has the theory that as a Jew in southern America (his immigrant Russian grandfather was, bizarrely, a farmer), he was out of step with the intellectual Jewish community in New York, and his very good brain found romance back across the Atlantic, in the intellectual movements of Oxford and Cambridge (bypassing the Whitechapel of his other set of grandparents, as he said when he heard this theory).

Moore had taken too long even for the publishers' large advance, and his money was running out. He got reviewing work, on subjects in his field such as the Bloomsbury Group. Terence Kilmartin of *The Observer* was the first to employ him. The Levy by-line also appeared in *The Times Literary Supplement, Books & Bookmen* and the *Literary Review*.

His first food writing came through two of his friends, Angelo Hornak and Mirabel Cecil, who separately recommended him to me when I was features editor of *Harpers & Queen*. His cooking was by then famous at Oxford. He did all the cooking for his household (first don flatmates, later his wife), and was very hospitable. This American who openly adored food, restaurants, names and parties was quite a surprise in pre-Yuppie days.

He had not done any cooking until he was eighteen. He was so ignorant he could not even boil eggs. His mother could not cook. But one of his family's black cooks, who worked for his Aunt Lola, had learnt Cajun cooking in New Orleans. She introduced Paul to French food. It was the beginning of the future. France is another of his passions. He used always to spend Christmas there. He still goes three or four times a year, and *tutoyers* all the important chefs. He says his liver is French, and he turns pink with pleasure if someone hearing him speak takes him for a Frenchman.

He looks back on his conversion to learning to cook with something like St Paul's feelings about the Damascus road. He was studying philosophy at Chicago and sharing digs with another boy. They lived on fried food, because when they turned on the gas oven and it didn't light they assumed it was broken. But the first time they invited girls to eat, one (called Dinah, says Paul reverently) struck a match and lit the oven. This made Paul feel so foolish that he bought a book by Louis Diat (of the Ritz Carlton) and worked his way through the stations of a large hotel restaurant.

So by the time he came to the attention of *Harpers & Queen*, at thirty-six, he was over-educated in food as in everything else. Combining his interests, he crowned his year's articles by a Christmas review of all the cookery books, a long article the publishers loved, because they could fillet his remarks and put the flattering parts on the jackets of their paperback editions: 'Vegetarians . . . will like it: Paul Levy', 'Best book on the cooking of Penang: Paul Levy', 'Breakfast section . . . can be recommended: Paul Levy.'

His name was in everybody's bookshelf, and suddenly, in January 1980, he was offered the two top food jobs in Fleet Street on the same day.

Introduction

Suzanne Lowry, women's editor of *The Observer*, asked him to do a column about food and eating and so did *The Sunday Times*, on identical terms. He accepted *The Observer*, out of loyalty, and that rather puritanical paper suddenly found itself not only with a food writer but a food writer who madly, passionately, unrelentingly believes in food, eating, shopping, a high standard of living and the pleasures of the flesh.

Paul did not know Fleet Street, but he rushed into it enthusiastically, saying *The Observer* was his fifth university. *The Observer* was also learning some things. In one year, Suzanne Lowry sent him on restaurant expeditions to Russia, America, France and China (which he added to France in his pantheon). He thought all journalism was like this, and was surprised to hear that his expenses were the chief topic of conversation in the bar at El Vino's. He laughs good-temperedly at suggestions that his policy was 'Never mind the subject – where's the plane ticket?'

But worldly as Paul is, he is also innocent and honest, and exhaustingly zealous. To confound his critics, he immediately won the prizes that have proved *The Observer*'s pre-eminence in food coverage – the readers of course knew already. In 1980, Corning Glass gave a prize (a trip for two anywhere in the world) for the best food writer in Britain and the best restaurant critic. Paul won the first and was runner-up for the second. A few weeks later he won the Glenfiddich award for his food writing. He has since won each of them again.

In 1982, he became *The Observer*'s wine editor as well as its food editor, and does the job of at least two people, as he keeps telling the paper's editor. In 1986 he was commended as a specialist columnist in the British Press Awards, the first time a food or wine journalist has scored in this category.

In the meantime he had brought out his fourth book, *The Official Foodie Handbook* (1984), in collaboration with me. This has a deceptive amount of research by Paul into the history and geography of food, reduced to a light-seeming mixture. The book grew out of a compiled article in *Harpers & Queen*, in August 1982, on 'Foodies', christening them in Britain (though we later discovered Gael Greene had also coined the term, in *New York* magazine). The subject whetted the typewriters of *Harpers & Queen* contributors, several of whom named Paul Levy as King Foodie. (He edited the article, but anonymously.)

Paul organised a dinner for the three-star chefs of Europe in the Dorchester to launch the book. The sight of Iris Murdoch sitting next to Pierre Troisgros must have warmed his heart almost to boiling.

The equanimity with which Paul takes jokes at his expense, and even attacks on him, is one of his nicest characteristics. The inedibility of someone's boil-in-a-bag *poulet*, or a Levy-bashing letter in the *Caterer & Hotelkeeper*, only incense him for a day. He fires off an over-educated, very cross letter, but can laugh about it a few hours later.

He is married to the British art historian Penelope Marcus (of half-Russian Jewish ancestry like his). She wisely refuses to cook as much as a mouthful (though when he is away, she produces delicious and ambitious dishes). But she is a redoubtable character, like him, which she does not hide. Paul does not resent it when he has earned a good verbal drubbing. He is completely un-neurotic, except for an occasional twinge of hypochondria. New every morning is his sunniness.

Paul's general kindness becomes deep loyalty in the case of his friends and people he respects. He has supported chefs in Britain such as Nico Ladenis, Anton Mosimann, Raymond Blanc and Sonia Blech, and introduced Continental chefs – Bocuse, Troisgros, Guérard, Girardet and others – to British readers. And he is a fearless campaigner, chivvying the supermarkets over additives, the Food From Britain campaign for having low standards, the Ministry of Agriculture, Fisheries and Food for not giving adequate guidance to the consumer during the Austrian wine scandal.

Paul Levy has run the *Observer* Mouton Cadet amateur cookery competition since 1980. It has thrown up several cooks who have become well-known food writers, as well as friends of the Levys'. Paul and Penelope Levy entertain constantly, though not formally. Paul thinks nothing of producing a Sunday lunch for twenty with all the vegetables having come from his garden, also a huge salad of different-coloured leaves (but, at least once, no main course). He had a special little greenhouse for basil until it fell down.

He became a father at forty. He has two daughters, Tatyana and Georgia, who adore Papa (pronounced Poppa) and can get anything out of him except normal food. They have been able to use chopsticks from the age of eighteen months. Paul presented them both at the Temple: he took Tatyana to Bocuse's restaurant near Lyon while still in her Moses basket, and Georgia's first meal out was at Auch, cooked by André Daguin. But they are allowed no sugar, salt, butter or sweets, and they talk snobbishly to other children about '*proper* food and naughty food'.

Paul meanwhile goes from fat to slightly less fat (at a health farm), outrageous to serious, lunch to dinner, hypochondria to euphoria. As he

said after a lunch in Anton Mosimann's private dining-room off the
kitchens in the basement of the Dorchester, 'I do feel strange. I can't make
up my mind whether I feel wonderful, or whether I'll have to go straight
home to bed.'

ANN BARR

HOME AFFAIRS

Gut reaction

Everything in excess. That's *our* motto. Ten people coming for lunch? Bring up a whole case of wine from the cellar, buy eight loaves from Maison Blanc, order four pounds of Toulouse sausages and a whole *chèvre* cheese from the Rosslyn Deli, and light the barbecue.But there is a case for refinement, and I suppose I have made a career of putting it.

What, I sometimes ask myself in a greedy mood, is the best meal I've ever eaten? Was it the first I ever ate at a French three-star restaurant? What I remember most clearly about that occasion, a mere fifteen years ago, was being shocked by Frenchmen in shirt sleeves at M. Barrier's temple of gastronomy at Tours. I also recall being bemused, not by the rich creaminess of the *foie de canard*, but by the specifically French bad taste of the Donald Duckish terrine in which it was served.

There I was, unselfconsciously present at the dawn of the *nouvelle cuisine*, and all I could register properly were the garish Guccis, Lanvins and Hermèses worn by M. Barrier's clientèle. (Is there a moral to the story? M. Barrier, having lost one of his three Michelin stars, has been convicted of removing from his tables the paid receipts left behind by his customers and effacing them from the cash book.)

Or was my best meal the one I ate nearly twenty years ago, when Henry Soulé still played the benevolent despot at Le Pavillon, making it the only world-class restaurant New York has ever had? *Billi-bi*, the silky, saffrony mussel soup, offered hot or cold, followed by fillet of beef *à la financière*, correctly garnished with truffles, cock's combs and kidneys. The raspberry tart was made with each perfect berry facing the right way. We could afford the '52 Chambertin, because my father was paying. His pleasure in the food and wine was slightly diminished by the apparent ease with which his son ordered it. Was this the sort of thing one learned to do at Harvard's philosophy department?

Since then there have been hundreds of meals – major meals, important meals, little suppers, big lunches, and cures for the liver. Lunch at Paul Bocuse's, with an infant in a Moses basket; 'Hein, but surely the little one eats also?' And the Master himself prepared *purée de pommes de terre* for the six-month-old, who spat it out, refusing to countenance the microscopic flecks of *petit salé* that seasoned it. At one year old, there was Tatyana again, seated on the *annuaire* and tied to a chair with a pink baby-sling. M. Outhier's waiters were concerned that we hadn't ordered anything for her. 'Bring an extra spoon, please.' *They* were shocked at her liking for *foie gras*; we were shocked that she obviously could pick out the chocolate *friandises* from the healthier strawberry *tartelettes* and Cape gooseberries.

My wife remembers a dinner at La Tour Rose in the *vieux quartier* of Lyon. After four or five meals at restaurants to which Gault Millau (more reliable than Michelin) gives top marks, our livers had become French. We washed them out with a litre each of sulphurous Vichy St Yonre, which had about half the desired effect. In other words, we were feeling *very* jaded. We should never have eaten again. But clever, generous Philippe Chavent, seeing our green faces, brought us a huge black truffle, a paring knife and a salt cellar, with which we repaired our appetites. And oh! the ravishing mouthful of salmon *mi-cuit* that completed our supper that night.

Country ham in Kentucky, soft-shell crabs in Maryland, thirteen different kinds of oysters at Grand Central Station, thick slices of pizza eaten on the street in Greenwich Village, *dim sum* further downtown; food that was both good *and* sophisticated at Alice Waters's Chez Panisse at Berkeley; Tex Mex in LA: you can eat *well* in America.

Closer to home, the Dorchester's incomparable Anton Mosimann has proved to me, between mouthfuls of his (technically difficult) lobster consommé and of his *rendezvous des fruits de mer*, that British bread and butter pudding can be liberated from the nursery. Sonia Blech of Mijanou (whose name and address Bernard Levin almost made the greatest mystery of 1984 when he wrote an entire column about it in *The Times* without disclosing either) does things with aubergines and yoghurt and with *fromage blanc* and vegetables that transform these fairly humble ingredients into very haute cuisine. The kerb outside her Ebury Street restaurant is littered with ministerial cars most lunchtimes – no one seems to have noticed that the only great woman cook of London is very popular with members of Mrs Thatcher's government. Then there is Nico's *mousse de foies de canard*, served Chez Nico, with a little salad. This classic dish, in its unchanging perfection, contrasts nicely with the impromptu creations of the boy chefs: Alastair Little, Simon Hopkinson at Hilaire, Pierre Cheviallard at Chewton Glen and Nick Gill at Hambleton Hall.

And how many glorious meals have I eaten at the absurdly young Raymond Blanc's Quat' Saisons, now translated to Great Milton,

Oxford, as the Manoir aux Quat' Saisons? It was for a dinner for my and Jane Grigson's readers that he invented his *aiguillete* of salmon wrapped like a green cigar in sorrel and spinach leaves, and Japanesely sliced. Pierre Koffmann invented a dish for us too, at Tante Claire: a pastry *croustade* with Roquefort, glazed with a reduction of Monbazillac wine. Very controversial – very delicious.

Eating in the East. Did I eat the last giant catfish of the Mekong? My companion, Alan Davidson, had long feared it was extinct. What did it taste like? *I* certainly don't know: it was served in one of those Thai soups redolent of lemon grass, and with so much chilli that your eyes sting.

Meals in China. I reckon I've eaten about 250. I like breakfast best. Bland *congee*, rice porridge, with salty peanuts and pickles, bits of smoked fish and lots of things with chilli, hideously stinky fermented bean curd, sliced fried chitterlings. Chinese soul food. Then this April I made up for lost time and missed meals. Willy Mark, the almost official gastronome of Hong Kong, arranged a marathon lunch, at which everything was aphrodisiac. Giant clams, with obscenely phallic necks. Three dishes, each made with three kinds of viper, and each exquisite. And at long last, a taste of durian, the forbidden fruit, so smelly that it is banned from aeroplanes and hotels. 'Like eating sweet, pink raspberry blancmange in the lavatory,' says Anthony Burgess's Nabby Adams. Mine was, in fact, yellow, and I found the taste addictive.

By the way, did you know that, in Macao, the wine drunk with braised dog is invariably Mateus Rosé? Yes, I did jot down the recipe. But that's a story for another time, perhaps when we are discussing *memorable* meals.

A *woman's place is in the office*

Are men really better cooks than women? It would certainly seem so, judging by the small number of female chefs. In this country there are only a pair of well-known lady chefs – the two Sonias – Sonia Blech of Mijanou, London sw1, and Sonia Stevenson of the Horn of Plenty, Gulworthy, Devon. And I have only heard of two notable American lady chefs of long standing, at Berkeley, California, and Manhattan's La Tulipe.

In France they used to order these things differently. Lyon actually had a tradition of women cooks, *les mères lyonnaises*. But the famous Mère Brazier is now presided over by the granddaughter of the founder, and she actually employs a male chef. The other well-known mère, Léa Bidaut of La Voûte, recently took herself off permanently to Canada, leaving – you guessed it – a chap in charge of the kitchen.

Paris boasts a few famous ladies in its kitchens. The most highly praised is Dominique Nahmias of the restaurant Olympe, followed by Georgette Descat of Lous Landès and Christiane Massia of L'Aquitaine. This trio practise the *nouvelle cuisine*; the other starred women chefs of Paris tend to be, like Fernande Allard of Restaurant Allard, what Gault-Millau describe as 'generous and ultra-traditional'.

In societies such as India, where there is almost no tradition of restaurants, virtually all the cooking is done at home, and by women. In China, on the other hand, where going out to restaurants is of great cultural importance, the principal cooks are usually men. I have often seen women cooks in hotel and restaurant kitchens in China, preparing foodstuffs and even making pastries. But I have never seen a woman presiding over the wok in a professional capacity.

Cooking professionally is, of course, not just a matter of native talent, but of stamina; and it is possible that it is not lack of skill, but the heat of the kitchen, that accounts for the preponderance and dominance of male chefs. We all know, too, that women cook at home because they have to, and men because – for the most part – they want to. That is not to say that I don't know any women who enjoy doing the cooking at home; in fact, most women of my acquaintance are enthusiastic cooks. And the best non-professional cook I know is a woman. But all the runners-up are men.

Kinder, Kirche, Küche may have done useful service as a motto describing the place of women in Wilhelmine Germany, and, *mutatis mutandis*, it certainly had the full endorsement of my Russian Jewish grandmother. However, speaking from my own purely personal culinary point of view, a woman's place is in the office.

The last room in the house where I want to see my wife is the kitchen. That is my domain and, in our house, a masculine preserve, my redoubt, as well as my retreat.

Some there are who say my wife is a closet cook; that before she met me she was capable of doing the cooking for an entire dinner party, and did not, as she does now, restrict her entertaining activities to setting the table and doing the *placement*.

I find this hard to believe. On the few occasions when illness has dictated that my wife feed me, she has always brought to my sickbed, on an elegantly arranged tray, the requested single boiled egg. It is always ravishing to look at, and it is always stone cold.

We men have much for which to thank Women's Lib. It has freed some of us to stay at home and mind the children while our wives go to work – whence, I am glad to say, mine has recently returned. I am not, myself, a stay-at-home father. And I am not really embittered by the battering my *batterie de cuisine* takes every time my wife cooks for the baby. But I am delighted at the prospect of the return to me of the one part of the house I can call my own. I know it's not exactly what Robert Louis Stevenson meant, but I look forward quite soon to saying to the missus: '*I* will make my kitchen, and *you* shall keep your room.'

This is the preferred style, I know too, amongst several of my friends. The reason usually is simply that the husband is the better (or more willing) cook. Domestic arrangements of this sort probably have no bearing on why there are so few female chefs, except for those that account for the difficulties of women with children holding down any job: the hours and the circumstances rarely make it possible to be a chef, wife and mother – all parties require dinner at approximately the same hour.

There is some merit, though, in the women-have-insufficient-stamina theory, for cooking professionally is an intensely physically demanding job, done in conditions that can never be more than just tolerable, and hardly ever comfortable.

Finally, there is the possibility that must be considered – at the risk of enraging at least half the readers of this piece – that, in the kitchen at least, women are actually less creative than men. Of course, I don't believe it for a minute; but could not this be the result of centuries of involuntary culinary servitude?

Fire in the kitchen

The horrible banshee wail of my wife was the first notice I had that fire had broken out in the kitchen. Its cause was outlandish. She had been melting beeswax in a saucepan, which was to be mixed with turps, and used to coat the large Barry Flanagan carved stone sculpture in our garden.

Of course I was certain afterwards that I had told her to put it on the Aga and allow it to melt gently. But it was taking too long, so she speeded things up by simmering it on the gas hob. When the saucepan caught fire, she panicked, dropped the pan on the stone floor, shrieked bloody murder and ran out of the kitchen. The sensible thing to do, the spokesman for the fire brigade later said sympathetically. I kept my head – at least, I gave the appearance of keeping my head. With the instincts of a proper bourgeois householder, I immediately went upstairs and began closing every door in the house, to minimise smoke damage, I thought. I also threw some blankets in the bath and turned on the tap, closed the door that shut off the front of the house, and slung the cats out into the garden.

Downstairs with the wet blanket, I paused to deliberate; I knew you mustn't use water if the chip pan catches fire. You smother a fat fire. But who can work out the chemistry of beeswax when it's blazing away on the kitchen floor? So I chucked the wet blanket on the flames, which had spread to a relatively small area that was probably accounted for by where the wax splashed when the pan was dropped.

There was a sizzle rather than a whoosh. The blanket neither arrested nor spread the fire. Its effect seemed completely neutral – but at least I was doing something.

Meanwhile my poor hysterical wife had dialled 999 and got quite a funny lecture about staying calm from the operator. But her shouts had the good effects of producing some neighbours. The neighbours, veterans of many a chip-pan fire not their own, had received six asbestos blankets in the post that morning. Into the kitchen I dashed with them, taking a deep breath against the growing fug.

After a fashion, the asbestos blankets worked. And my wife found our foam fire extinguisher in the front hall cupboard where we irrationally kept it, along with posters and drawings awaiting framing and the Christmas wrapping paper. I was able to break the seal and use it without reading the instructions.

It was quite effective. I felt I had the fire under control now. So I shut the door to the kitchen and went out to the back garden to join my wife and neighbours waiting for the fire brigade.

Of course I had failed to notice that the fire was still smouldering inside a cupboard. I tried to go back with the fire extinguisher, but the fumes from the melting Magimix made re-entry out of the question. Its twisted remains were practically a sculpture in itself.

The fire brigade were marvellous. They not only put out the fire, in seconds, but they wore gas masks to do it, which confirmed the correctness of my failure to go in a second time with my dinky extinguisher. Mess was held down to the minimum; the fireman even waited for my wife to produce the key to the window locks instead of breaking windows.

The firemen told us that the first thing we must do, now that the fire was under control, was to drink *several* cups of tea. Not so much for its soothing properties, as for its use as a liquid remedy against smoke inhalation. They also stayed on for a few minutes while I re-lit the Aga (we'd had the sense to shut off the gas and electricity at the mains), and to assure us that the tiny explosion it made was perfectly in order. The oxtail *ragoût* in the simmering oven was undamaged, and did much to restore morale.

I shall never forgive my lack of charity the next morning, when I found my visiting mother-in-law scraping away helpfully at the toasted polythene on the stone floor with my best carbon steel knife. 'But darling,' she said so reasonably, 'its blade was all rusty.'

The damage is incredible. I am not surprised that the just-redecorated kitchen is black, or that an entire cupboard of kitchen machines and gadgets has simmered to nothingness, or even that one of the world's larger collections of cookery books is covered with black grime.

But I am astonished that the rest of the house is coated in an invisible film that turns black on your fingers when you touch the walls or surfaces. I feel certain, and so did the fire brigade, that this is the price of plastic kitchen utensils. The fumes that nearly overcame me, and that have necessitated re-decorating the entire house were largely the result of smouldering plastic dustbin, compost bucket, and assorted melted Moulinex blender goblets, plastic saucepan handles, smart plastic egg timers from Bloomingdales, etc.

I now know for certain that the plastic is the enemy of the good. We shall replace all the plastic in the kitchen for which there is a substitute, starting with the swing-top dust bin and covered compost bucket, which will be replaced with aluminium or stainless steel hospital-type bins and buckets, or even with galvanised metal if we cannot find the more sightly kind. And six asbestos blankets and two fire extinguishers will live permanently in the kitchen.

Naturally (but quite wrongly) I expected resistance from the insurance assessor, who called the Monday after the Saturday of the fire – in the middle of a business luncheon party (the Show must go on). (I was unduly nervous about his good will. I got the whole house redecorated, the *batterie de cuisine* replaced, and the cookery books cleaned and rebound in a uniform blue.)

The chief problem after the fire was what to give Saturday's guests for their first course. I thought of a warming soup. There was a beautiful ham bone in the fridge, and dried green pea soup suggested itself to me. But the Magimix, the liquidiser, the mouli-légumes and even the large sieve were all casualties of the conflagration. No purée today.

Sorrel soup, however, can be made with only a sharp knife. So out of the ashes arose lunch: soup, poached salmon trout (from the deep freeze) with Sabayon sauce, spuds, braised leeks with mint, green salad and cheese. And it was only one and a half hours late.

———

Melt down

Ask about Great Culinary Disasters and the other person always thinks of Vatel, who threw himself on his own sword in 1671 when the fish didn't arrive in time for dinner, and his employer, the Prince de Condé, was entertaining royalty. Or else people mention the loss (or unjust award) of Michelin stars to restaurants.

But real culinary disasters, like the best tragedies – think of those of Lear and Oedipus – are domestic affairs. Like the day my wife unplugged the freezer.

It was perfectly innocent. She was making some frozen banana yoghurt for the children, whose diet at home does not include sugary things. Though we actually have a Gelato Chef, which will whip up a concoction such as this in 20 minutes flat, she chose not to use it. In fact, she had removed its plug and put it on the iron or the tumble drier, and not replaced it.

So she used the little £10 job that has to be put in the fridge-freezer, with its flex trailing out. Of course, it had to plug in somewhere, so she plugged it into the place normally occupied by the plug of the enormous chest freezer.

Exactly a week later, I was preparing dinner, as is normal in our household, and I went to the freezer to draw out a cube or two from my bank of home-made stock, which I always freeze in ice trays and turn out into polythene bags.

She had forgotten to plug the freezer in again. The 'on' light was extinguished and the bottom of the cabinet was awash with liquid. There it was: stock made from last autumn's grouse, partridge and pheasant, the winter's turkey and beef, and a whole year's collection of chicken and turbot, sloshing around inside and mingling their flavours.

Pounds and pounds of tomatoes, frozen whole as they ripened in the greenhouse, now collapsed like pricked balloons. A whole salmon joined an entire baby turbot in the dustbin. The basil that we harvest all summer and fast-freeze on trays before storing it in aluminium boxes had all turned to green slime.

There were made dishes, too. January's overproduction of *cassoulet*, with its genuine *saucisse de Toulouse* and beans called *belles de Soissons*, which – if you can get them at all – are the most expensive in the world. A carton or two of chilli con carne made in a burst of enthusiasm was spoiled, alongside a similar amount of *soupe au pistou*.

And out went the odds and ends. The pair of Seville oranges that were being saved up against a *sauce bigarade*, the precious calf's foot that was to enrich a *daube*, and the many emergency loaves of bread and packets of pitta – they all had to go.

So, I noted in a spirit of vengeance, did all my wife's sorbets and ices, as well as the remains of last summer's soft fruit, which she was hoarding for this spring's premature summer puddings.

We are, however inadequately, insured against loss by reason of the freezer's malfunctioning. (I say 'inadequately', for how do you value your home-made stock cubes and home-grown produce?) But I hadn't the cheek to put in a claim. What would one give as a reason for the malfunction? Absent-mindedness?

Here is the good news: the lid of the freezer hadn't been opened for the entire week, so there were still ice crystals in the frozen birds. We were having a huge party that Saturday night (to whom we fed the forty cobs of sweetcorn that had thawed out), and there would be many guests left over for Sunday lunch. It made an impressive show: three pigeons, a brace of grouse, a pheasant and a guinea fowl. And I have given the chest freezer to the daily and bought a second-hand upright from a friend who's hardly ever used it.

Ode to UFOs

The season of mellow fruitfulness is upon us. The mists are agreeable enough, but the rain is playing hell with the late apple-picking and I am depressed about our chances of seeing the maturing sun much before next June. My problem is not the fruit-laden 'vines that round the thatch-eaves run', but loading the freezer with the surplus veg that linger on in garden and greenhouse.

There is ample time in the winter and spring for fancy lightly to turn over the pages of the seed catalogues, but in autumn we poor drudges, who are enslaved by vegetable gardens and allotments, turn our thoughts grudgingly to the heavy task of clearing out the deep freeze. And there is no time to waste; space must be made before the o'erbrimming clammy cells actually rot.

Probably the best freezer-clearance method is the most radical one: top to bottom or, in the case of an upright freezer, front to back. This results in the expulsion from the hidden depths of dozens of UFOs. (Katharine Whitehorn, I think, first christened the evil 'Unidentified Frozen Object', which makes a mockery of last year's autumnal labours.)

It was a phenomenon that demanded a name. I have seen them much too oft amid my store of carefully labelled and dated polythene bags and plastic cartons. Usually, in my experience, the UFO is a soup or a stew – something that, when thawed or heated, will be largely liquid.

Our most recent excavations turned up five of these, in identical, lidless, two-pint Tupperware bottoms, covered over with cling-film, and bearing no identifying marks. 'Fish stock,' I ventured. 'Vegetable soup,' guessed my wife. The colour gave us no clues, but I thought I could smell something aromatic and winy.

Unable to bring myself to devote an entire lunchtime's labour just to clearing up this single mystery, I decided to kill two birds with one cold stone, and put whatever it was into the bottom of the steamer, the top of which contained the newly defrosted bit of chicken for the baby's lunch. That way, if it turned out to be edible, it would do service as a first course; but if it was not itself to be eaten, at least it would have contributed to cooking something that could be consumed.

It was delicious, thick soup. I rather agree with my wife that it was basically a purée of white haricot beans; but I still thought I detected a fishy note. I wonder if it could have been left over from the time we all agreed that making *potage de légumes* with fish stock was *highly* original, and that the wine gave it a particularly subtle added zip. Well, it really was *quite* good, and there are only four more containers of it to use up.

As UFOs go, this really wasn't much of a challenge. It was, after all, definitely savoury. It is much more interesting when you can't tell in advance whether the large cube or rectangle is going, upon thawing, to turn out to be raw, grated celery root, which Katharine Whitehorn remembers leaving her husband for dinner in the belief that it was creamy vegetable soup, or whitecurrant sorbet. My wife was only deterred from throwing away a vast tub of some orange-red substance, with a cry of 'Oh God, not more tomato soup,' when she spotted the tell-tale presence of kidney beans that signalled 'chilli con carne'.

The offal problem is probably the worst one of all. They languish at the bottom of the freezer: sets of calf's brains, pairs of lamb's sweetbreads, calf's feet and pig's feet. Covered in their layers of hoar, survivors of heaven knows how many power cuts, it is impossible to tell which is which.

In the upper left-hand basket we have collected the candidates for becoming the ingredients for Freezer Soup. 'Broad beans, June 1981' is clear enough. But are those frosted dark green things overgrown French beans? Or are they that odd variety of mangetout peas that we grew last year? They couldn't be asparagus peas, left over from the year before, when we last grew them? And the crumbly, rather separate green leaves in a polythene bag. Is it spinach? Sorrel? No, it's basil, quick-frozen on trays, then tipped into a bag and forgotten.

Recently I discovered that our daily help must have run out of high-gauge polythene freezer bags, and used flimsy 'food bags' to store the whole tomatoes that we always shove straight into the freezer without bothering to pulp or purée them. I cursed her and them as the cheap bags split at the seams, and their contents spilled all over the freezer, bouncing like insanely large marbles.

As I repackaged them I took an inventory: cling-filmed trays bearing this year's basil leaves, and one of fresh coriander; ice cube trays filled with snipped chives. The entire right-hand compartment is filled with sorbets. The peach and the nectarine sorbets are the result of my arriving with a tray of each for the August bank holiday weekend. 'Very clever,' said my wife, 'but we don't have any guests and we're invited out ourselves.' I couldn't bear to tell her that I'd bought them with her Luncheon Vouchers.

Face – and the fruit – was saved by Jane Grigson's rule-of-thumb recipe for firm fruits: to each 500g of peeled and stoned fruit, use 125g of sugar and water to cover. Bring to the boil, cool, purée and freeze, putting it through the food processor a second time before it is frozen all the way through. This last task can be made easier by the addition of some alcohol, either the appropriately flavoured *eau de vie* or vodka, which will lower the freezing temperature.

There are also many, many Tupperware pints of pear sorbet, enterprisingly made from the same recipe on the initiative of our daily help (whom I forgive for the tomatoes), when she could see that otherwise this year's entire crop of pears would go sleepy and perish. The pink stuff in the same corner of the freezer is raspberry sorbet made from last year's fruit, which we used up only this summer to make room for this year's.

But I grow cynical, and begin to doubt the value of it all. There is an old *cassoulet*: I should like to see it eaten up, as I'd like to reclaim the earthenware gratin dish that contains it. Will anyone ever taste it? Or the chilli con carne? How can one use up all that nameless stock? As I consign this year's produce to the depths of the freezer, I cannot help questioning whether any of it will ever be resurrected.

Sleep tight

The world's most comforting drink is called a Brompton cocktail. The recipe differs according to which doctor prescribes it; but, basically, it is a mixture of morphine or heroin and cocaine in a sweetened alcoholic base. It goes without saying that the circumstances in which it is administered are pretty drastic.

Still, human beings are accustomed to drink in order to be comforted, as the original and most soothing nightcap is, of course, mother's milk. Doubtless it is the atavistic memory of this common mammalian experience that gives the hot, milky bedtime drink its kick. Medical researchers were even tempted for a time to think that cocoa, Horlicks and Ovaltine out-performed Mogadon in scientifically controlled knock-out tests. But now, as Dr Kirstine Adam reported in 'Dietary Habits and Sleep After Bedtime Food Drinks' (*Sleep*, vol. 3, 1980), medics feel 'normal dietary habit is the predominant influence on the response to bedtime food'.

With her husband, Professor Ian Oswald, Dr Adam has written a riveting book for a non-medical audience, *Get a Better Night's Sleep* (Martin Dunitz). Reading it kept me up most of one night. There they report the findings, for example, of two American scientists during the 1930s that a pre-bedtime snack of, say, cornflakes and milk seemed positively conducive to less restless sleep.

In the course of the famous Chicago sleep study, the great American sleep researcher, Dr Nathaniel Kleitman, found that there was less squirming about during the night after a nightcap of Ovaltine before going to bed. Ovaltine is a malted product made from milk and cereal, so Kleitman's finding bears out the cornflakes and milk results.

At Edinburgh Oswald and Adam themselves conducted experiments with Horlicks. The young people in the study 'slept so well . . . that nothing could have improved their sleep anyway, so no difference showed up with the Horlicks. The middle-aged people, however, slept quite a lot better after they had had Horlicks.' But before you buy shares in companies that manufacture malted milk drinks, read on.

There was a flaw in the Edinburgh experiment; they realised that the correct correlation had to do with whether or not the subject was in the habit of having a food drink before retiring. The important thing was to continue as you began: Horlicks helped the sleep of those who were used to having a little something before bedtime, and wasn't much use for those who weren't. The moral is that you'll sleep better if you stick to your own bedtime ritual.

Unless, that is, your own routine involves smoking, taking sleeping pills or drinking a lot of alcohol before bed. Nicotine is an upper, like caffeine, and those who smoke in bed not only risk setting themselves on fire, but also a bad night's sleep. Alcohol, by contrast, is a downer. The reason it gives an immediate uplift to the spirits is that the first thing it suppresses is inhibitions.

Some doctors, Oswald included, advise against the nightly tot of whisky or brandy that is most people's favoured sleep-aid. Nocturnal boozing, they maintain, causes *bad* sleep. And there is no difference between taking your whisky neat and cool or diluted in a hot toddy – they will both be at the same temperature when they reach the stomach where they start to work. You get to sleep more quickly, perhaps, but you pay for this later when the organs of the body break down the alcohol. Gastritis, poor appetite in the morning, and even a headache are all possible side effects. Here we are speaking of small amounts of alcohol;

large quantities can lead to that regrettable condition, the hangover.

The hangover-making properties of sleeping pills are due to the same phenomenon. Most of the drugs used for their snooze-making effect linger in the body's tissues, and are still being broken down and eliminated at breakfast time.

Malted milk is thus the favourite of many conscientious doctors. In the words of the poet, however, 'Candy is dandy, but liquor is quicker', and there are those in the medical profession who would not sneer at a few tablespoons – or more – of Scotch in the hot chocolate to speed up its soothing action.

Personally, I'm a tisane-freak. I drink a hot infusion of *Verbena officinalis* (which the French call *verveine*) on cold winter nights. At the very least it warms me up, which really does have an effect on falling asleep, as it is notoriously hard to zizz if your nose or toes are freezing. (There is precious little scientific evidence for the efficacy of herbal infusions. So your tisane might have exactly the same effect poured into a hot-water bottle as it does poured into your mouth.) Country people also swear by the sedative qualities of tea made of the slightly soapy-tasting lemon balm, and camomile, peppermint and lime (French *tilleul*) all have their night-time adherents. Proprietary 'herbal teas', unless they bear a label stating all their ingredients, should probably be avoided by those seeking a calmer night's sleep, as it is always possible that they contain something madly over-exciting.

The Loaves of Academe

The Oxford Food Symposium 1980

The ancient University of Oxford was the setting for some pretty peculiar academic activities in May 1980. Food celebrities, famous dons, well-known gastronomes, publishers, literary agents, booksellers and even a star-spangled chef met at Saint Antony's College to participate in a symposium on the history of cookery books.

It would have been a first, were it not for the fact that this was the second year in a row that Alan Davidson, formerly HM Ambassador to Vientiane, whose most recent book is *North Atlantic Seafood*, and

Theodore Zeldin, the brilliant young historian of France, have collaborated on this project of treating food as an academic subject.

Davidson, a deeply eccentric man in his mid-fifties, is the ringleader of a group I call the scholar-cooks. They have their own magazine, the zanily pendantic *Petits Propos Culinaires*, their own publishing company in London, Prospect Books, and their own source of inspiration, Elizabeth David.

Now, thanks to Zeldin's imagination and Davidson's organisational verve (and his appointment for 1979 as Alistair Horne Research Fellow at Saint Antony's), they have their own annual seminar at Oxford – surely the only great university in the world to treat the study of food with the seriousness it deserves.

Dr Zeldin gave the opening address to the seventy or so symposiasts, and welcomed them by pointing out that what they were doing at Oxford was actually one of the ancient functions of the university – to reflect on their daily activities: writing, editing, publishing, selling and using cookery books, in this case.

The first speaker, Kai Brodersen, a young German from St John's, launched into his subject: cookery writing before the era of the printed book. He was very cautious, and raised the question that was to dog us all day: before the age of widespread literacy, whom were cookery books written for? It seems unlikely that, until relatively recent times, those who cooked were able to read, and that those who could read had any need to cook for themselves.

Claudia Roden spoke next on early Islamic cookery manuscripts. Mrs Roden, the justly celebrated author of the Penguin book of Middle Eastern cookery, so charmed and captivated her audience that we tacitly agreed to suspend the ten-minute rule; and she spoke for forty-five minutes on the culinary literature of the Arab world.

I was enchanted to learn that food was held in such high esteem by the caliphs that at their banquets they often commissioned poets to recite verses in praise of the food as it was consumed, or even musicians to sing the recipe for the dish being eaten. Mrs Roden's contribution was seminal, for subsequent speakers made it clear that the tradition of cookery writing in the West, at least, was transmitted by the Arabs.

Alan Davidson had asked the participants from the UK (there were many from abroad) to bring enough food 'for about one and a quarter people, the additional element being to cater for overseas visitors'. With Davidsonian precision he went on to gloss his own test: '"Food for one and a quarter people" should be interpreted as food for two and a half people for *one* course.'

The lunch was spectacular. Sonia Blech, formerly chef of the Crown Inn at Whitebrook, made an avocado *bavarois* and a mango tart. Claudia Roden supplied aubergine-stuffed pastries. Josephine Bacon from Time/Life Books made an elaborate travelling picnic pie of braided buckwheat bread dough, which enveloped cheese, cooked sausages and unshelled hard-boiled eggs. Elizabeth Evans, who had come from the Channel Islands, brought smoked scallops and Jersey cream. Elizabeth Lambert Ortiz, who is famous for her books on Caribbean and Latin American food, no doubt brought something extra delicious, for it had disappeared completely by the time I got to the buffet table.

Nicholas Kurti, Professor Emeritus of Physics at Oxford and a dedicated amateur of food, brewed coffee in his own replica of Count Rumford's coffee pot, and served a *bombe* he had invented twenty-five years earlier for the annual Diamond Conference 'devoted to the discussion of certain topics in Solid State Physics'. 'The name of the dish, *Bombe Allotropique (Graphite–Diamant)*, alludes to the then recent news of the experimental realisation of the graphite–diamond transition (the production of artificial diamonds) at the General Electric Research Laboratory in Schenectady.'

After lunch Jill Norman, one of the two most important British publishers of cookery books (the other, Caroline Hobhouse of Macmillan, was also present), made some pessimistic remarks about the present state of affairs in which 2,000 mostly worthless cookery books are published every year in this country alone.

I have no doubt that, at this venerable seat of learning, with Alan Davidson and Theodore Zeldin as the unlikely midwives, a new academic subject has been born. Any day now I expect announcement of the foundation of the world's first chair of gastronomy.

1981

Meeting in solemn conclave, the scholar-cooks – that band of gastronomic intellectuals inspired by Elizabeth David and organised by Alan Davidson – held their third annual deliberations in September 1981. They call themselves the Oxford Symposium, and they meet at St Antony's College.

This year nearly 150 of them gathered to discuss 'National and

Regional Styles of Cookery'. Twelve of them came from America, one from Canada, two from Australia and two from Japan; one each from Germany, Switzerland and the Netherlands; and there were seven distinguished scholars from France.

A good many academics specialising in the new subjects of food habits and 'foodways' were present, and most of the really serious American and British writers and publishers of books about food were there too. It was a glittering *galère*, replete with celebrated and familiar food and wine world names.

Elizabeth David sent a message containing a subject for discussion. She suggested that cookery books very often reflected the practices and habits of the generation of cooks *before* a book is published. It follows that cookery books are, therefore, unreliable evidence for those who are interested in the history of eating habits.

There were only two categories of food freaks noticeably missing. Too few chefs came, a fault that Alan Davidson hopes to rectify next year. And for a company engaged upon such amiably eccentric pursuits, there was a dearth of cranks. I rather missed the presence of crazed vegetarians, evangelical *tofu*-ites and brown rice maniacs.

Nevertheless, the actual sessions were agreeably dotty. The topic that appeared the most *recherché* of the day turned out to be the most dramatic. Maria Johnson's paper in the volumes of published proceedings was called 'North Balkan Food, Past and Present', and I expected it to be just that tiny bit more obscure than, say, Helen M. Leach's (actually, riveting) 'Cooking without Pots: Aspects of Prehistoric and Traditional Polynesian Cooking'. But when Maria Johnson spoke to the group, she presented a photograph of a model of a bread oven and another of a loaf of bread from Bulgaria. She went on to argue that the model was 7,000 years old and represented a loaf made of wheat and barley – the first leavened loaf of bread in history. The only other person present who seemed to be in a position to know about these matters found this conclusion stunning – and appeared to disagree with it.

I myself hope Maria Johnson is right, and find it difficult not to put implicit trust in her carbon dating techniques, as I have very little idea what they involve. The Bulgarian loaf was decorated with acorn impressions, incidentally; one of the symposiasts said she had seen a loaf just like it in a Camden Town market that very week.

Raymond Sokolov, the celebrated New York author of *The Saucier's Apprentice*, contributed a witty and telling paper on 'Sunbelt Food:

Southern Cooking, the Major Surviving Native Cuisine in the USA'. In it he pointed out that the popularity of deep-frying in the deep South is no accident – it is an ideal method for the restaurateur: 'The process is quick and ideally suited to modern fast-food situations. You can, moreover, deep-fry almost anything. A friend of mine ran a fryolator at a chicken joint in the Southwest. . . . To relieve the boredom of the job, he took to methodically southern-frying old sneakers [plimsolls]. They came out golden brown, looking like giant fritters.'

'The best grits I ever ate,' Mr Sokolov wrote, 'were the baked cheese grits served at a fund-raising event in Lexington, Kentucky.' I felt honour-bound to tell Mr Sokolov that I was born and brought up there, and have never tasted baked cheese grits in my life. But, as he gives the recipe at the back of his article, it is possible to remedy this. (Grits are 'corn leached out of the kernel with a lye solution' – identical to Italian *polenta*.)

The symposium ended with the *rapporteur* of the session on 'bogus cuisines' telling us that his group had failed completely to agree on how to distinguish non-genuine from authentic regional styles of cookery.

A clear instance of the bogus is, of course, fast food such as Kentucky Fried and Big Macs, when transplanted from their native land, their wrappings serving only to litter the streets of Paris, Tokyo and London. And the food of the international hotel dining-room, it was agreed, is nothing if not bogus. But these are not notes towards a definition.

Professor Nicholas Kurti reported a promising sighting of the definitely bogus, though: a label that read, 'Dad's Cookies, Like Mum Used to Make. Untouched by Human Hands'.

1983

Every 18 months or so, Alan Davidson, the world's leading expert on fish and fish cookery, and Theodore Zeldin, the celebrated historian of France, gather together an ever-increasing band of scholar-cooks. In June 1983 the tribe convened in solemn but light-hearted symposium, to discuss the papers some of their number had written on the theme 'Food in Motion'.

In fact, what they were devoting their collective attention to was the burning issue of 'the migration of foodstuffs and cookery techniques'. The most famous example of this is what has come to be called 'the Columbian exchange'. Following Christopher Columbus's 1492 adventures, the New World gave the Old maize, potatoes, tomatoes, a great many other vegetables and the turkey; and the Old World gave the New in exchange cows, sheep, chickens and venereal disease. (Details can be found in Alfred W. Crosby Jr's *The Columbian Exchange: Biological and Cultural Consequences of 1492*, Greenwood Press, Westport, Conn., 1972.)

In his introduction to the symposium papers, Davidson points out that all the contributors have dealt with 'assisted migration', though he gives several important examples of 'natural' migration, such as the common gourd, which 'was present in both hemispheres long before the period of European expansion'. It probably originated in Africa and reached America by floating. There is at least one fungus 'whose spores can be blown across oceans', one fish whose eggs seem to have drifted from the Mediterranean to the Caribbean; and, as we know, edible migratory birds do it.

Even within the category of migration assisted by man, however, there are distinctions to be made. Davidson singles out 'unwittingly assisted migration', as when de Lesseps's construction of the Suez Canal resulted in 'such a diminution in the salinity of the Great Salt Lakes, through which it passes, that certain fish from the Red Sea' were 'able to migrate through it to the Mediterranean'. And, muses Davidson, 'the stewards on transatlantic liners who threw overboard, in Southampton harbour, American clams which had not been eaten on the voyage thought they were consigning them to oblivion, not ensconcing them in a new habitat.'

The most obvious – and sometimes startling – example of food in motion is the growth and popularity of immigrant cuisines. The reflection of this in British restaurants was closely analysed by Christopher Driver.

Symposiasts came, as usual, from all over the globe. There was a particularly strong Australian contingent this year, though the Japanese presence appeared to me to be diminished. As usual, the Dutch greatly outnumbered the French, and Americans positively abounded.

The contribution that appealed most to my sense of humour was by Raymond Sokolov of *The Wall Street Journal* (the journalist who so annoyed the French Minister of Culture earlier in 1983 when he spoiled Jack Lang's cultural jamboree by asking questions about contemporary French fiction). During the discussion of his paper, 'New American Cuisine: Japonaiserie in Sarasota', Sokolov revealed that he had, almost by chance, been present at the beginning of the culinary revolution we call the *nouvelle cuisine*, when he interviewed Paul Bocuse in 1972. Indeed, since Sokolov regards the movement as one in which press agentry is as important as gastronomy, and, as his was the first article to appear in an American paper, he might be said to have been present at the birth, as a midwife, if not as a parent.

Sokolov accused himself of contributing to the confusion between the new movement and the minor branch of it – called *cuisine minceur* by its inventor and sole expositor, Michel Guérard – which is only an elaborate set of recipes for slimmers. The *real* movement, Sokolov claims, proceeds from Fernand Point and Bocuse, via Guérard's *Cuisine Gourmand* and the Troisgros brothers' book, and its chief apsect is the visual appearance of the food. In this, whether they were aware of it or not, the new chefs were indebted to Japanese food: 'The *nouvelle cuisine* rapidly evolved into a feast for the eyes, *à la japonaise*.'

But the most serious – and scholarly – paper I heard discussed was 'Ireland without the Potato: Short and Long-Term Solutions' by Jillian Strang and Joyce Toomre. I had not before realised that, during the Irish potato crop failures of the 1840s, in consequence of which 'nearly one and one-half million people died', the Irish ate virtually nothing else.

'It was not unusual for an adult to consume ten to fourteen pounds of potatoes a day,' say the authors; and these were eaten boiled, without the addition of butter or any condiment. Indeed, it emerged in the discussion that, once they had discovered the potato a hundred years earlier, the Irish could not be persuaded to eat anything else.

Though the shores of Ireland, then as now, teemed with fish, the catch was often left to rot on the quay. It was almost impossible to transport it inland, but the fishermen themselves valued fish as food so little that they strangled the infant industry by selling their nets to buy potatoes in times of shortage.

Did the Irish, I asked Dr Toomre, have beer to drink? She thought they did, though more research will be necessary to confirm her views. Certainly, something like beer would have to have been there to prevent a whole host of diseases in anyone who ate nothing but ten to fourteen pounds of potatoes a day. Which proves that Guinness, or at least its ancestor, really was good for you.

1985

'Alan and Theodore seem to think there should be a chair of Gastronomy at Oxford, but I don't believe the dons will think it's an important enough subject,' said one of the three unbelievers at the fifth Oxford symposium, on 'Science, Tradition and Superstition in the Kitchen', held in June 1985.

The 150 delegates were deeply serious about food. They had come from Ireland, France, Spain, Belgium, Holland, Norway, Germany, Australia and the USA. There were more than at any previous Oxford symposium, more than the organiser (Tom Jaine, who until recently ran the Carved Angel in Dartmouth) had bargained for, but he and the symposium's founders did not want to turn away the faithful. Of those early enough to appear on the attendance list, there were six cooks/hoteliers, thirty-one journalists/writers, thirteen publishers/editors, nine historians, seven booksellers, one film-maker, two broadcasters, two marketing people and twenty-three academics, plus sixty who gave no occupation. Each was paying £32 including dinner.

The delegates looked happy. For many of them, it had been an almost annual party (1980, 1981, 1983, 1984) since the symposium went public. The first one, in May 1979, was just a gathering of Alan Davidson's chums (including Elizabeth David, Jane Grigson, Richard Olney, Jill Norman and me) to discuss the history of cookery books.

The atmosphere at Oxford was buoyant for a second reason: the Oxford symposium has whetted the world's appetite for food get-togethers. The American Institute of Wine & Food, founded in 1981 in California, held its first 'Conference of Gastronomy' last January at Santa Barbara, in the presence of Julia Child and Danny Kaye. There were AIWF conferences in Boston in October, San Diego in January and Dallas in April. Turkey has held a gastronomic conference. Australia had its second gastronomic conference in Adelaide in September.

In June 1983 I went to a conference at Radcliffe College in Cambridge, Massachusetts, sponsored by the Culinary Historians of Boston. Food historian Karen Hess was fierce on the history of johnny-cake and American *Vogue*'s Barbara Kafka was savage on how to break into food journalism.

Basically, these events are attended by academics or those with an academic turn of mind, and have the pedantry, bitchery and politics of all academic gatherings. But there is one improvement on normal university life: the meals. At Boston there was a 1621 dinner, surprisingly good, cooked and served by actors who work in a Pilgrim Fathers' village (like an intellectuals' Disneyland) called Plimoth Plantation. As forks had not been invented in 1621, we ate the capon with the tips of our knives off wooden trenchers.

At Adelaide, they held an 'after-meal drinking party of ancient Greece'.

At Oxford this year, for dinner we ate Parson Woodforde's menu for 3 July 1788: 'Soals fryed, Ham and three boiled Chicken, a large piece of boiled Beef, Beans, a Couple of Ducks roasted and Peas, Gooseberry Pies and Current Tarts.' It was delicious, but tasted like 1958, actually.

But the most fun meal is the lunch at Oxford, when delegates bring their own specialities. This year, there was the buried salmon (*gravad lax*) that figured in Dr Astri Riddervold of Oslo's paper about the tradition of burying fish in Norway, Sweden and Iceland (mysteriously, it does not go off); the anti-allium stew prepared by a lady who is allergic to garlic and onions; the chocolate-covered garlic cooked by one of the three women whose paper was on aspects of garlic (Lynda Brown, of Yorkshire, Alexandra Hicks of Ann Arbor, Alicia Rios of Madrid); and modern Californian cuisine by Sally Clarke of Clarke's restaurant in London.

For the 'keynote' address to start the proceedings, an exotic foreign Foodie is the form. At Boston, Alan Davidson bemused for England when he promised that his talk would end with an important surprise announcement. This turned out to be that the Early English Text Society had inadvertently produced an edition not of any old old book but of the earliest known cookery book in English, *The Forme of Cury*. We were all bowled over.

The Oxford conference was opened by American academic Harold McGee, a trained scientist with a Ph.D. in English. His book *On Food and Cooking: The Science and Lore of the Kitchen* has sold out in America.

Dr McGee disproved a few old cooks' tales, e.g. that searing meat keeps the juices in. He has proved the efficacy of copper, though: while egg whites beaten in a copper bowl take three times as long to mount as those done in a glass bowl, they hold their foam much longer.

The conference then dispersed into groups, and in the two days of discussion, several interesting ideas were thrashed out.

Yan-kit So, author of the *Classic Chinese Cookbook*, told about the diet of pigs' trotters and ginger a Chinese woman eats for a month after giving birth.

Alan Davidson asked why yoghurt and fish are a prohibited combination in many countries of south-east Europe and the Near East, although yoghurt and meat are common.

Sami Zubaida cast doubt on 'instrumentalist' views of the Jewish and Muslim food taboos that credit them with a medical rationale.

Jill Tilsley Benham described how Persian food is traditionally divided into 'cold' (*sardi*) and 'hot' (*garmi*): these the Iranians balance, like Yin and Yang and also like the Hippocratic theory of humours. For instance, if Iranians make the Middle Eastern dish cucumber and yoghurt (both *sardi*) they put raisins (*garmi*) in too.

Dr Tapan Raychaudhuri described India's attitude to the Western food introduced by the Raj (they adopted the biscuits and the omelettes).

Valerie and Gerald Mars annoyed many of the food faithful by proposing to classify them as Epicures, Isolates, Mess-mates or Cultists, using anthropologist Mary Douglas's 'Grid/Group' indices. Foodies came out as Epicures – refusing to be ranked on a Grid, refusing to act with a Group, and refusing – in Oxford – to admit that anyone could look at them from the outside and imagine they used 'food primarily as a weapon to demonstrate superior awareness of the latest and newest cuisines, diets and current health fads'. This suggestion wrung indignant protests from the audience.

Many of the delegates, led by Claudia Roden, had something to say about aphrodisiacs. These come in several forms: organ-shaped food, suggestively textured food (mushrooms, oysters), body-strengthening food for men, body-scenting food for men and women, genital-itching food (Spanish fly, *cantharides*). Two doctors in the audience tried to keep the travellers' tales in proportion.

An untoothsome novelty was the paper on cynophagy (eating dog) by Professor Bruce Kraig of Chicago. In a food column he writes for a Chicago paper, he made a half-joking reference in 1983 to the meat walking around in starving African countries in the form of dogs. He received hate mail, obscene telephone calls and a death threat. In his paper given at Oxford, he traced his Swiftian idea in the archaeological record and in Chinese, Hawaiian, Mexican, Philippine and Plains Indian practices.

Professor Kraig thinks that we in the West personalise our dogs to such an extent that eating one would be cannibalism. His paper obviously broke a formidable taboo. (I do not endorse his views. Please, anyone who wants to send me another copy of the pamphlet about dog-eating in the Philippines – send it to someone new.)

In the closing moments of the symposium, when all the academics had patted each other on the back and the audience had gratefully clapped Tom Jaine for his organising power, another Chicago academic, Dr Rachelle Dubnow, suddenly spoke up to praise the 'joy' of the weekend, but to denounce as 'sad and decadent' Dr Kraig's joke, attributing to him the idea that 'starving Africans should go to the dogs'. Some of the academics smirked at the non sequitur. The rumour went round that this Chicago academic had actually *followed* Dr Kraig here to nail him (they did not know each other).

More characteristic of the weekend's proceedings was an exorcism carried out after Saturday lunch by Alicia Rios, Spanish food historian and proprietor of the Los Siete Sardines restaurant in Madrid. On a table heaped with cloves of garlic, she poured bottles of something clear into a metal bowl, lighted the liquid and sang a casting-out song with the refrain 'Bim, bim'. One sip was enough for most delegates, as also of the Chinese three-penis wine on offer the next day. They were both sixty per cent proof, forty per cent wish for a spiritual experience. Like the conference.

Cooking: the books

The sale of the Marcus and Elizabeth Crahan collection of books on food, drink and related subjects in New York on 9 and 10 October 1984 was an occasion when the interests of scholars and the interests of collectors were shown to be divergent. Books on food and drink have hitherto been prized for their contents; they are the very stuff of social history, however neglected they have been by past generations of historians. The tremendous prices – $25,300 for an Apicius, $31,900 for André Simon's copy of Pietro Crescentio's *Ruralia commoda*, the first printed work on agriculture, and $39,600 for a Platina, even though it was the first dated edition of the first printed cookery book – show that this has become a field for collectors as well as for scholars.

The latter, of course, are served just as well by microfilm and other reproductions, less pleasant though they are to handle than objects made of vellum and calf skin, (and lovely bindings such as those Marcus Crahan did himself). For the scholar of these matters, completeness is the thing, and the quality of individual books with strong claims to be considered as works of art – of which the Crahan collection contained a good many examples – has little to do with his professional concerns.

The study of cookery books and other works on food and drink can tell us something about the history of everyday life that we do not yet know in detail – how and what did people actually eat and drink in the past? Answers to these questions can open many new avenues for researchers in several disciplines. For example, the importance of the history of the nutritional aspect of diet is only just becoming apparent, as the concept of nutrition-related disease now seems to have a great deal to do with the ills of the affluent part of mankind, as well as with those whose problem is not having enough to eat. But knowing *what* people actually ate will also reveal facts about international trade and about the movements of foodstuffs. The trouble is that cookery books are not always reliable witnesses to history. It is essential, for purposes of scholarship in this new field, to assemble somewhere a complete collection of texts.

Some examples will make clear why this is so. The history of cookery books from La Varenne in the seventeenth century through the present day has displayed one odd and consistent practice: plagiarism. To quote Anne Willan on La Varenne (from *Great Cooks and Their Recipes*, 1977): 'La Varenne's name . . . did not appear on any of the early editions of *Le Pastissier françois*, and there is some reason to doubt that he wrote it. The profession of *pâtissier* was completely separate from that of *cusinier*, and it is hard to believe that two years after writing *Le Cusinier françois*, the same author could turn out a second book so different in style and content. Several of the same recipes appear in both books, but *Le Pastissier* is much more detailed; its author gives precise instructions, while La Varenne writes in a shorthand that assumes a thorough knowledge of cooking.'

In another country and another century, the same problem persists. The most famous of all English cookery books, Hannah Glass's 1747 *The Art of Cookery made plain and easy*, scarcely differs from half a dozen contemporary books of recipes. Whole sections were lifted from other books, such as the chapter on creams, which, says Anne Willan, 'is taken word for word from the first (1727) edition of *The Compleat Housewife* by Eliza Smith'.

In our own time an action for infringement of copyright was initiated by Richard Olney in 1983 against the author and publishers of an American cookery book, who admitted liability and settled out of court. The offence was to have reproduced thirty-nine recipes, almost word for word.

Before the study of the history of cookery books and diet can go any further, it is of paramount importance to assemble a complete set of texts, so that comparisons can be made and the network of borrowings untangled. A completely false impression is given by the activities of the plagiarists. They make it appear that through the ages, especially from the sixteenth through eighteenth centuries, there was much greater culinary stability than was actually the case. With every scholar's contribution, it becomes clearer that cookery books from these periods must not be taken as a record or reflection of what was actually happening in the kitchen.

We have much more to learn from the genuinely original cookery and food writer than from the copier. But until we can detect the plagiarist, it is hard to recognise the novel thinker such as Richard Bradley, whose value to the scholar is much greater than his value to the collector. (Lot 254, Bradley's *New Experiments and Observations relating to the Generation of Plants* . . ., 1724, made only $275 in the Crahan sale.)

It seems clear, then, that this is a field in which the interests of scholars and those of collectors are different, and the very high prices commanded by the best lots in the Crahan sale might make one fear that such books will eventually become inaccessible to those who actually use them. Fortunately, a conflict of interests in this area has been averted. The needs of scholarship, as we have said, are well served by reprographic texts. St Antony's College, Oxford, in collaboration with Prospect Books Ltd, the firm run by Alan Davidson that specialises in the publication of facsimile reprints of old cookery and food titles, is assembling a collection. There are sixty-seven important printed books in the English language dealing with cookery and food history that were published before 1699. Twenty-one of these titles were contained in the Crahan collection. St Antony's and Prospect Books already have fifty-four titles, mostly in reprographic form, and hope to have sixty by the year's end. Thus scholarship is made independent of the marketplace. The co-operation of the owners of important books can only enhance the value of their collections, and the day draws closer when the ambitions of scholars to have a complete set of texts will be realised.

For the collector, the reward for his co-operation with the scholar is bound to be even higher prices than those realised in the Crahan sale. This is a field in which scholarship is new; there is not yet a chair of gastronomic studies at either of the ancient universities, though there will be some day. Systematic connoisseurship is also a relatively new phenomenon. How fortunate it is that they can both develop together.

Why is this night different?

Sometimes Easter Sunday is also the first day of Passover, when Jews all over the world celebrate the holiday with the traditional Passover supper, the *Seder*. It is not unusual for the two holidays to coincide, as the Last Supper was a *Seder*.

Most Jewish festivals involve food, almost always in the form of a special meal, prepared and eaten at home, often with invited guests as well as family members. The Passover meal has the most elaborate ritual of any Jewish feast, and is a treat for the kids, for whose benefit the story of the Exodus from Egypt is retold, with many sorts of food as visual aids, graphic symbols of aspects of the age-old tale.

But it is a pain for the observant housewife. She not only has to cook within the normal constraints of the Jewish dietary laws, but has to deal with special Passover prohibitions against 'leavened bread'. This last is usually interpreted as any food containing yeast, and is merely a symbolic gesture to the Biblical account of the Exodus, when the Hebrew slaves had to flee on such short notice that there was no time for bread to prove in the normal way.

The laws of *Kashrut* prescribe what foods and practices are Kosher. They are complicated and, I think, responsible for the mediocrity of much Orthodox Jewish cooking.

Meat and dairy products cannot be served at the same meal — a condition that makes most European cooking wildly difficult. Pork and shellfish are prohibited altogether, making oriental food out of the question. For meat meals, margarine or (intrinsically delicious but lethal) rendered chicken fat is in lieu of butter.

As you will have gathered, though I was always told (falsely) that both my grandmothers were good cooks, I don't really rate Jewish food. In fact, the sight of a hot salt beef sandwich with its slightly melting fat makes me feel distinctly queasy — despite its traditional rye bread and pickled cucumber garnish. Even with a side-order of absolutely impeccable *latkes*, the Jewish potato pancake that is easily the best version of that wonderful dish, it is not my idea of a light lunch.

None the less, I feel nostalgia for the *Seder*, with its food that is totally symbolic (until the meal gets down to business with the first course proper of chicken soup with matzo ball dumplings) and its obligatory four glasses of wine.

The beauty and the *fun* of the Passover dinner were recalled to me by *The Home Book of Jewish Cookery* by Judith Jackson. The table (and the stage for the re-telling of the Passover story) is set, she reminds me, with three matzot (the Hebrew plural of 'matzo' and 'matzah', both of which spellings are correct). They represent not only the unleavened bread of the Israelites' journey, but also 'the poverty they suffered both in Egypt and in the desert'.

A roasted lamb bone is on the table, Judith Jackson says, 'to commemorate the paschal sacrifice which every family brought to the Temple in ancient times'. Boiled eggs are on the table as 'symbolic of the festival sacrifice which was always additional to the paschal lamb'.

Bitter herbs, usually horseradish, are eaten to remind the *Seder* participants that the lives of the slaves in Egypt were bitter. A mixture of nuts, apples, sweet wine and spices, *charoset*, commemorates the mortar used by Jews at forced labour to build the Egyptian 'treasure cities'.

Green herbs such as parsley and watercress are eaten to symbolise the return of spring and the renewal of life; but they are dipped into salt water in memory of the tears shed by the enslaved Hebrews.

The best part of the evening is the compulsory four glasses of wine – of which even the youngest member of the party takes a sip. An extra place is laid at the table for the Prophet Elijah, who is supposed to visit every Jewish home during the *Seder*. And his glass of wine is always poured out too.

In addition to ensuring that the feast is a jolly one, the wine plays its symbolic part in the proceedings. At one point in the ceremony ten drops of wine are poured out to represent the Ten Plagues suffered by the Egyptians before they would agree to Moses leading away the children of Israel. I well remember the look of malicious pleasure on my grandfather's face as he conducted the ceremony, and visited locusts and boils on the Egyptians. It was just after the war, and even the children knew that the 'Egyptians' he had in mind were German.

Into the mouths of babes

Infant nutrition has not always gripped my attention by its intrinsic fascination as a subject for conversation and bedtime reading. But

Tatyana, the apple of her aged first-time parents' eyes, is eight months old. Her mother doesn't really cook, and her father, who does, imagined that she would require no more culinary attention than to put the grown-ups' *boeuf bourguignon, bouillabaisse* or *cassoulet* through the Magimix.

Dr Spock was not much help on the subject. His limited remarks about this method of bringing up baby did lead me to suspect that it was not entirely orthodox, or even conventional practice. But then, the good doctor's book, though it has reprinted so very often, has not been reissued recently enough to do more than hint at the newest received truths about infant gastronomy.

This is hardly surprising in a field in which half-truths and untruths are still believed by those whose job it is to know better. As elderly, and therefore highly suggestible parents, we suffered from the misguidance of those who told us that Tatyana, who weighed in initially at only 5 lb. 3½ oz., wasn't gaining weight rapidly enough. It was suggested that her diet of mother's milk ought to be supplemented by powdered muck. Tatyana showed what she thought of this by being sick for the first (and almost only) time in her life.

A distressing, and medically unnecessary, but brief return to hospital proved that the only thing that was wrong was our adviser's knowledge of infant nutrition. And after someone else who should have known better suggested that we ought to fatten Tatyana up for the winter, we decided to learn the elusive 'facts' for ourselves.

The 'facts' of infant nutrition are always related to a theory. At the moment there seem to be basically only two. The first is that mother's milk is the only perfect food for a baby, and that it almost never needs supplementing until the baby is ready for its first solid food. This time varies greatly, from two to six months.

The second theory is more startling. The *number* of fat cells in the human body, an American nutritionist told us, is determined in the first twenty-four months. After that, they expand and contract, but do not increase in number. Fat grown-ups are (or at least can be) made by indulgent mothers. Sugar, apart from that which occurs naturally in fruit, is not only unnecessary for children, it is harmful. Those who give babies sugar – even whole-food honey or brown sugar – are not only cultivating the bad habits and dental problems associated with a sweet tooth; they may be condemning their infant to an adult life of overweight and misery and a painful and premature death from heart disease.

I am sorry to have to give Tatyana's doting godfather so public a warning, but anyone who gives her a sweetie before she has achieved the age of two years will have a very cross father to deal with. Salt, the consumption of which is implicated in hypertension, is also counter-indicated on the infant menu, and animal fat should be avoided. For example, there is no point in giving a child a taste for silver- or gold-topped milk. In fact, it is better not to give children past their infancy whole milk at all. Skimmed milk, which is now widely available, contains *all* the nutritional goodness, vitamins included, of the milk, except for the butterfat and the fat-soluble vitamins that they normally get elsewhere. Skimmed milk is also cheaper, and, I think, tastes nicer in coffee and tea. (When heated it forms less 'skin' than whole milk, and is perfectly suitable for cooking.)

Tatyana's fare consists largely of vegetables, root and otherwise, cooked in as little water as possible, whizzed up and strained. Lately she has enjoyed the addition of a little white fish or breast of chicken to her lunchtime purée. Baby rice and similar stodge is not in the store cupboard. But Familia for infants is allowed. Stewed fruit – apple and pear – has long been on the menu, and scraped, ripe banana is her invariable teatime snack. Tatyana first tasted (and adored) avocado pear at six months; and at Christmas I did my culinary duty by seeing that she had a mere molecule of *foie gras* and a splinter of truffle. (Last week Tatyana actually had lunch expressly prepared for her by Paul Bocuse himself, at his Lyon restaurant. It consisted of purée potato with just a *soupçon* of *jambon*. So she is well and truly embarked on the culinary life in the style to which her papa would like to see her become accustomed.)

In fact, Tatyana spent her first Christmas in France, where we naturally took her to have her first solid food. It was then that we learnt the naughty tricks the French use to get their babies to *manger* their vegetables. Every *pharmacie* has expensive jars of salt- and sugar-free purées of almost everything imaginable. Tatyana, however, disapproved of their basic *mélange* of veg. It *was* strange. The sneaky Frogs feed their *enfants* on globe artichokes. Globe artichoke makes everything eaten after it taste sweet. So after a meal of mixed veg with artichoke, *bébé* can even be persuaded to swallow cod-liver oil without making a face.

I haven't much experience of British baby food in jars and tins, but I understand that the brand leaders no longer lace their products with salt and sugar, or with the evil (and I think taste-addictive) monosodium glutamate. MSG is banned, as are most other additives, in baby food made in the United States.

Moreover, much American baby food is salt- and sugar-free. As Tatyana was about to make her second journey to France, where she was going to stay in a hotel, I had reason to look for food in jars. A culinarily literate friend, who is another feeding father, tipped me off about an American brand called Beech Nut. The labels on their jars boast, 'We add no salt, sugar, preservatives, MSG, flavour enhancers, nor artificial flavours or colours.'

Beech Nut baby foods are widely available at north London chemists' shops. Can it be that the burghers of north London are more nutritionally aware than their southern neighbours? No, there is an easier explanation to hand: Beech Nut baby food is kosher.

How can I lose?

My mother says I started putting on weight when I had my tonsils out at the age of four. When I was twelve, a paediatrician gave me a year-long course of Dexedrine, an amphetamine appetite suppressant. This would now be considered unorthodox treatment for a young boy, but it worked. Fat melted away, my weight plummeted, and the plump boy who had well deserved the horrid nickname 'Fats' was now, at a new school, as popular with his peers as he had been with his teachers. Of course I was energetic and charming; I was speeding for a whole year.

I kept the weight off. But, as I had been a fat child, I never knew that I was a normal-sized adolescent, and never consciously enjoyed being that slender, blond creature old photographs reveal. My 'body image' was formed in childhood, and never recovered from it. I think I was twenty-three before my weight started ouncing its way upwards; through my twenties it crept up from nine and a half to eleven stone. I weighed eleven stone 7 pounds until my late thirties. I am now 45, and I have seen the bathroom scales touch the thirteen stone 7 pound mark on a bad day.

Others find it impossible to forgive (but certainly not to overlook) this failure to control my weight. 'It's your job,' they say; 'how can you expect to maintain your weight when you eat and drink professionally?' Even my wife takes this line. 'You're not *really* fat,' she always maintains, 'just – larger.' I long ago lost interest in clothes, I hate sunbathing, I have not gone gay and I'm not having an affair. So I don't have any of the usual strong motives that cause newly middle-aged men to want to lose weight.

From time to time I have paid obeisance to the routine wretched excess of my job by taking myself off to the fat farm. (By the way, I think I have a claim to have coined this expression, in a piece published in 1977.) I enjoyed being pampered at Ragdale Hall; and I never deviated from the very low calorie, but sensible diet they asked me to keep to. But at the end of my eight-day stay, I had set a negative record by losing only a couple of pounds. After my return home, I lost another eight pounds without even trying; so it was evident that the regimen worked, but that to observe it working, one needed the medical equivalent of time-lapse photography.

Another year I tried the fasting programme at smart Forest Mere. It didn't suit me. Something was wrong with my blood sugar level, and I conked out and had to be rescued with glucose tablets as early as day two. (It was my fault. I should have remembered that, years earlier, doing the infamous Dr Atkin's diet with two friends from Oxford, I ended up going feet first into the Radcliffe Infirmary. At least I didn't need to have my gall bladder removed, as did one of my co-slimmers.) I think I lost half a stone at Forest Mere, and had a very pleasant time. But I put the weight back on, plus a little more, immediately I resumed my – ahem – professional duties.

As these latter include taking an interest in nutrition as well as gastronomy and, as I have occasionally done some research into patho-logical modes of eating, such as anorexia and bulimia nervosa, it dawned on me and more than one editor that I was really quite well placed to take myself in hand. So I embarked upon a vast programme of research into the business of banting, with myself as subject and the reduction of this self as object. To my spiritual as well as physical profit, I spent several hours with a psychiatrist who is interested in eating disorders. We tried hard to discuss and discover the psychological causes of my particular weight problem.

We failed. I was born in America in 1941, just as America entered the war. I was brought up during a particularly benign form of rationing, and got a very sound nutritional start to life. After my mother weaned me, she had less to do with feeding me than did the southern American black ladies who brought up me and my brother. I owe my life-long interest in food to the fact that my mother couldn't cook. Several of the nannies/cooks/*bonnes à tout faire* who ran our household were really first-rate at the kitchen range.

Though I suffered from the normal eat-up-think-of-the-starving-chil-dren-in-China maternal nagging, I was not subjected to the threat of withdrawal of mother's love or the promise of it in exchange for a clean plate. Mother wasn't feeding me.

My personal shrink (as I fondly came to think of him) also acted as my personal physician; he was interested himself in the physical and medical aspects of the treatments I planned to undergo. But what started in a larky enough fashion soon became earnest. I wasn't very well.

The results of my first physical examination showed that my blood pressure was elevated; so was the glucose level in my blood – we even feared adult-onset diabetes. There were high-ish levels of urea in my blood, and other signs that not all was well with my kidneys. All three free fatty acids were at unpleasantly high levels for a middle-aged man with a family history of near-universal heart disease. Normal thyroid-function tests removed any possibility of a physical excuse for the shape I was in. It was my own fault, not a cause of metabolic malice.

We had just had a new baby. I began to brood upon the orphans I was creating. Then I went to consult a psychologist who is interested in 'body image'. She subjected me to tests usually used on anorexics and bulimics. In a darkened room, the subject stands at a distance determined by his height from a rail, along which a pair of sliding lights can be brought together or made to move apart by a remote control device.

The object is to move the lights to the width of various parts of the body – shoulders, waist, hips and thighs. People suffering from eating disorders can't do it: they consistently over-estimate their own size. Overweight people, on the other hand, mostly under-estimate the volume of space their bodies fill. Six weeks later, the results of my test were analysed. I had been uncannily accurate – plus or minus one inch. The retrospective conclusion drawn from this was that I had been unusually aware of the dimensions of my body – and of my problem – and was particularly well-motivated to slim.

First I went to a gym. I chose Body One near Baker Street in London because it advertised an intensive weight reducing, for men only, in the *Standard*. I reckoned most people who did not have a word-of-mouth recommendation would find their gym or exercise class in this way.

It pleased me at first because it was exactly what I had pictured from the advert. Sleazy without actually being dirty, it was a whole world apart from the gentility of Ragdale Hall and Forest Mere. Hard-sell techniques and a deep anxiety about being paid in advance were more obvious at first than any real concern for the health of their clients. But all that changed as I got to know the personnel in the six weeks that I attended.

Though the only person with any medical knowledge was the truly splendid nurse who acted as masseuse, and though I received some minor injuries from my first work-out, caused by over-enthusiasm on the part of the beautifully muscled iron-pumping instructor, I soon came to find all the staff sympathetic. And my fellow gym-users were a very funny mixture of elderly retired stockbrokers, middle-aged fatties like myself and extremely narcissistic young men.

A pretty young woman with no qualifications but 'lots of experience' attempted to prepare a diet sheet for me, but gave up when she understood fully the nature of my job. We settled that I should try to eat no more than 1500 calories a day. This was to include a high fibre breakfast (without which I tend to suffer from irritable colon).

The programme should have been diet plus thrice-weekly work-outs, along with one massage a week and a one-hour heat treatment called 'PDR'. No one I asked could remember what the initials stood for; but the treatment consisted of being tightly wrapped in a number of electric heating pads that fastened around the trunk and thighs. I was normally weighed after PDR, and it was claimed that the weight loss was fat as well as sweat, but that the magic would be undone unless one refrained from eating or drinking for three hours following treatment.

I started out with really good intentions about exercise. But the torn ligaments of my triceps and a 'flu-like cold that lasted for weeks militated against me getting much further than fifteen minutes on the 'bike'. I hated the PDR, though I did it five times; but I loved the massage, both because the masseuse was excellent and personable, and because it was obviously psychologically good for me to have my attention drawn to my body. I think I have slight mirror-phobia and my vanity is certainly not bound up with the shape of my body. It's difficult for me to pay attention to what I look like; and the knowledge that, in gym apparel, I look like a slob gives me only momentary twinges of unhappiness. So having my mind concentrated on my shape by the whack of the masseuse's palm on my tum was probably an essential adjunct to my dieting.

On Body One's scales I began at 83.5 kilos (13 stone 2 pounds) and finished at 77.5 kilos (12 stone 2½ pounds). They were quite pleased with me, in spite of my being a shirker about exercise. Was it worth the £186 special discount price for the 6-week programme? Hard to say.

The advice on dieting was sensible, but less detailed than I required. On the whole I ignored it; but I kept a diary of my food and drink intake for the first few weeks, until I was certain that I could judge whether I had taken in only my 1500 calorie allowance. I could have profited from the counsel of a qualified dietician on the subject, particularly, of fibre; and I could have done with more competent guidance about drink. (I started by allowing myself half a glass of wine with each main meal; sometimes I gave up drink altogether.)

How, the experienced reader will now be asking, did you stick to your diet? The answer may surprise you. I went for four sessions to a hypnotist. Dr Carpenter (not his real name) came highly recommended by friends who were old hands at the slimming game. He is a Harley Street man and comes at Harley Street prices – a pound a minute.

For me, at least, it proved cheaper than psycho-analysis at the same unit cost. At the first and only forty-five-minute session (all subsequent ones are thirty minutes), Dr Carpenter took my history and my blood pressure – a mildly sinister elevation of 170/100.

He was very thorough, and I knew I was in competent hands. But that does not account for the ease with which he put me under. I had never been hypnotised before, though I knew what to expect; and though I wanted to co-operate, I somehow thought it my duty to resist a little. Dr Carpenter asked me to recline in his comfortable chair, and stare at my right hand, which he prophesied would begin to move, the fingers to splay, and then rise of its own accord. When it touched my face, my eyes would close, and I'd go into a deep hypnotic state.

How silly, I thought, just seconds before my fingers began to twitch, and, though I tried to prevent it, my right hand flew up and I nearly struck myself in the eye. From then on, I was a goner. 'Imagine yourself walking down the stairs to a lovely garden . . .' Dr Carpenter intoned soothingly. No sooner said, than imagined. When I later asked why I was such a good subject for hypnosis, Dr Carpenter replied, 'Journalists always are'. Then, perhaps seeing the loss of self-esteem in my eyes, he softened the blow by explaining, 'It's the creative aspect of the job that helps.' Oh.

In hypnosis you are completely relaxed, as if asleep, though fully conscious. You always know exactly what is going on, but, as when I could not manage to scratch my itchy nose, not always able to do anything about it.

By means of implanting post-hypnotic suggestions in my memory, Dr Carpenter attempted to deal with what I agree is the real problem: eating habits. He tried to undo the conditioning my generation received in infancy that compels us to finish everything on the plate. He tried to get me to understand sub-consciously what I have jolly well consciously known to be the truth since the age of four: that the problem of starving children in foreign countries is to do with the world-wide distribution of food and is not affected one jot by the disposition of the food on my plate.

Further dietary commandments, couched in calm imperatives, were: eat slowly. It makes food taste better and gives the brain a chance to tell you when you've had enough to eat from the blood sugar level messages it's receiving. Put down your knife and fork between each bite, and your glass after each sip. Use a smaller plate for your own food; it satisfies the eye, and helps the portions look big, whether they are or not. Never eat except when sitting down. Food that can be eaten standing up is generally finger food with high calorie values, starchy, fried, sweet – or, as in the case of doughnuts, all three. Always leave some food on your plate – it can become a habit that will ultimately obliterate mother's teachings.

Shun sweets, and never eat anything that isn't part of a meal, continues the slimmer's litany. These were easy for me, as I usually do the first and never do the second.

It was, as they say, uncanny. I became a difficult dinner companion, eating at the pace of a snail munching his way through a whole row of my garden's lettuce crop, putting knife and fork on the plate between enormously long and thorough sessions of mastication, and savouring each sip of my half glass of house white.

Dr Carpenter recorded one of my treatments. I played the cassette to myself at night. I don't know if it did any good: he counted to fifty; I always seemed to be asleep before he reached ten. He taught me to hypnotise myself. I can do it.

'Never eat because you're upset or bored,' the good doctor preaches. We worked a bit on boredom. I think cooking, even for oneself alone, is one of the most interesting things you can do. On my very rare nights at home, alone, I cook a little something for myself with as much ceremony and care as if I had guests or was feeding the family (my wife doesn't cook). To my surprise, Dr Carpenter does not disapprove of this obsession. 'Thinking about your meals gives you the chance to plan them carefully so that you eat the right foods. It gives you *more* control over your diet.' Too right.

This account of hypnotism as an aid to slimming makes it sound terribly unromantic. But I do think it was probably the most useful treatment I undertook, and I plan to see Dr Carpenter for a top-up after he and I have both returned from our holidays. On his scales I weighed in at 13 stone, 4½ pounds and out at 12 stone, 5 pounds again, only 8 ounces short of losing a whole stone. More importantly, perhaps, my blood pressure, before hypnosis, had gone down to a nicely normal 145/85.

I can't decide about acupuncture. After I finished hypnosis, I took myself to the charming Dr Lily Cheung, a qualified practitioner of both Western medicine and acupuncture, both of which she studied in her native Canton. She began by taking a medical history; and, having assured me that the metabolism can be 'speeded up' by acupuncture, which can encourage the body to burn its own fat reserves, and that her average overweight patient loses several pounds a week, we proceeded to treatment.

Don't let anybody tell you acupuncture doesn't hurt. The thirteen needles inserted into my legs, belly, arms and ear at each session did not give me sensations of pleasure. My psychiatrist has some time for the idea that acupuncture has something to do with the endorphin system, whereby the body produces substances with molecular structures similar to opiates.

Once or twice, when Dr Cheung had inserted the needles and fastened electrodes to them that made each needle give me a tiny electric shock, I felt uncomfortable and wanted attention; but she was busy with other patients and I did not like to bother her. I noticed that after a few minutes the discomfort subsided totally, and I began to experience euphoria. I have had morphia in hospital; it was very similar.

I went to Dr Cheung at a point in my diet when my initial weight loss had tailed off, and I expected to remain on a plateau with no further loss for some time. (This is a phenomenon universally reported by slimmers, and has to do with the fact that the rate of metabolism itself gets lower following weight loss, so that even the maintenance of vital functions requires less energy than before the diet began. This has obvious advantages in case of famine – one cannot expect the body's adaptive responses to distinguish between famine and a mere slimming diet. The book *Dieting Makes You Fat* turns entirely on this fact.) In spite of this I lost three pounds after my first week of acupuncture. But, perversely giving me some gratification, I *gained* one pound after my second week. After four weeks I had lost six pounds. I continued my diet throughout the acupuncture treatment, but I lapsed a good deal more than usual.

Acupuncture was the first method of slimming that claimed to act on its own, without any help from me, and to act directly on fat, rather than by altering my eating habits. My experiment was conducted so unscientifically that it is completely useless to anyone who wants to know whether acupuncture can make you lose weight. (It would be easy to design a scientific trial of acupuncture as a slimming therapy. When the body burns its own fat reserves, it excretes ketones; it would be simple to give acupuncture to a population whose diet is not changed, and to see whether they become ketotic.) At £12 an hour-long session, acupuncture was the least expensive therapy I tried.

Really I have nothing to say about this aspect of the treatment. But there is another, to do with appetite. At the end of each session, Dr Cheung taped a stud inside one ear, and said that if I waggled if for twenty minutes before each meal, or when I was hungry, it would suppress my appetite. It is supposed to reactivate the meridians affected by the treatment. My impression is that it works – though it disturbs fellow passengers on the tube to see me vigorously playing about with my ear. But it might be that anything, including the saying of prayers, done for twenty minutes before meals, would dampen the appetite.

Most people in search of a radical slimming cure think first of chemical will-power aids such as tablets and injections. Many drugs have been tried as slimming helps, and even bizarre remedies such as swallowing tablets containing a bit of a tapeworm have been used by desperate people. Mechanical and surgical techniques exist too. The *very* obese can have their jaws wired together so they are only able to take liquids; they can have part of their stomach stapled shut, so that they feel full on much less food; they can even have their gut altered, short-circuiting the process of digestion.

Though I was medically obese, using the definition of weighing more than twenty per cent in excess of one's ideal weight as given in actuarial tables, I was not a candidate for anything so extreme. Most private practice doctors who specialise in slimming now treat patients like me with the tried and true method of a rigorous diet combined with an amphetamine drug, to suppress appetite and induce a feeling of well-being, along with a diuretic, a 'water pill', which, of course, leads to instant, observable weight loss. Both these drugs are not good for you, and the resulting weight loss is almost never permanent. Still, we all know people who go regularly, once a year or more, to the Harley Street equivalent of a slimmer's Dr Feelgood, and swear that they are keeping their weight under control by means of injections, despite the cost of treatment, which can range from £40 for three weeks to £350 for six weeks.

So I went along to a doctor, recommended by friends, who treats slimming patients with injections. But with a difference. Phillip Lebon, FRCS, believes passionately in the therapy he administers, and has written several journal articles about it. Mr Lebon, who has pointed out in print that 'obesity is a killing and crippling disease' and then gone on to criticise his profession because 'medical schools teach nothing about obesity as a disease in itself', uses 'Simeons' programme' for the treatment of obesity.

This was first described by A. T. W. Simeons in a *Lancet* article in 1954. It consists of injecting patients daily with small doses of human chorionic gonadotrophin (HCG), a hormone derived from the urine of pregnant women. This, it is claimed, enables patients to stick to a remarkably low 500 calorie, high protein, no fat diet, such as would normally require a stay in hospital, and still do a full day's work.

I had only four days free before the deadline for writing this piece in which to undertake Mr Lebon's treatment; but he sportingly agreed to let me give his therapy a not very fair four-day trial, provided it was not medically inadvisable. He took a very thorough history the day I saw him, and asked to be sent the latest results of my glucose tolerance, urea and free fatty acids tests. My GP and 'my psychiatrist' obliged, and the results delighted and thrilled me. I had already lost about twelve pounds. All the test results had retreated to within the boundaries of normality. I was no longer an unhealthy wreck, but a suitable case for treatment.

It was a challenge to stick to Mr Lebon's diet, but I did it. My culinary ingenuity was taxed to the full sometimes to find three ounces of a protein without any fat, suitable for eating, without cooking, at my desk. The first injection was a double, 250 i.u. On day two I was so weak I could scarcely sit up in the taxi taking me to get my injection; but on having it I perked up immediately and did a full day's work thereafter. On days three and four I felt high, and occasionally was sure I was speeding. The fourth injection was another double.

The results were disappointing – I only lost two pounds. Still, it was by no means a fair test; at least I did not *gain* weight, and, as at Ragdale Hall, lost another four pounds the next week.

In 1973, Drs Hirsch and Van Itallie, in a letter published in the *American Journal of Clinical Nutrition*, criticised daily HCG injection therapy (and a study by Drs Asher and Harper supporting it that had been published in that journal earlier in the year): 'We think it is fair to conclude,' wrote the critics, 'that individuals who received more injections may adhere better to a low calorie diet than those who do not, and it makes little difference what the injection is.'

At the moment of writing this, I have lost a little more than a stone. Though I have taken off five inches from my waist measurement and can almost button a jacket made for me in 1967, I am not thin. The psychologist I consulted gave me a set of questionnaires before and after my weight loss, the Repertory Grid test, based on George Kelly's Personal Construct Theory. I was asked to indicate what I thought of my character and bits of my body in several dimensions, and also to indicate what I should like the answers to be.

Following weight loss, my 'actual self is now much more positive in all aspects, particularly on the "pleasant–unpleasant" axis; you also see yourself as stronger and slightly smaller than before. On the "kind–cruel" axis you are willing now to admit to the odd "cruel", perhaps showing that you wish to think of yourself more as a potent person than as a potential saint. You also see yourself as a more "whole" person, in the dimension in which patients with eating disorders see themselves as "damaged".

'Your ideal for yourself is now more openly emotional and more active, less passive. Before losing weight you were ambivalent about whether you wanted to be gentle or tough. You are now totally changed in that dimension, and show a desire to be consistently gentle.'

What is the prognosis for my figure? Alas, it is not good. Most people who lose weight inevitably gain it back. This is in part due to the changes in metabolic rate emphasised by Geoffrey Cannon in his book *Dieting Makes You Fat*. His solution is a life-long regimen of exercise. Unfortunately, all the doctors and researchers to whom I spoke were scathingly dismissive of this approach, which they found logically unsound and even silly.

Exercise may be a good thing in itself. But its uses in slimming are limited. 'On balance', said Dr Nigel Benjamin, Research Registrar at the Obesity Clinic of St George's Hospital, 'as a therapy, exercise causes more problems than it solves' for the more than mildly obese. 'If you exercise, it is very hard not to eat more.' And finding a suitable form of exercise is particularly difficult: 'cycling and swimming are good, but running is just asking for joint problems'.

Dr Mike Stock, the physiologist who along with Nancy Rothwell did pioneering work on brown fat, agreed about the lack of utility of exercise. But his work holds out the future promise of a cure for fatties like me, in the form of the discovery of thermogenic drugs, which alter the metabolic rate without affecting heart or brain functions. O brave new world, that has such pills in it!

The incredible shrinking Levy

Controlling one's weight is the chief difficulty of any professional Foodie's job. I continue to go to the fat farm at least once a year, and ordinarily shed enough avoirdupois to make it possible to return to my real job – eating. I've tried every known method of painless weight loss – hormone injections, acupuncture and hypnotism – and the painful one, dieting plus exercise, as well.

It had been my ambition, since the publication of *Cuisine Minceur* in 1977, to experience the most pleasant and sybaritic means of losing weight. I had a great longing to do a 'cure' at Michel Guérard's Les Prés d'Eugénie at Eugénie-les-Bains. Following a stay there last summer, my resolve strengthened.

So off to Eugénie I went.

Friday 5 October   Arrived late after missing plane. Though too late for normal service of *cuisine minceur*, they made an exception. Drank only water with first meal, which was: 1) tomato soup with *pistou* – delicious; 2) *rouget* grilled *à l'écrevisse* with *sauce Choron*, gâteau of aubergine, courgettes, tomatoes, onions, garlic, basil cooked in steam, with olive oil – very strongly flavoured; 3) compote of apple with apricot.

It is Friday night; the clientèle is dressed up. As a mark of favour, Christine Guérard sat at my table and made conversation. I was flattered.

Saturday 6 October   Slept very soundly. Awoke 7.30, breakfast at 8: a four-minute boiled egg with *minceur* breakfast of pop rice cookie (*galette de riz*), thermal water, coffee (*au lait*). Eager to begin cure proper.

To Dr Revel at 9 a.m. (Every *curiste* has a medical. Eugénie is a registered spa, recognised by the French medical establishment as having therapeutic powers; you can even be sent here on the French 'National Health'.) Problems: digestion, back and neck pain. Weight 79 kilos.

Treatments fabulous and alarming. A cross between Thomas Mann's *Magic Mountain* and an establishment like Iris Murdoch's in *The*

Out to Lunch

Philosopher's Pupil – hot springs, baths, showers, pipes and caverns. Identity is shed by exchanging hotel guest's beige towelling peignoir for *curiste's* pink one. Given a badge of identity: a calibrated glass for the water, plus personal wicker case for the glass.

'Treatment' begins with a fifteen-minute warm bath. Private and luxurious, slightly sulphurous smell. Then the exercise pool with the other *curistes* and an instructor for underwater gymnastics, holding on to bars. Followed by fifteen minutes of underwater massage you control yourself. Wonderful but very tiring.

Then scheduled for twenty minutes of steam. Then a high pressure hosepipe, held by a youngish woman with a good aim. Then *cataplasme* heat pads. Then a penetrating shower that sprays you gently with eight to ten heads while you lie down. Then an older woman stands you in the corner and sprays needle-fine high-pressure jets at you. *Then* you put your legs in a machine that sprays feet, legs, knees, followed by hot mud bath.

Followed by lunch: 1) marinated salmon with tiny slices of fresh ginger and a puddle of *fromage blanc* with chives; a *salade mesclun* and a *galette de riz*; 2) *confit* of duck leg and thigh with *julienne* of carrot, orange peel and green onion in sauce of *ceps* – heaven; 3) banana with fresh strawberries cooked *en papillote*. Fragrant and good. Coffee on terrace. Put in one lump of sweetener, though I don't take sugar.

About *les soins*, Christine Guérard said last night: 'Most of the people taking the cure are French. Our viewpoint is Latin: we do it all for you. Anglo-Saxons like to do it for themselves.'

4 p.m. Went for a walk; looked for wild mushrooms. Saw eight to ten different species. There was a handsome crop of what *looked* like parasols in the back lawn. Then a pot of *tisane d'Eugénie* in the salon, with a log fire blazing.

Dinner: Starving by 7 p.m. Held out till 7.30, but still first in the dining room. Then came three other *curistes*: the single French lady, and the curious couple from next door – late middle-age – he bearded and seemingly amicable. She had stared at me very directly in the *piscine*. Two American ladies are not on a cure despite last night's appearance to the contrary. They pigged it up beautifully. 1) *Soupe des toutes les légumes du marché*. Hearty and good. 2) *Goujonettes de sandre et écrevisses au beurre de cerfeuil*. 3) *Oeufs à la neige, coulis de cassis*. Artificially sweet; could have skipped it. To drink – Badoit. And decaffeinated coffee. Everyone else in jackets and ties and several large parties. Mostly Americans.

Felt I had had a real *bouffe* and could hardly finish. But by 9.30 p.m. thinking of breakfast – hungry again.

Sunday 7 October   Slept extremely soundly. Even more than normally obsessed by food.

Breakfast: not desperate after all. *Café au lait* seems more like food than does tisane. But I put *faux sucre* in. It was so horrid that I drank the rest black.

Last night told the maître d'hôtel that I couldn't possibly follow house rules. There is no *minceur* menu on Sunday (and the baths are all shut). *Curistes* have vegetable bouillon in their rooms. This keeps tables free for serious eaters in the dining room (there are a million cars in the car park now – 2.15 p.m. but complete silence reigns: they are all making their devotions at table), and aids the cure, naturally.

But can't *jeûner* (fast) because of low blood sugar: mustn't swoon in my lovely room. After bouillon, strongly flavoured and full of vegetables, had two pop rice cookies and a salad of avocado slices. Best thing I've ever tasted. NB: Bread is forbidden but I crave toast.

Unfortunately, I've got a backache.

3 p.m. Surprised by a bowl of bouillon. Another follows at 7 p.m. I think the fast is designed to induce ketosis – I am surely already ketotic. (Ketones are excreted when the body is burning its own fat reserves. Though I don't think my breath smells, my urine does a little.)

8.20 p.m. Desperately hoping they'll remember to bring a salad for dinner. Not because I'm hungry but because I'm so *bored*. They didn't.

Monday 8 October   7.30 a.m. Slept beautifully again. Not particularly hungry for breakfast. Definitely ketotic, can smell it on the breath.

Feeling less creaky, but emphatically more out of shape. *Very* conscious can no longer touch toes without bending knees. Resolve (weakly) to do something about it. (Took a short walk.) Weather glorious – much sunning of self sans shirt on balcony. *Booze*. Until today had actually *not noticed* I wasn't drinking. Didn't even think of drink on Saturday or Sunday. But today, envied those who had wine at lunch.

Lunch was quite satisfactory: 1) *Salade d'haricots verts vinaigre de Xérès* – with *batonnets* of raw mushroom in lemon and shallot and tomato *concassé* and chervil. 2) Boned veal chops, grilled, served with salad. Good. 3) Sorbet of strawberries. *Lovely* coffee – better every day.

Treatments are getting interesting. More spraying of jets by older women in white uniforms and younger ones in one-piece bathing costumes. Plus, new today, powerful near-total immersion underwater massage and proper massage on a table under eight shower heads – strange, wonderful.

Purpose seems to be to firm up the flesh and remove cellulite. Staff all swear that the water, even taken externally, reduces fat cells.

Bath and change for dinner – out of tracksuit into jeans. Would *love* to *taste* a gin Martini.

Dinner: 7 p.m. Apéritif, just to try to be a bit social. But the cold tisane was a bit too sweet. In to dinner at 7.30 p.m; out by 8.30 p.m. 1) *Crème* of wild mushroom soup, strong, hearty. 2) *Raie* with cabbage in *vinaigrette* – a vinegary sauce with microscopic bits of tomato *concassé* and truffles – 4 vast slices of truffle, rounds of carrot, savory cabbage. Truffles pointless, except for texture. But someone is taking one's need to eat quite seriously. 3) Apricot tart, fruit seemed fresh, the pastry flaky and deliciously thin. I feel stuffed; *bouffé* and *gonflé*: might just have been the laxative effect of my 4.30 p.m. tisane.

9.15 p.m. It's difficult for those on cure to pass an evening. Should take up billiards. Interesting people in the dining room. Two very rich Indian ladies in western dress and diamonds having *cuisine minceur*. Two boys, film stars at least, are dining. I thought they were English, but they spoke French to each other. One drank water only. The other had G & T and smoked English cigarettes.

Tuesday 9 October　　7 a.m. Upset tummy last night. Woke feeling creaky and in need of limbering up. Which I did. Changed my breakfast: yoghurt and fruit, plus *tisane d'Eugénie* and lemon, instead of an egg. Felt better, but still suffering from a slightly upset tum.

Les soins. Two or three good-looking ladies around. Especially the larger of the Indian ladies. I fancied her. She has begun to enjoy herself and giggles a lot with her companion at lunch. Contrary to my first impressions, the set up here is very un-*Magic Mountain*: there is scarcely any opportunity for the guests to fraternise.

Lunch, a classic: 1) *Gâteau du carotte* – delish. 2) *Aiguillettes de boeuf* – four tiny blue slices of tender beef with three purées and a strong sauce. 3) *Granité de chocolat amer* – wonderful with iced coffee crystals as a garnish.

There was so much sun this a.m. they put out mattresses and parasols. But have headache and smell of thermal waters.

Dinner: 1) *Crème d'artichaut* very delicious. The *fond* so strong though, I imagine the taste of stock cubes – in deference to the rumour. I'll find out when I visit the kitchen. 2) *Pot au feu de mer, sauce persil.* Very simply, pretty easy. 3) *Clafoutis* of apple.

Christine sat with me for a few minutes. She told me my clothes were 'floating' on me, that I'd certainly already lost 2 kilos.

Diuretic effect of the water is very noticeable; so is the laxative effect of something. My wife's phone call found me in the same place as her call the night before. Thank heavens there is a phone in the loo.

Wednesday 10 October   8 a.m. Exhausted, I had slept particularly well.

Breakfast: yoghurt, pear and green grapes with tisane. Some exercise before breakfast had loosened my back. Treatments included a massage. Most enjoyable. Felt better today.

Lunch: 1) *Oeufs en cocotte aux poireaux grandmère*: sensational lightly poached egg with crunchy *julienne* of leek in truffled rich brown sauce. It *did* taste of truffle. 2) *Aiguillette de canard sauce poivrons frais.* Delicious, rare. 3) White peach poached in Sauternes.

The Indian ladies had a flash English-speaking French boy at their table and giggled a lot – until his main course of duck arrived and made them reflective, as it was twenty times bigger than theirs. He was the non-drinker, one of the pair of boys who had dined on Monday.

Dinner: sip an apéritif of *jus de tomate assaisonné* to stretch out the dinner hour. 1) *Soupe aux truffes noirs de Caussade.* Excellent deep-flavoured stock *plus* several large slices of Caussade truffle. 2) *Daurade* steamed on a bed of just cooked veg, with a thin veg purée for sauce. Very clever. 3) Pear poached in red Graves.

Thursday 11 October   Thought I'd got over the nightly diarrhoea. But it struck immediately after I put down the phone.

Exhausted, I slept till eight. A little creaky this a.m., but some limbering up exercises before breakfast did the trick. Breakfast: egg, apple, coffee. Coffee disappointing – tisane tomorrow.

Found myself alone with my pin-up this morning in the steam room, then again the mud bath. Spoke to her and learnt she is from Arabia. Her card says she is 'Princesse J'. A bit shy about being spoken to. Promised her an article about a Paris hospital slimming cure, which I gave her later. Do you suppose her husband wants her to slim? *I* shouldn't. The other woman is her lady-in-waiting and the boy is her 'secretary'.

Out to Lunch

At lunch I asked Christine to get Michel to plan a diet-breaking menu for Friday night. Really more interested in what I am going to drink. Am not at all hungry any more, except just before meals and two to three hours after. But I retain a strong *academic* interest in food.

This solitude and atmosphere, European and de luxe, engenders: 1) punctilio 2) curiosity and 3) introspectiveness. As for 1), it becomes hugely important to be correct: to get to the dining room before the 1 p.m. and 8 p.m. deadlines, to be on time for treatments, to be out of the way when non-*curistes* are eating. 2) *Dying* to know who the other guests are, and what they're having to eat. 3) Every cure induces the desire to reform. How *could* I let myself get this way especially when the remedy seems so easy?

But I also *know*, actually *know*, that if I let myself get out of shape again, I'll either get crippled with back trouble or have a coronary (as everyone in my family always has done). Or both. Trouble is, I *will* relapse, I always do. Perhaps one cure here a year will repair the damage for another whole year.

Lunch: 1) *Salade de prés aux ciboulettes.* 2) *Ris de veau, braisé aux champignons de bois.* Heaven. 3) *Ananas givré au kirsch*, garnished with raspberries. Good.

p.m.: Tour of kitchen, during the service. Didier Oudill, Guérard's chef, is only thirty. Guérard attends to details himself: spots a tiny tart missing from a plate of *petits fours* and replaces it. A small compact kitchen, eighteen cooks, separate *pâtisserie*. A lot of preparation is done in the courtyard.

There are several maîtres d'hôtel. The one I like best – with the most *gravitas* – is Patrick Charbonneau; he lived for years in the States and speaks perfect English.

But there is little occasion to speak at all, still less to speak French; my French is not improving. I spoke *much* more fluently three weeks ago.

Friday 12 October p.m.: Very honoured, after the treatment, to be invited to the Guérards' château which they are restoring brilliantly. They give me a glass of champagne – own label. Naturally it seems the best I've ever tasted; all my senses were concentrated on that one glass. We gossiped about friends in common. Then gulped down my best *minceur* meal: 1) *tarte aux oignons*; 2) *blanquette de veau*; 3) pink grapefruit sorbet.

Then off to Dr Revel to be weighed. He was mortified that I had only gone from 79 to 78 kilos; I'm unperturbed. I weighed 79 kilos at 9 a.m.; this was immediately after lunch, which means another kilo. Also: my tension, blood pressure, had gone from 150/90 to 135/75. Have certainly lost inches around the waist. Skin is clear and glowing, eyes unusually bright. Can bend easily from the waist; lumbar vertebrae crack much less. Knee flexes more than it has for fifteen to twenty years; senses of smell and taste are more accurate.

Dr Revel predicts I'll have lost another kilo by the fourteenth. Who cares? It's been a great success, I look forward to returning.

Dinner: Michel had prepared a wildly special menu for me. Had a *coupe champagne* on the terrace then Château Beauregard 1970, by Raymond Clauzel. Luscious, full, mature. Damn near knocked me out of chair. Spoke to nearly everyone in dining room; fluent in French again. It was bread I wanted most. Wolfed down the *pain grillé*.

Michel Guérard's Menu Surprise: 1) Creamy cabbage soup with *julienne* of truffles and slivers of hot *foie gras* on toast. Less interesting than it sounds, soup lacked guts. 2) Home-smoked salmon wrapped around *langoustine*, garnish of *trois caviares*: black, red, hen's eggs – flavoured with chives and chervil, a good combination, if too elaborate. 3) A plate of small birds: in the middle an ortolan on a canapé of stuffed and herbed jacket potato, surrounded by four tiny fig-peckers with a salad of bacon and cubes of *foie gras*, lettuces, *frisé*. Spectacular. 4). Poached white peach in fresh *verveine* ice cream with *confiture des prunes*. Wow!

Saturday 13 October   Breakfast: ordered the 'gourmand'. All I wanted was *bread*. *Pain grillé*, a tiny crusty bread roll, a brioche, a croissant; no butter, no jam. And I drank my mineral water, though it will very likely have dire consequences during the journey to Bordeaux. Don't feel terribly well. It is not a hangover, but worse. Ironically, a cold.

Dr Revel was right. By the fourteenth I had lost another 3 kilos. I wonder how I can arrange to go back this year – and stay three weeks?

────────

Eating your cake and not having it

At this time of year [January] nearly everyone has some recent experience of over-eating. Most of us are only now repenting of the extra avoirdupois we acquired during the ritual excesses of the Christmas feast.

For some young women, however, Christmas presents a more sinister threat. These women are victims of a double obsession: their weight and food. They eat compulsively and diet with fervour. Every Christmas some of their number, spontaneously made sick by too much turkey and Christmas pudding, discover a means of having their cake and eating it. They have found that they can consume vast quantities of food, but control their weight by vomiting immediately after eating.

They keep quiet about their discovery – nobody shouts from the roof-tops that she regularly sicks up her meals on purpose. But such women tend to think, at first, that they have learned a secret that will make life easier. The knowledge can turn out to be deadly.

Women whose eating habits and preoccupation with their body images lead them experimentally to disposing of their meals in this way are at risk from a 'new' disorder which psychiatrists, who are encountering it with increasing frequency, call bulimia nervosa.

The Times for 10 November 1981 carried a brief story summarising the verdict of a Liverpool coroner that a recently dead twenty-four-year-old fashion model had suffered from bulimia. Surgeons had operated on Pauline Seawards to remove 'three litres of partially digested food from her stomach'.

Obsessed with the need 'to keep her tummy flat', Pauline Seaward's eating behaviour alternated between feast and fast. Her last meal was a binge of grotesque proportions. 'It included two raw cauliflowers, two black puddings, one and a half pounds of raw liver, two pounds of kidneys, a piece of cheese, three pounds of raw carrots, two pounds of peas, a pound of mushrooms, ten peaches, four bananas, two apples, four pears, two pounds of plums, two pounds of grapes and some home-made bread.'

Pauline Seaward died from 'gastro-enteritis caused by intestinal damage due to massive ingestion of food'. Because she had breathing difficulties, an emergency operation failed to save her.

Other deaths have been recorded of women suffering from bulimia. But the more often seen physical ill-effects of the disorder are severe damage to the enamel of the teeth from the acid of the vomitus and bowel damage from laxative abuse by the smaller group of bulimics who purge rather than vomit.

I have deliberately gone into the unsavoury details of this disorder to reinforce the point that, to sufferers from it, bulimia is not funny – despite the ignorant sensationalism with which some headline writers have treated it and the nervous humour some journalists have displayed when writing about it recently.

Actually, the physical effects of bulimia are less painful to its victims than its social consequences. Binges, by their nature, are private affairs. The bulimic, who, says one source, may eat food containing as much as 55,000 calories in an hour or so, then vomit or purge, and repeat the entire cycle several times in one day, suffers silently and by herself. Every aspect of her illness is anti-social, and most bulimics cannot bring themselves to tell anyone else about their habits. It is usual, when a bulimic finally does seek help, for her to tell the doctor that she thought she was the only person on earth who behaved in this fashion.

Reports are coming in from America, according to an article in the *International Herald Tribune* of 29 October 1981, that some studies 'indicate that 15 to 20 per cent of college women occasionally purge after binges'. Reports such as this terrify psychiatrists who deal with the disease, especially since some of them fear that a study of British schoolgirls going on at this moment will result in similar figures. What worries them most is the prospect that there is an element of learnt behaviour – a copy-cat mechanism – in the origins of the disorder, and that bulimia, which many doctors saw for the first time in the '70s, is actually epidemic.

The first reference to it in the medical literature of this country appears to be the 1979 article by Gerald Russell, formerly of the Academic Department of Psychiatry at the Royal Free Hospital. He called his piece 'Bulimia nervosa: an ominous variant of anorexia nervosa'.

But bulimia is not new. The name itself can be found in Liddell and Scott, which cites a reference in Aristotle. It is made up of the particles 'bous' (from the word for ox) meaning something monstrously large, and 'limia', the sort of hunger associated with famine. The OED finds the first instance of it in English in 1389, and cites another use of it, in which it is coupled with anorexia, two hundred years later. The word itself has been around so long that it even has a figurative use (e.g. 'the French king has had . . . such a Bulimy after money').

Doctors are now less certain about the association between the two eating disorders. Anorexia nervosa was seen earlier, and more frequently, in the Sixties. The typical patient is a female in her teens, and the three essential diagnostic criteria are clear ones.

Professor Russell gives them as 'self-induced loss of weight with severe

inanition, persistent amenorrhoea (or an equivalent endocrine disturb-
ance in the male), and a psychopathology characterised by a dread of
losing control of eating and becoming fat'.

While many patients being treated for bulimia do exhibit a history of
anorexia, and have in common with anorexics the determination 'to keep
their weight below a self-imposed threshold', the bulimics 'tended to be
heavier, more active sexually, and more likely to menstruate regularly and
remain fertile. Depressive symptoms,' Russell adds, 'were often severe
and distressing and led to a high risk of suicide.'

The anorexic patient is usually identifiable by her appearance. Not so
the bulimic. In fact, I was told by a psychiatrist at the Royal Free who has
a special interest in the disorder, that his bulimic patients appear to be
better-looking, more self-assured, successful and intelligent than one
would expect a group of women of the same age chosen at random to be.

(There is, of course, another very common eating disorder that involves
compulsive, sometimes incessant, eating, which may or may not alternate
with bouts of dieting or fasting. It is distinguished from bulimia by the
absence of vomiting or purging.)

It was arranged that I should meet one of the bulimic patients being
treated by the team at the Royal Free. (Both doctors and patients welcome
sensible publicity. One of the greatest difficulties is that no one knows the
extent of bulimia in the population as a whole. And from the patient's
point of view, the isolation and solitude from which she has suffered can
only be ameliorated for others by sympathetic publicity.)

Juliet Capulet is twenty-eight, a lecturer in anthropology at a provincial
university, terrifically attractive, and, though not a pound overweight, a
famously good cook. There was a lovely irony in our situation: we were
having lunch in one of my favourite restaurants and Juliet found the food
so light and delicious, she said, that even a near-cured bulimic could eat it
all without guilt feelings. Eating in restaurants – even eating meals with
one's family – is for most bulimics an impossible social ordeal, not
improved by a furtive trip to the loo at the conclusion of the meal.

Juliet told me about her earlier isolation and how her depression
(possibly a separate illness) had increased until it resulted in a suicide
attempt. But the shame and unease engendered by bulimia is so great – the
sufferer from it feels so repulsive – that Juliet could not bring herself to
mention it even to friends who knew of her depression and suicide
attempt.

Gastronomic bulimics such as Juliet are rare, but in most other respects she presents a typical profile. It is a disorder that attacks the daughters of the well-off middle classes. Juliet learned her cookery skills as an *au pair* in Switzerland; her bulimia started when she was at Cambridge. She had always worried about her appearance – she is very small, and an extra pound or two makes itself felt very quickly on her petite frame – and at Cambridge she began to fear that she was not attractive to men. This was in spite of the fact (true to type for bulimics) that she had had a happy and satisfying undergraduate romance quite early on in her career.

She also had a lot of girl friends, and gave very popular dinner parties. But while she gave every outward appearance of success, Juliet was bingeing and vomiting so frequently that she has had to have all her teeth capped. Even a close observer could hardy have guessed that anything was wrong – except that Juliet failed to get the first her tutors had predicted for her.

Later, in London, Juliet led a life of increasing dietary chaos (a telling synonym for bulimia used by some American sources). Most bulimics do not care very much what they eat when they binge. Carbohydrates, and foods considered 'fattening' and therefore forbidden, are most popular. But Juliet was more particular: she told me that she had visited as many as four Chinese restaurants a day, when in the grip of her illness, and eaten a complete meal in each one.

After the suicide attempt, Juliet was treated at the Royal Free for depression. And eventually she came to the attention of Dr Adrian Yonace and Miss Alex Macleod. Dr Yonace is studying the question of whether bulimia is a depressive illness – his research is not yet concluded – and Miss Macleod, a psychologist, specialises in behavioural therapy. The Royal Free has long been noted for its interest in eating disorders (an interest shared at the Maudsley, St George's and Oxford's Warneford Hospital) and the Professor of Psychiatry of the Royal Free's School of Medicine, Anthony Wakeling, is noted for his expertise in this field.

Juliet joined the out-patient group run jointly by Dr Yonace and Miss Macleod, and found, as many patients do, that merely *knowing* there were other sufferers was the greatest help and incentive to get better. In the group, Juliet learned how to eat all over again.

This may sound a ridiculous enterprise for a group of attractive, successful young women. But someone who has suffered from bulimia for a long time may genuinely not know any longer how normal people eat, or what a normal meal consists of. So Alex Macleod gets her patients to keep a food diary in which they log every morsel that goes into their mouths. This works a treat. Who, after all, could bear to re-read a menu such as the one that Pauline Seaward ate at her last supper?

All Miss Macleod's efforts are directed at altering the patient's behaviour; and in many cases, this works wonders. Of course it rather side-steps the issue of the origins of the illness, and whether it stems from some other psychiatric problem, and whether *that* problem ought to be treated. But the facilities of the Health Service are already stretched to the utmost: it is hard to find time to consider the question of the psychogenesis of an illness that may prove so widespread. Juliet feels the need of some psychotherapy. But at the moment, so little is really known about bulimia that it's difficult to see how a therapist would set out to treat her.

The diagnostic criteria for bulimia are: 1) a constant preoccupation with losing weight; 2) incessant dieting; 3) uncontrollable urges to eat followed by vomiting or purging. Implicit in these criteria is the notion of a 'healthy weight'. Juliet told me that she felt that there was sometimes a small measure of disagreement between the therapist and the patient as to what constitutes the healthy weight. She felt that treatment would perhaps be made easier if the therapist would be more willing to accept the patient's view of her own ideal weight, which is usually lighter than the therapist's sometimes robust vision of the patient.

Of course, we know where at least some of the blame lies. It is the fault of the emphasis our society puts on slimness as an element of sexual attractiveness. One villain is the 'slimming industry', which has exploited the consumer society's destructive urge to diet.

In this connection, the organisers of competitions such as 'Young Slimmer of the Year 1981', the disgraceful, but pathetically funny proceedings of which I attended last September, have much to answer for. Girls as young as eighteen were encouraged to acquire the obsession that enriches the publishers of magazines devoted to slimming aids. The occasion itself acquired pathos because most of the finalists appeared – to me – still to be plump.

It may be that this obsession with slimness is the reason why both anorexia and bulimia nervosa are principally disorders found in the female half of the population. Of course, chaps are concerned about their weight, and have even been known to be vain about their appearance: I wrote this piece at Forest Mere health farm. But, in some totally unscientific way, we all seem to *know* (or at least feel) that a man's sexual being is not so closely related to his *shape* as is a woman's.

No one actually knows whether the incidence of bulimia among males is statistically significant (though more than one bulimic male has been seen at the Royal Free). This is part of a more general problem, touched upon earlier: the extent of the disorder in the population as a whole is not known. As a result it is not yet possible to assess the most efficient or efficacious way of treating bulimic patients.

Note: Following the original publication of this article on 17 January 1982, hundreds of sufferers wrote to the researchers named in the piece, which allowed them to do valuable statistical studies. Several self-help groups for bulimics were set up as a result.

FOREIGN AFFAIRS

China syndrome

Some people want their dream hotel to be as like home as possible; others demand of a perfect hostelry that it be as unlike their home as anything in this world can be. Until I awoke one May morning in a dingy hotel room in Canton, racked with excruciating pain, I had no idea at all what I should require of my dream hotel. The three doctors who were among the members of the group I was leading on a gastronomic tour of China diagnosed kidney stones, pooled their analgesic tablets and managed to bundle me on to the Hong Kong express.

The tablets worked. I alit from the train in a distinctly good state of mind, and was still euphoric when I saw again the front door of the Peninsula Hotel. One enters via the drive in which is stationed the hotel's fleet of Rollers – green Silver Shadow IIs – and passes the pair of door gods, the traditional Tang dynasty protection against evil spirits, before approaching the reception desk, with its small private army of formally dressed attendants.

'I'm afraid I need a doctor,' I said feebly to a six-foot-two, square-jawed Chinese. Resplendent in his black jacket and striped trousers, his own appearance simply mirrored the gilt and marble magnificence of the Peninsula's lobby. I was perfectly – acutely – aware of the bathos of my situation.

Still, I thought I must be mis-hearing. He seemed to be saying: 'Take the lift to the lower ground floor and turn left.' 'No,' I replied, 'I'm so sorry for not making myself clear. It's a doctor I need.' 'Yes,' smiled the Oriental Apollo, 'the clinic is on the lower ground floor. And when you are finished with the doctor, Mr Levy, your bags will be in room 902.' Funny, I'm certain I didn't give him my name.

The clinic had an X-ray machine, a dispensary, Chinese receptionists and nurses, and at least one Scottish doctor. In the course of the next few days I only had to leave 902 once, for a slightly complicated X-ray.

That's how I discovered what I required for my dream hotel. In a pethedine-induced stupor, I sat or lay in the L-shaped mini-suite, looking at the view of the harbour from my windows, or at near first-run movies on the hotel video. When I was hungry (almost never), room service appeared with a tray. I thought I fancied the Chinese menu more than the Western one; but I discovered that, in spite of the popularity of the

73

Chinese take-away and the dizzying speed of the Peninsula's room
service, the stir-fries never really travelled well.

The club sandwiches were delicious, though, and the mini-bar well-
stocked. But both these were irrelevancies to a man with renal colic. The
real wonder of the telephone, so far as I was concerned, was that it could
be used, any time, day or night, to produce a Chinese male nurse with a
syringe of ease-conferring medicine. Day followed agreeable day, as I
waited for my wife and the rest of my party to return from Taiwan to
catch our Gatwick-bound Apex flight.

Between injections I carried on the normal life of a tourist in Hong
Kong. I shopped. But I discovered the bonus of being a guest at the
Peninsula – I was able to shop from my bed. I remember that Mee Yee
even agreed to bring a bag full of swatches round, so I could choose some
new shirts. He even had them ready for my departure. (I must, though,
have had a fairly druggy time that day; I was slightly surprised to find that
I had ordered six shirts, of which three were red or pink.) And I had a pair
or two of spectacles run up by Victoria Optical, who have a shop in the
hotel.

Two or three times a day I removed my nightshirt (I had two with me,
and the laundry saw to it that there was a clean one for me each morning),
climbed into the oversized black marble bath, and had a good scrub with
the Lanvin, Dior or Givenchy soap that is the management's gift to every
guest.

Then perhaps just a sliver of the mango or snow pear from the bowl of
fruit that comes at the same time as the soap. I don't think I felt much like
drinking the champagne in the discreetly hidden mini-bar. Though I knew
perfectly well that the insurance would pay for that, just as they were jolly
well going to pay for the extra days in the room and the room service I
would have used with reckless abandon if only I'd felt like eating. (The
price of French wine in Hong Kong makes it a *wicked* extravagance, even
for a self-indulgent valetudinarian. The claim made by a famous cookery
writer in another magazine in autumn, 1983, that French drink is
particularly good value in the Crown Colony, must have been intended to
be provocative, like those competition cod-guidebook entries of the
order: 'Visitors to London should always go to the head of the bus or
ticket queue, lest they give offence to the natives' sense of hospitality.')

The Peninsula boasts that it will try to do or supply anything a guest
wants or needs. The 'floor boys', who are in reality extremely dignified
and often venerable Chinese men, routinely unpack and pack for the

guests, clean and polish their shoes, replace broken luggage straps, and lend them bathroom scales and hair driers.

Even so, I think I stretched the system just a little when I told them I wanted to make my will. In the event, I supplied my own solicitor (another member of my group – one who had chosen not to go to Taiwan); but I feel sure they could have dealt with that problem too. Urs Aeby, the genial Swiss General Manager, graduate of Lausanne's famous hotel management school, veteran of the George V's kitchens as well as those of three Swiss establishments, headwaiter at a couple of smart addresses in Bermuda, sometime manager of the Repulse Bay Hotel, the Empress Hotel and a couple of others in Hong Kong and Penang, lent me his secretary, Katie. Katie took it in her stride – she obviously does a couple of last wills and testaments every morning before breakfast, and sends copies of them off to the executors and trustees by lunch. It was quite complicated, arranging to leave property in America to an infant in England, in a document drawn up in Kowloon. But not in Katie's book. The first draft was letter-perfect. There was no charge and Katie, who was patently the Hong Kong equivalent of a Sloane Ranger, was certainly not going to accept a tip. I sent her some flowers.

When I left the Peninsula after this visit, it was in one of the Rolls. The driver had arranged for a wheelchair at the airport *and* for a hotel employee to wheel me on to the plane. I had my last injection at Bahrain, and left Gatwick on a baggage trolley. I've never had such a comfortable journey.

That was my second stay at the Peninsula. I've been there again since (though room 902 and the clinic have reverted to being the flats they formerly were and seem to have disappeared utterly) and shall go again as often as I can. I used to take the *Observer* tour group there for at least one night, to wash off the dust of China and to experience the sort of cultural shock that highlights just how much work it still is to travel in China.

Oddly enough, the Chinese have built what ought to be a mainland analogue to the Peninsula near Peking. It has been written about often, and I went there in May, 1983, to check it out. The Fragrant Hills Hotel, one and a half hours' drive from Peking, had been open twenty-three days when I arrived. The staff of its Chinese-American architect, I. M. Pei, had departed, leaving behind a purely Chinese management and staff. None of them was yet fully trained. The delightful manager of the extremely up-market souvenir shop (it sold antique theatrical costumes and old cloisonné beads in contrast to the more usual offerings of Chinese hotel shops) spoke some English and became my guide.

Fragrant Hills Hotel – Xiangshan in Chinese – certainly ought to have fulfilled my fantasies of the ideal hotel. Ieoh Ming Pei, the architect, away from China for forty years, was determined to make a permanent architectural contribution, to set an example which, God knows, Chinese planners need desperately. He started by getting records of all the trees growing on the site, and allowed them to dictate the shape of the building plot, and thus of the hotel itself – a sort of dendronic *feng shui*.

The overall design is that of a *siheyuan*, a compound with houses around a courtyard, a typical structure of northern China. The lobby, a particularly splendid open three-storey space with a glass roof, is called *yixiangting*, 'overflowing fragrance hall'. The trouble is that, less than a month after the official opening, its white terrazzo floor was already scuffed and stained where the pot plants drain directly on to it. The management did not seem to realise that the floor was meant to be white and polished.

After abandoning me for some minutes in the lobby, an assistant manager joined my shopkeeper interpreter and I was shown to room 371, with its wonderful view of the lake and water-maze. It was spacious and seemed worth every *yuan* of the £46 a night it cost me.

That turned out to be a superficial impression. There was no hot water or tea (and thus nothing to drink, as no one ever drinks tap water anywhere in China), no tissues in the built-in tissue holder, no writing paper, an empty basket beside the sink (I later learnt that it was put there to hold shower bonnets and other bath paraphernalia) and, more seriously, no hotel telephone directory and no dining-room schedule.

On the way up, I had noticed that poor Mr Pei's specially ordered stone-coloured carpet had already worn out on the stair treads. (I later discovered that the management did not know there is a difference between domestic and commercial grades of carpet, and had naturally ordered the less expensive of the two.) The bedroom carpet was pilled, scruffy, had loose threads and was dirty. A panel hiding the air-conditioning works was smudged with thumb-prints. The drawers were badly made and the formica veneer was already peeling off the tops of the units.

A very friendly room-boy, dying to practise his little English, brought everything rapidly, though he was surprised to think anyone could need *both* tissue and writing paper. Among his offerings were the first tea bags I ever saw in China.

The view from room 371 I found almost moving; but it was marred by the streaks on the huge picture window; and the casement of the cleverly double-glazed side windows (which open on diamond-shaped screened lattices that let you feel the breeze and hear the artificial waterfall) was chipped and scarred. Everything is in severe good taste, and this is revolutionary in China. But it's heartbreaking. Twenty-three days after the official opening, the entire hotel was shoddy and beginning to disintegrate. It would soon reach the state of the horrid Qianmen Hotel that I had just left behind me in Peking itself.

It is easy to explain why this should be. The management and staff have been recruited locally, from peasant families. They are, quite simply, non-urban people. They have, mostly, never *seen* carpets before – of course they don't know how to care for them. They genuinely don't know how to recognise dirt and disrepair.

Things began to look up when at lunch in the *à la carte* dining room (they do not serve lunch in the coffee shop – they serve coffee in the coffee shop) I had the best fish I've ever tasted. 'Suzhou fish in vinegar and pepper' was one half of a silver carp, scored in a diamond pattern, floating in rich stock, perfumed with coriander, and peppery enough to bring one out in a light sweat. It made me feel tipsy, though I drank only *laoshan*, mineral water.

In the evening a transformation took place, and I began to feel that perhaps this was a dream hotel after all. The other guests began to trickle into the bar about six, and I had the electric feeling of being where the action is. Whereas the bar had been occupied earlier by Chinese cadres, party members being shown around or just having an outing, it now began to fill up with the sort of Europeans who populate the movies of Josef von Sternberg.

A Greek talking to a Gitane-smoking Turk or Bulgarian sat at a table next to a youngish German, who drank gin and tonic and spoke into a tiny recording machine, which he switched on and off after each clause, and before and after the final verb. A French table of four also drank G & T. An overseas Chinese couple, terribly sexy and wearing contrasting primary colour T-shirts, took each other's photographs in front of Pei's pool.

Suddenly it was dinner time, and the entire hotel filled up with Americans, on extremely expensive package tours. In the dining-room three stunningly drunk American kids asked me to join them. They were students on an exchange and they hated the food. One of them said he had chronic diarrhoea and I gave him enough Imodium to cure him.

Back in the lobby the canned music played Schubert and 'Santa Lucia' indiscriminately, and I talked to an Englishman called Ron who sells sophisticated X-ray equipment to the Chinese. The bar began to hum as a dozen Japanese businessmen ordered drinks. Another dozen American kids joined my three and stood around the pool drinking beer. An Egyptian couple did a loud business deal with an American young woman whom they had just met, and insisted she write down the address they gave her in Cairo.

I don't think I. M. Pei intended his Fragrant Springs Hotel as a backdrop to a Thirties film of international intrigue, but it fills the role brilliantly. As I re-read the journal I kept during my stay there, I feel that *it*, not the hotel, was almost a dream. If the hotel is still standing in two or three years' time, I should like to return – perhaps via the Trans-Siberian railway.

Lotus eaters

The smell of China is impossible to forget, but difficult to recapture. It is utterly unlike the pervasive disinfectant odour of the Soviet Union. To Western nostrils it is not altogether pleasant, connected though it is with memories of delicious meals and the sensations of tasting exotic things for the first time.

The pungent deep scent of sesame oil is the most easily identifiable part of the Chinese smell, but it has many other components – the related one of pickled vegetables, the spicy aromas of ginger and garlic, a whiff of fish, the dull, stale pong of re-used cooking oil and the unmistakable undertone of vegetable decay.

Everywhere in China where food is served or sold the smell is present, even in the air-conditioned dining rooms in which foreign guests are segregated in hotels and restaurants; in private houses; and in open-air markets with their huge heaps of yard-long beans, mounds of watermelons or whatever has been harvested the day before. The streets themselves are redolent of the cooking smells produced by the ubiquitous street vendors of food and by the People's Restaurants that, in summer, have no shop front, but give directly on to the street.

Though the smell is not entirely hungry-making, the traveller to China feels nostalgic about it almost as soon as he leaves. It can be re-experienced in Chinese markets and food shops in the West, but, curiously, not in Chinese restaurants. It is an odour that sets China apart from everywhere else in the world. It either gets up your nose or into your blood; merely trying to recall it or analyse its composition makes you pine to return.

I first went to China in 1980 on a semi-official tour with a group of American nutritionists, whose brains the few Chinese nutritionists who survived the Cultural Revolution hoped to pick. My own purpose in going was not only to 'eat Chinese', but to see the Chinese eat.

I did not feel a total fraud for masquerading as a nutritionist, as I was genuinely interested in learning what and how the Chinese eat. This did not prove easy to accomplish. But it led to moments of rich comedy, as when an elderly lady in our party, whose life is devoted to promoting 'alternative proteins', learnt with bewilderment and disbelief that, in Peking at least, bean curd (*tou fu*) is not universally or even commonly eaten.

We learnt this fact during a visit to the School of Public Health of Peking Medical College, from the director. A distinguished and cultivated woman in her sixties, she had acquired her fluent English before the revolution, and, beneath her professional white coat, she wore the traditional female dress of the north, matching coloured blouse and trousers.

Obviously as embarrassed as we were astonished, she told us that bean curd, at least in some regions, was rationed. In the hour that followed, a lot of our cherished ideas about what the Chinese eat bit the dust.

Take monosodium glutamate (MSG), for example. I, and all the other members of our party, believe passionately that MSG (*ve-tsin*) is nasty and bad for you. We hoped to find that the vicious powder was not used in Chinese cookery – or at least not in the north.

But, said the director of the public health programme, 'when added to vegetable soup it imparts something extra to the flavour. I use it myself in everything.' Every Chinese in the crowded room nodded or murmured agreement. At first they appeared stunned by the claim that Westerners experience evil reactions to MSG – the well-documented 'Chinese restaurant syndrome'. On recovering, the director proposed that there are 'impurities in American MSG that cause the problems', or that Chinese restaurants in the West use it in too great a concentration.

Thus she, with all her colleagues assenting, gave further currency to the idea, which I'm sure is wrong, that MSG is 'merely a flavour enhancer'. Our presence was a great event for them. They were polite, even deferential. But they obviously thought the entire discussion silly.

The room was hot and sticky despite several large electric fans. We supplemented them by our own fans, thoughtfully provided on their first jumbo jet by Air China. We drank not very good tea from lidded mugs that were topped up regularly from pastel-coloured thermos jugs, and we heard more that was disagreeable to us. It was as though our Chinese hosts had to *force* us to listen to the truth, the telling of which seemed to give them exquisite pain.

This table, which they drew up for us on the chalk board, shows the composition of the Northern Chinese diet, as compared to the typical American diet, in percentage by weight:

	N. China	US
Cereals and beans	65	25
Veg. and fruit	27	20
Fats and sugar	1	14
Meat and fish	4	18
Eggs	1	5
Milk and cheese	0	15
Other foods	2	3

(*Most adult Chinese have lactose intolerance and cannot digest milk. There are practically no cattle, and therefore no cheese or other dairy produce, in China.*)

Two problems are obvious: there is not enough high-grade protein and there appears to be a calcium deficiency. 'Aha,' said out alternative protein lady, 'those are both catered for by bean curd, which doesn't appear in the table.' That was how we came to learn about food rationing.

The director seemed to me actually to squirm with embarrassment as she told us, in a choked voice, that the bean curd ration in the Peking region is half a catty (1 catty = 500 grams, just over 1lb) per month, though elsewhere it was a whole catty. Sugar – two catties a month; edible oils – half a catty. Rice and wheat flour are rationed too.

Rationing is also used as an instrument of social policy. For example, as a negative inducement to restrict families to the one child per couple that the State strongly urges, the rice ration is not increased proportionately if there is more than one child in a family. And the price per catty of meat increases with quantity bought.

In fact all rationed foods, though in short supply, are freely available at higher prices without restriction; rationing is a device to distribute them fairly at a low price.

Nutrition is an infant science in China. It was not encouraged during the Cultural Revolution, and the Chinese are, quite rightly, more concerned with the distribution of food than with its nutritional properties.

Before our eighteen days in China were up, we were to learn many more disillusioning and unpleasant things about Chinese food and eating habits. We all know that the Chinese eat more fresh fruit and vegetables than even Americans do. But, in hotel kitchens all over the land, we saw tins being opened – sometimes they even contained foods that we had seen on offer in the markets that same day; and in dining-rooms and restaurants we were served not only canned button mushrooms as a substitute for the delicate straw mushrooms (which were available fresh in Hong Kong) but tinned bean sprouts.

Everybody 'knows' that one reason the Chinese diet is so healthy is that it is low in fats and sugars, as the table shows. But unhealthy lard, as opposed to vegetable oils, is not rationed, and its use is increasing. Everywhere in China we saw dense crowds whose size it is impossible to describe, consisting of grown-ups as well as children, sucking on ice lollies. Their flavour varied from region to region, encompassing both ersatz chocolate and synthetic vanilla, but everywhere they had in common their sticky, sickly sweetness. More than once we were given iced drinks made by shoving an ice lolly into an already revoltingly sweet glass of plum juice or tea. At every public place and on every street buns, sweet 'moon cakes' and candies are sold.

At the conclusion of banquets and restaurant meals, we were routinely given a choc ice. So much for the idea promoted by Chinese cookery books published in the West that the Chinese don't have much of a sweet tooth.

We travelled more or less from north to south from Peking to Nanking (one of the five 'furnaces' of China, and appropriately hot), then a slight north and east deviation to the small city of Chenkiang, also on the Yangtze River. The Yangtze is the north-south culinary divide of China, but we were not in a position to notice great differences (except for Peking), because our route lay along the river itself. Next we went to Soochow, the city of canals, gardens and famously pretty girls. Then we went to the great sophisticated metropolis of Shanghai, at the mouth of the river. We flew to Canton, our final destination in China, and left at Hong Kong. (I have called these cities by their pre-Pinyin names because

English-speaking Chinese use the older names themselves. For those whose maps are too up-to-date to follow my itinerary, the new names are Beijing, Nanjing, Zhejiang, Suzhou, Shanghai – unchanged – and Guangzhou.)

Northerners and southerners profess to loathe each other's cuisines. The distinction between them is no longer the simple difference that the first is a wheat-eating culture and the latter a rice culture, for in modern China both rice and wheat flour are used everywhere.

As you go south in China the reliance on sugar as an ingredient of savoury dishes increases (though the unappealing sweet-and-sour sauce is universal) and, oddly enough, the use of chillies decreases. But the real culinary rift goes deeper. The scurrilous old *Punch* doggerel: 'With . . . their diet of rats, dogs, slugs, and snails,/All seems to be game in the frying pan/Of that nasty eater, John Chinaman' unpleasantly reflects the northern Chinese's view of the eating habits of his southern compatriots. At the Guanfeng Canting restaurant in Peking, the menu features what the Pekinese think of as typical Cantonese dishes, snake and dog.

Chinese food is inextricably mixed up with folk medicine; every foodstuff is thought to have a medicinal aspect, and almost every living thing is regarded as potential food. Thus southerners certainly do eat dog meat, and find that of black dogs particularly tasty. Eating dog, says Frederick W. Mote (in *Chang, Food in Chinese Culture*, Yale), is thought to confer upon the eater 'the quality of hot-blooded animal energy'.

France, the only other nation with a gastronomic civilisation as advanced as China's, gave up eating her citizens' pet animals after 1870. Dogs are, very sensibly, banned in China's urban areas.

The relationship between food and medicine was brought home to us most forcefully when one of my travelling companions, a teetotaller, bought himself a bottle of tonic, whose action was 'promoting the brain and recovering memory', and one of whose indications for use was 'overburdens of the brain'. After he had tasted his tonic, with a grimace that showed it was doing him some good, I found a table of ingredients on the bottom of the carton: 'Penis Cervi 5 per cent, Penis Otariae 1 per cent, Penis Canitis 1 per cent, Radix Ginseng 7 per cent, Cornn Cervi Pantotrichum 5 per cent, Radix Astragali 10 per cent, Radix Angelicae Sinensis 6 per cent, Other ingredients 65 per cent.' It was not necessary to read either Latin or English to be able to tell from the taste and smell that the last category of this health-giving tonic, the fabled three-penis wine, manufactured by the China National Native Produce and Animal By-products Import and Export Corporation, Shantung Branch, was alcohol.

The Chinese not only eat every*thing*, they eat every*where*: at market stalls that sell slices of melon or bowls of herbal tea; at the snack bar at the Great Wall of China that sells blissful *chiao-tzu*, steamed and pan-fried crescents of dough filled with minced pork and ginger, very cheaply, but also sells Coke and Fanta for a fortune to American tourists; at the railway food kiosk, where there are salted watermelon seeds, and a dozen varieties of sweets, but nothing to sustain the body on a long journey.

Even so, it is not so simple to see the Chinese eating. Tourism has bred a race of camera-toting snoopers, who stick their lenses into everything, eating places not excepted. This is clearly one of the reasons for segregation in restaurants, which are mainly patronised by the locals.

I hope they got to eat the same food we were served, for some of it was superb. Most of the restaurants were closed during the Cultural Revolution, and the chefs sent to work in the countryside. Many of them have now been called back from retirement to train the brigades of new chefs needed to cope with the tourist invasion.

Of course, very few Chinese eat the sort of diet given to tourists. The Chinese word for food, which also means 'a meal', is *fan* (rice – though it also applies to other grains, such as sorghum and millet, and to wheat products). Cooked foods, whether of animal or vegetable origin, are called *ts'ai*, and their purpose is simply to help the *fan* slip down. The *fan* is the real food, the *ts'ai* merely a necessary accompaniment. Children are praised for the numbers of bowls of *fan* they can eat, and the less *ts'ai* the better.

At Nanking I inadvertently interrupted a group of workers having their evening meal. Earlier in the day we had been moved from one hotel building to another; about 5 p.m. I returned from building five to retrieve the bottle of Wild Turkey I had left behind in building eight. The service room was crowded with small, slender young men and women, all wearing white shirts and blouses, standard-issue electric-blue trousers, and black cloth slippers with red rubber soles. In sign language they attempted to get me to take a seat.

Each had a rectangular metal case, like a giant soap dish, full of imperfectly polished boiled white rice. (We had seen these metal boxes in the department stores and wondered what they were. And thank heavens the rice was not so well polished as what we were getting, or they would have had a constipating shortage of roughage, and a B-vitamin deficiency to boot.) Each portion of *fan* had three to four teaspoons of *ts'ai*, just enough to help the rice down, and no more.

Every diner also had a mug of thin soup, and there was the ubiquitous thermos of hot water for making tea. Everything I saw and heard in China confirmed that this was an average evening meal.

By coincidence our tour leader, Jackie Newman, who teaches courses in Chinese food habits at Queen's College, New York, had gone wandering about the streets that led to the entrance of our hotel, which was some distance from the centre of Nanking. There she saw, at about 6.30 in the evening, the pavements, such as they were, lined with family groups having their dinners al fresco. To escape the heat, it was the universal practice to set up table and chairs on the streets.

Jackie saw one family that had five serving dishes on the table. One of them was a great delicacy, Nanking Lake crabs. Jackie is not shy. The family beckoned to her to join them at table. Curiosity and freshwater crabs were sufficient to persuade her to accept the invitation. 'The woman of the family,' Jackie said, 'wore an arm-band indicating that she was a block captain. Their food seemed *ten* times better than what the rest of the people on that block were eating, much more like our food at the hotel than like the peasant food being eaten by the others.'

Jackie Newman knows more about food in China than anyone I have spoken to or read. Her sad conclusion was that the block leader and her family are members of a privileged group, in consequence of which they enjoy food that is almost extravagantly better than that eaten by the average Chinese family.

Manners and scrutability

The Chinese are a strikingly lean people, many of them as slim as our Peking guide, the diminutive, boyishly charming Mr Wen, who told us, to his own huge amusement, that his friends call him 'Little Wen'. His new leather belt went around his waist one and one-half times.

In perfect English he told our newly arrived coach-load of mostly American nutritionists that the knots of people gathered under every street lamp at regular intervals along the main road to Peking were 'playing Chinese chess'.

Perhaps they were. But it was my first introduction to Chinese scrutability. The sweetly open expression on Little Wen's face as he explained away the presence of hundreds, perhaps thousands of people on this swelteringly hot night showed that he did not mean to deny that the people on the road were escaping the heat of their (then) invisible hovels, where they cook and sleep in the same room. Nor did he mean us to overlook the fact that the crowd was taking advantage of the free electricity provided by the State to light the way from the airport.

Maybe this helps to show why everything you've ever been told about China is probably wrong, though it may well once have been true – or partly true – in one single city or region.

This law is of particular importance if one is trying to understand Chinese food and eating habits. In Peking I was laughed at for enquiring about factory canteens and communal dining facilities. Mr Wang, our helpful 'national' (as opposed to Mr Wen, our 'local') guide told me, in a tone of voice that managed to convey his unmalicious hilarity at my ignorance, that most Chinese took most of their meals at home. But in Canton I was told, with equal amusement at my innocence, that most factories had workers' canteens and that it was the exceptional commune (such as the one I saw, the Evergreen Commune, near Soochow) that did not have a communal dining-room. Though it can be difficult to observe the Chinese eating, our tour leaders, Jackie and Leonard Newman, were returning to China for a second visit, so well endowed with names and addresses that they were twice invited to dine in Chinese homes.

I had reason to be grateful for their second invitation, as it forced the cancellation of our visit to Canton's infamous snake restaurant, where the front window is filled with writhing serpents. You choose your viper, and the waiter brings it to the table, dispatches and skins it in front of you, then removes it to the kitchen, usually to be simmered in chicken broth.

The Newmans' first meal in a Chinese home was at Shanghai, where, they told me, their hosts' factory had brought them a new dinner service on which to serve their guests – Americans are very popular in China just now – and supplied electric fans to cool them. The factory may also have contributed some money, for there appeared to be 200 US dollars' worth of food on the groaning table. The excellent dinner consisted of fifteen courses, all cooked under the most primitive conditions. In Canton the food was less good, but there the cooking was done by enthusiastic young people entirely on two wood fires, with no running water and no sanitation facilities.

This bears out what Mr Wang told me one day during a long coach ride. Again amused by my innocence, he said that of course he and his student friends entertain one another to dinner parties. In fact, the form for his age group – early twenties – is to do both the shopping and the cooking co-operatively. The food, good by Wang's account, is consumed with a lot of beer and accompanied by singing.

Also I have seen both urban and rural private kitchens, and can confirm the Newmans' reports of primitive conditions. At the commune near Suzhou, all cooking was done on a single-burner charcoal stove; and, as was the case in the Shanghai apartment I saw, there was no refrigeration or hot water supply.

With the exception of hotels catering to foreign guests, where Western standards apply, Chinese kitchen and food hygiene is not impressive. Yet China has never had 'national epidemics such as the Black Death of western European medieval history', Frederick W. Mote in *Chang* says. This owes less to chance than to cultural preferences: since ancient times the Chinese have boiled all drinking water and cooked all food, excepting only fruit, pickles and preserved food.

The thermos jug of boiled water is an important furnishing of every hotel room in China.

The Chinese are at one and the same time the most fastidious eaters on earth, insisting that their food be so fresh that fish and poultry is usually bought live, and capable of eating almost anything (except dairy products, which, owing to lactose intolerance, most adults cannot digest). Thus the system of food distribution ensures that vegetable produce is harvested by peasants in the afternoon and transported in huge bicycle baskets to the 'wholesaler', who sees that it has reached the urban market by midnight. The market is organised and ready for trading between 3 and 5 a.m. I reckon that most vegetables in China have reached the consumer by about twelve hours after harvesting.

The manner of eating one's family-style meal is of great importance (most meals in Western Chinese restaurants are served family style, except for the usual omission of the cold dishes and incorrect service of the soup at the beginning of the meal). Everyone helps himself with his own chopsticks, moving the food from the serving dishes to his own plate. Rice is ladled into the *fan* bowl. A smaller bowl is used to serve the soup. Food is picked up from one's own plate and transferred to the mouth with the chopsticks. The rice bowl is held in the left hand and kept in constant movement under the chopsticks, so as to prevent your spilling food down your shirt front. It is *rude* to leave your rice bowl on the table, as it shows that you are not interested in your food and not enjoying your meal. Burping, on the other hand is not necessarily rude.

Etiquette requires that the host press food upon his guests, and insist at every course that they cannot possibly have had enough to eat. Moreover, he must himself serve his guests with the best morsels of each dish. Conversely, the good guest constantly demurs, insisting that he has eaten far too much, that he has never seen such a magnificent lot of food on the table all at once, and so on. It follows that the guest should not help himself to the last bit of food on the serving platter, but should allow it to remain there, to show that there is enough food; to take it would imply that he has not had enough.

And finally, food having been accepted, it should be eaten with the appearance of relish. Thus soup is slurped, not sipped from the side of the spoon, so that the guest's enjoyment of it is made audible.

Chillies for breakfast

There is only one trick to getting the most out of your package tour to China: be an early riser. Chinese social life is conducted as it was in the days before there was electricity (of course, in some rural areas, there still isn't any). Up at dawn and to bed with the sun is all too often the maxim upon which the Chinese act.

In Peking the parks and public squares fill up between five and six a.m. with masses of people. They are doing their calisthenics, practising the ancient art of shadow-boxing, playing musical instruments, giving their caged birds an airing or just going for a walk around the block. By eight o'clock there are traffic jams, as there are in any capital city, but the hum of everyday life going on in public places has disappeared and given way to the incessant sound of the car hooter.

The worst aspect of the Chinese early-to-rise syndrome, at least so far as the Western tourist is concerned, is that meal-times are geared to this schedule. Even in restaurants.

Breakfast at seven is normal and six a.m. is not out of the ordinary. It's worth getting up for. And for heaven's sake, insist on *Chinese* breakfast. There are always a number of non-experimenters on every tour and, for some reason that I cannot comprehend, they all draw the line of culinary daring at breakfast.

It's the meal most unlike our own, and I find it perfectly delicious. To start with, the Chinese consume virtually no dairy produce. So there's no butter for the soggy toast, and no milk for the decaffeinated coffee. Or rather, the butter and milk that are offered ought to be treated with the greatest suspicion. The toughened, dried-out egg mixture and the squishy steamed 'cake' that are invariably given to the masochists who ask for Western breakfast are what they deserve for their lack of imagination.

They could, after all, be eating what the Chinese eat: rice gruel, called *congee*, watery, unsalted and bland. Horrid by itself, but don't worry, it is intended as a vehicle for bits of spicy pickle, smoked fish, fried peanuts, chicken with chillies, deep-fried bites of meat or bean curd, or even tiny portions of some of the best dishes of last night's dinner. You've never lived until you've had chillies for breakfast – you wake up, and you stay awake.

Many hotel dining-rooms will also serve *dim sum* for breakfast – steamed or fried savoury dumplings with the most delicious fillings of minced pork, ginger and garlic or prawns and water chestnut, for example. Sometimes there are even sweet steamed buns. And, in the North, deep-fried crullers, like long doughnuts, to be dipped in sugar and soy milk.

All wonderful. And an early breakfast makes it possible to eat lunch – and be grateful for it – around noon. (I've more than once been asked to have lunch at eleven.) Lunch is often a substantial meal, and it is useful, anyway, to be on the same time-table as your hosts.

This is most evident in the evenings, when dinner, even in smart restaurants, begins between five and six, and is over by seven. More than once I have been pleaded with by our Chinese guides to get our group out of the restaurant by 7.30 at the latest, as the comrade waiters will have to be up very early the next morning. So if you don't rise with the lark, you risk spoiling your own day and your digestion as well.

Most package tours are not strong on restaurants, which is a pity. The Chinese are a nation of diners-out, and their restaurants are very import-ant, sometimes historic institutions. Every tourist has a Peking duck banquet at one of the vast restaurants in the capital that serve nothing else.

But there are restaurants in every small town in China; and though standards vary so much that no Westerner who wasn't starving could bring himself to eat at the least inviting of the people's eateries, you can tell simply by looking whether the food will be disgusting.

Every restaurant that caters to tourists has a less salubrious room where the natives themselves eat, excepting only those few restaurants that are too small to segregate the visitors. But, as the experienced China-traveller will tell you, this really is for your comfort and is less sinister than it sounds.

If you stop first in Hong Kong, you can buy a little guide, *Eating out in China* by Harry Rolnick. I recommended it, so far as it goes. But it is a pity to leave China without having made a fair sampling of its restaurants, especially in Canton, where there are some of the most beautiful dining rooms in the world. And the food is famously good in the eastern cities of Suzhou, Yangzhou and Hangzhou, as well as in Canton, and almost everywhere in the provinces of Sichuan and Hunan.

A final word of advice concerning 'evening entertainment'. This euphemism covers everything from the Peking opera to regional acrobats. The acrobatic shows are wonderful – but the Chinese seem unable to distinguish between acrobatics proper and what we would call magic shows. So unless you've a passion for seeing flowerpots produced from silk scarves, you'd be well advised to ascertain that your *second* and any further lot of 'evening entertainment' really is tumblers and tightrope walkers.

'Evening entertainment' precludes eating out; and there is usually much more fun and enlightenment to be got from going to a restaurant than from witnessing even the best tricks of another nineteen conjurers.

The face on the plate

11–12 February, 1985 We set out for Hong Kong – press from all over the world – the extremely lucky British contingent, Robert Carrier, Fay Maschler of the *Standard*, Shona Crawford-Poole of *The Times* and myself, in the first class of the Cathay Pacific flight. We are to join Christian Millau, Luigi Veronelli (who writes the only reliable restaurant guide to Italy), American journalists Fred Ferretti and Corby Kummer, Joan Campbell of Australian *Vogue*, Violet Oon (who is *the* food journalist of Singapore), Harry Rolnick (author of the only restaurant guide to mainland China), Shizuo Tsuji (chief Foodie of Japan), Louis Outhier (*chef-patron* of Restaurant L'Oasis at La Napoule, to whom Christian Millau, in his guide, gives 19.5 out of 20 points for his cooking) and Rémi Krug, who is going to give us all a little of his own champagne.

This is definitely the Foodie first eleven. The reason for our convergence on Hong Kong is that the Mandarin Hotel is celebrating its 21st birthday with a reconstruction of an Imperial Banquet (see Hong Kong Foodie), and we are the fortunate guests. Under the 'technical direction' of the amazing Willy Mark, who must know as much about Chinese cuisine as anyone now living, the Mandarin's Chinese Head Chef Lam Sing-Lun has been working for months. He is recreating the sort of menus served to the Ching Dynasty Emperor Kang-hsi (who started the custom of banqueting during his tours of southern China – he made six between 1684 and 1707) and to his grandson, the Ch'ien-lung emperor. Compared to the stifling protocol of the Imperial Court at Peking, these were relatively informal affairs, often held in a tent. These provincial banquets combined some aspects of the ruling Manchu 'Man banquet' with the native Han Chinese 'Han banquet'; the full three-day number was mostly restricted to Peking. It was from these Imperial tours that a national, as opposed to strictly regional, Chinese cuisine developed, as chefs were recruited and ingredients gathered from the whole of the Middle Kingdom. These oriental *grandes bouffes* were of real importance, since they were the means by which the ethnically different Manchus – who were men of the north – discovered the culinary superiority of the south, particularly of the Cantonese chefs.

We arrive at the Mandarin fuddled and exhausted, but revive considerably when we see the suites we have been given. Robert Carrier is, appropriately, in the flamboyantly wonderful Persian Suite. I am next door, in the Howorth Suite, which is done in exemplary good taste; it is restrained and elegant. Can the management really have matched the rooms to the characters of the guests? I hope so. Anyway, we all seem to have views over Hong Kong harbour, as well as a bar stocked with ten full bottles of hooch. By God.

13 February   We assemble, in black tie, for the First Repast reception. Still feeling both sophisticatedly Western and a little abstemious, most of us drink a glass or two of champagne. Then we ascend seventeen floors to the Man Wah restaurant which has been closed several days for redecoration – and so that the staff can rehearse the preparations for the banquet.

The room has been newly laquered in black, and there is a huge red silk hanging behind the 'offerings' table. The offerings include coloured dough sculptures of the Four Ancient Men, the Three Fortunate Men, the Eight Immortals of Taoism, the Five Auspicious Animals, and tableaux of the Carp at Dragon Gate (symbolising that the humblest person in the land could rise to the most exalted position – through success in the Mandarin equivalent of the civil service examinations) and the Ceremony of Investiture (representing nobility, wealth, ceremony and royalty). Elaborate verbal and visual puns are involved in this display of edible sculpture and calligraphy, and each object has an esoteric numerological connotation.

There is a lion skin on the floor, and after our host, Peter French, the Mandarin's General Manager, dots the lion's eyes with paint, the musicians begin to play and the lion comes to life and dances – a lovely, unselfconscious performance by two members of the local boys' club. The table setting is breathtaking: in the centre is an entire garden of mostly white flowers, through which peep groups of *blanc de chine* figurines. The arrangement is about three feet in diameter. The chopsticks are, of course, real ivory, and the plates and bowls of exquisite blue, red and gold porcelain. Boom – a gong sounds, announcing the first dish. (The gong boy, costumed as are the waiters and musicians, is expected to sit – without fidgeting – through three nights of this.) The first platter is shown first to Peter French, as number-one host. (The others, each with a table of ten guests – 'any more than that, and we would be into mass catering' – are Willy Mark and Eric Waterhouse, managing director of the chain that owns the hotel.) It is a cold plate with the ingredients made to form a peacock, and very aesthetically superior to the normal, maraschino-cherry-decorated Chinese restaurant version.

When the gong boomed twice more for the next two of the evening's twelve courses, we really felt like applauding; for served with the Mondavi *Fumé Blanc* 1982 was a spinach-green dish of prawns with green tea shoots added at the last moment. Its four-character Chinese name (its poetic or euphemistic name) was something like 'jade and pearls'. To follow there was a very unusual dish of 'stir-fried fresh milk with crab coral and olive seeds'. Unusual, because lactose intolerance is so common among the Chinese that milk is almost unknown. (And, it transpired, when we visited the kitchen to see the dish demonstrated, 'fresh' is a euphemism for UHT.) Something like an omelette made only with the white of egg, cream, milk and a lot of oil, the dish was garnished only with the crab roe; and the olive seeds had similarities to pine kernels. But it was magnificent, as was the really expensive combination of dried abalone with dried King Garoupa skin. The latter, when rehydrated, had that slippery, chewy texture the Chinese adore. Steamed coral fish was firm in texture and so fresh it must have died on the way to the table; and we all loved the 'Imperial Noodles', *al dente* triangles of pea starch dough in a rich broth. Indeed, the surprise of the evening was the number of soupy dishes – three – served for serious feasting. At precisely midnight, the gong sounded and we took our leave – extremely grateful that the Mandarin had chosen not to repeat their earlier, 1969, Imperial Banquet, which also included lunch and breakfast. And so to bed – with real linen sheets that had been changed after my mid-afternoon snooze.

14 February   With clear heads and, amazingly, no jet lag, Fay Maschler and I set out to do some demon shopping. My shirts are already ordered from Mee Yee, so it only remains to get to the tailor. We discuss last night's do, and agree we were both very honoured by the seating arrangements: to the right of the host, facing the door, a subtle signal of rank, which only hardened Sinophiles would recognise. Also, how generous and forgiving Bob Carrier is, when I have practically made a career of being rude to him in print. As for the food, it is clear that we are being treated to Willie Mark's choice of the most refined and aristocratic dishes in the Chinese culinary repertory; and we both wonder whether the audience is capable of appreciating these exquisite historical recreations. After all, the Spaniard has hardly ever tasted Chinese food, and even the Italian, Luigi Veronelli, whom I know to have a good deal of knowledge and superb taste, is innocent of any previous acquaintance with Chinese nosh. Wouldn't it have been more sensible to have started them with a hearty bowl of noodles before dropping them into the superior shark's fin soup?

Tonight is Rémi Krug's great triumph. We are to drink six Krug champagnes, including two great rarities, their new single vineyard Clos de Mesnil 1979 *blanc de blancs* and their vintage 1961, of which very little remains. Also their rosé and the 1976 and 1969 – hardly any of these are even for sale in Hong Kong.

The table setting is unbelievable. Suffice it to say that in the centre of each table there is a pond, with full-size water lilies and goldfish, all surrounded by cymbidium orchids.

In the event, most of the 'marriages' of the food and the champagne were really good, and proved Rémi's point that champagne is suitable for good Chinese grub. The outstanding dishes, though, were not necessarily the ones that tasted best, but the ones we are more likely to remember because they are bizarre, or because they are made from endangered species. Thus, tonight, we had shredded turtle with bamboo shoots and black mushrooms, which Harry Rolnick (author of the as yet unpublished *Endangered Species Cookbook*) said he could not eat, even though he knew this particular turtle was farmed. I had never before encountered the odd phallic-shaped bamboo fungus that we were served steamed and 'filled with Superior Bird's Nest topped with Crab-Coral'. It was good. But of the next three game dishes, shark's fin with pheasants and lobster with partridge, it was the 'Braised Civet Imperial Court Style' that none of us will ever forget, alas. It was very interesting in texture and taste, both gamey and chewy; and it was served with a redeeming sauce of pungently stinky fermented bean curd that had the resonance of (and a strong resemblance to) Gorgonzola cheese. But it was served with its head on the platter, and its little face stared at us with reproach. I have heard that it is farmed for the table. But that begs the question of what it actually is. Is it a fox? I hope so, as I do not relish the thought of having eaten a pussycat – even a pussycat's cousin.

The dishes were gonged in, one by one, and were becoming absurd: 'Sea Cucumber stuffed with Shrimps and Sturgeon Maw', 'Steamed Unicorn Fish' and, best of all, 'Double-boiled Chinese Crane and Cordyceps'. No one had any time to worry about the poor crane; we were too excited by the cordyceps, which Willie described as 'a vegetable in summer and a worm in winter'. It rang a bell. I remembered Alan Davidson telling me about a biological mystery organism that could not be classified, as it appeared to have all the characteristics of a vegetable, except that it also appeared to have the power of locomotion. Well, this was it, and, reader, we ate it. I only wish I could describe it accurately; unfortunately, by that time of the evening, Rémi's elixirs had taken effect. All I recall is being very, very happy.

15 February   The preparations for Chinese New Year are hotting up, and all my Chinese friends are getting ready for it, either by buying new refrigerators, cookers and kitchen sinks at the very last minute, or else by trying to get in the right frame of mind for going home to Mother (that is, the very few who don't actually live at home). There are great bargains to be had in the shops and in the lanes, and I show Fay some pretty fancy haggling techniques, which she admires the more as I am dreadfully hung-over.

Now comes the last Repast. We are to come in Chinese costume, i.e. Mandarin drag. In my room is a satin, electric-blue gown. It is hell to get into, and, as I mount the steps to the swimming pool where drinks are to be served, I tread on my hem and all the poppers open. I must learn to lift my skirts when climbing the stairs.

The wine is Chinese grape wine, and almost undrinkable. My dining partner, the famous jewellery designer Kai Yin Lo, says she will not drink the Great Wall and insists on a bottle of champagne, which they serve us awkwardly in white porcelain tripods.

The theme of this night's banquet is obviously air (obviously, because we have already had earth and water). So there are bird cages suspended from the ceiling and the table flowers, in chaste good taste, might be found at the edge of a bird sanctuary.

I think it will make the point if I just list some of tonight's twelve dishes: 'Poached Sliced Fresh South China Sea Conch'; 'Sautéed Wild Duck's Tongues with Pine Seeds and Wood Fungus'; 'Braised Bears' Paws with Game Birds'; 'Stir-fried Shredded Fillet of Deer with Bamboo Shoots and Fine Herbs'; 'Steamed Cabrilla Mouse Garoupa'. And to finish there was 'Double-boiled Snow Frog with Fresh Gingseng', which turned out to be my old friend, frog's ovaries. Oddly enough, the best dish of the whole three dinners was served tonight: it was called 'Superior Vegetarian Platter', and it consisted simply of fresh lotus root and a few perfect snow peas. It was served as though it were the sorbet, to freshen the palate after the gelatinous, chewy and strongly gamey bear's paw, which was served, surrounded on the platter by its claws, in thick slices with halves of quails. I am pleased to think I have eaten bear's paw at last, and can now refuse it without feeling ignorant.

What's the conclusion? The Chinese and Singaporean newspapers are full of how much the Mandarin spent on this exercise. (The Chinese *adore* discussing money, and seem not to be envious about the good fortune or the fortunes of others.) I know the figure that is being mentioned, but I cannot even bring myself to convert it into pounds or US dollars, for fear I might feel guilty (i.e. hypocritical) about it myself. I am relieved that this sort of thing can only happen once in a lifetime; but I am awfully glad that it happened in mine, and I am keenly aware of the privilege of having been invited. I feel wildly honoured and flattered that the Mandarin asked me, and am swanking with pride that I knew enough about Chinese food and etiquette to be able to appreciate it. And dismayed: the menu practically amounted to a list of endangered species. It is comforting to think that this event is unlikely to be repeated.

———

Hong Kong Foodie

Of the many memorable meals I've eaten, the most remarkable have all been in Hong Kong. Not long ago the Mandarin Hotel celebrated its 21st birthday by flying in the world Foodie first eleven for a historical reconstruction of an Imperial Banquet. It lasted three days, and culminated in us honoured guests wearing Imperial drag to eat the last of the dinners in the Man Wah restaurant, the decor of which had been completely changed for each of the meals. The menus, being historically accurate, read like a list of endangered species – the Chinese adore what they think of as 'game'. The bears' paws and the odd heron were not nearly so interesting to me, though, as the cordycep, which, we were told, 'behaves as though it's a mushroom in summer and a worm in winter'.

This information was imparted by Willy Mark, the man who did the research for the Mandarin banquet. Financial journalist and restaurant consultant, Willy is the more or less official mouth of the Hong Kong Tourist Association – the ultimate authority on Chinese food. On another unforgettable occasion, Willy Mark arranged a lunch for me at Kowloon's Sun Tung Lok Shark's Fin restaurant. Willy had been tutoring me in Chinese food appreciation for a whole week, and the object of this meal was to complete my education by introducing me to the few dishes we had not eaten earlier in the week. Well, that was agreed to be the ostensible purpose of the meal.

I began to realise early on that there was something special and *unified* about the meal. It began with a steamed dumpling served in a bowl. An ordinary enough looking dumpling; but, when pierced with chopsticks, it spurted shark's fin soup, the rarest and most expensive, but everyday delicacy of the Chinese. Next the waiter brought to the table a live, Giant-neck Clam. It was more phallic even than its name suggests. Under the waiter's ministrations, with Willy beaming approval, the bi-valve tumesced, and , as the waiter manipulated the halves of its shell, released some liquid. 'It is very good,' said Willy, 'eaten raw.' In fact, it came back to the table, minutes later, in paper-thin slices that we dipped into boiling stock.

Though the raw materials were really out of season in summer, when we were eating our lunch, the next three courses consisted of poisonous snakes. We were served three sorts of viper, done as three different dishes. All were peculiarly delicious: the uninitiated would have mistaken the ingredients for chicken and prawns, and possibly lobster or squid.

Pudding was the forbidden fruit of the Far East, durian. I had enquired closely about tasting this fruit, which, looking like a cross between a pineapple and a grenade, was displayed on all the fruitmongers' stalls of Hong Kong. It was out of the question simply to buy one, for there was nowhere to eat it. Because of its extraordinary smell, it is strictly forbidden to carry the durian across the threshold of a hotel or aboard an aeroplane. Some find the smell excremental, some find it reminiscent of sick. Orientals adore it. One of Anthony Burgess's characters says that the experience of ingesting it is like eating sweet, pink blancmange in a lavatory. I thought I'd never find out for myself; but Willy can fix it. The Chinese at the neighbouring tables not only did not object – they looked on admiringly at people whose status was so high that they could be served durian in a public place.

I liked it. Actually liked it. I'd eat it again with pleasure, which is more than I can say for a great many things I've digested in my professional lifetime. At the conclusion of the meal, a benevolently smiling Willy addressed our all-male company. 'What all these dishes have in common,' he chuckled, 'is their aphrodisiac properties.'

Of course, one eats superbly almost everywhere in Hong Kong, whether it's a banquet at the Mandarin's Man Wah or a dinner eaten off jade and silver at the Chinese restaurant of the Regent Hotel, or a modest *dim sum* at the Luk Yu Teahouse or in the more commercial surroundings of the United Restaurant on the 5th and 6th floors of United Centre, which is so useful because it accepts reservations for *dim sum*.

And, of course, few people other than food journalists actually get force-fed civet cat, birds' nests and other gastronomic tit-bits. But for the culinary experience of a lifetime, the intrepid Foodie (or the hardened tourist) will take himself off to the fishing village of Lau Fau Shan, in the New Territories. There you see dozens of stalls and vivariums, where the fishermen are selling their own catch (the Chinese have a thing about freshness). Buy whatever you fancy – but be warned that the highly coloured Parrot Fish doesn't come cheap. It will be given to you still alive.

Take it across the road, to Oi Man restaurant, at 4 Ching Street. The man in the back room will take your fish away from you, and return it braised with ginger root and bamboo shoots – or whatever he thinks most appropriate for what you've bought. Now that's what I call going out to lunch.

———

Wokking the dog: a rendezvous with gastronomy in Macao

Northern Chinese insist that the Cantonese will eat anything with four legs except the table, and anything that can fly except an aeroplane. At Canton's Qing Ping market, I have myself seen dog already butchered, as well as house cats, pangolins, owls, barking deer, and even live kingfishers awaiting sale and execution.

On this trip to the Orient, I was commissioned to eat a Cantonese dog dinner. But here in the crown colony the practice is illegal. So I asked where I could taste dog meat without giving offence or committing a misdemeanour, and was advised to take a day trip to Macao, where 'funny food' such as dog and cat is tolerated by the law's blind eye.

William Tong, a 30-year-old, Macao-born Chinese, agreed to look after me, and he kindly took a day off work to make the elaborate arrangements. We also needed a few more mouths, as there was no way for a restaurant to order or prepare dog for only one pair of chopsticks. So I invited a family friend, a 17-year-old, Anglo-American schoolboy who was idling in Hong Kong waiting for the visa that would allow him to visit China for a month, and my cicerone invited his old friend, a Macao building contractor named Lim.

Mr Lim was in direct charge of the arrangements after the three of us alighted from the jet-foil catamaran in the seedy Portuguese enclave. The engaging Mr Lim said that the first thing for us to do was to have some lunch. In the yin-yang scheme of folk nutrition, dog is considered a very warming or 'heaty' food, and is only served for dinner. So we had an excellent lunch of fish-maw soup, steamed sole and deep-fried conch at the elegant Macdowell Restaurant. We spent the remaining hours in traditional Macao pursuits, losing a little money at roulette at one of the casinos, watching the mourners play mah-jong at a Buddhist temple.

Shortly after 5 p.m., we met up with Mr Lim again. He led us down an alley and into a workingman's restaurant. 'This,' said Mr Tong, 'is the most famous place for funny food in Macao.' It is run by an elderly man with a cigarette permanently dangling from beneath his wispy moustache, by his longhaired son, who strongly resembles a skeleton, and by a grandson. The standard of hygiene is identical to dozens of grimy one-room restaurants in China itself, and the standard of dress wasn't much different. The chopsticks were sealed in paper and the bowls clean, which was all that mattered.

From an alcove at the back came the whoosh of a butane gas jet, on which a large metal cauldron was boiling ferociously. In another alcove a clay stove, filled with charcoal and ignited, was placed in front of an electric fan to make the coals glow. The stove then was put in the centre of our table, and immediately made clear why one did not eat dog in the heat of the day. A clay pot was brought and balanced precariously on the stove. Little bowls of mustard and chilli sauce were placed on the table, as is the Cantonese habit, and the longhaired, death's head son used his asbestos fingers to lift the clay pot lid. Inside were chunks of brown meat with thin but substantial slices of ginger in a brown sauce. The meat had dark skin attached to it, was quite fatty and looked like pork. It was chewy, and had a very strong, though not disagreeable, flavour, like mutton, venison or goat. The matchstick-sized bones made it clear that it had come from a young animal.

The meal was completed by bringing plastic bowls of shredded Chinese leeks, yellow chives and a green spinach-like vegetable for adding to the clay pot. Those ingredients greatly improved the dish, and with the judicious application of mustard and chilli sauce, it was possible to eat enough to avoid disgracing oneself. Messrs. Lim and Tong seemed to relish the meal, and my young friend's appetite did not falter. The sight of the clay pot on our table attracted passers-by from the street, who knew that this meant dog was on tonight; and while we were there, two family parties came into the sleazy restaurant and ordered it.

(Willy Mark, the celebrated Hong Kong gastronome who had arranged for Mr Tong to take us to Macao, said later that this is a very provincial way to serve this admittedly rustic dish. While dog meat is not refined enough to serve in a first-class restaurant, gourmets occasionally serve it. If Mr Mark were to acquire a whole dog, he said, he would prepare it in four courses. First, the fillet shredded and stir-fried, with shredded bamboo shoots and black mushrooms, garnished with finely shredded lime leaves. Second, a double-boiled soup made of the bones and meat scraps, plus the penis and testicles, if the dog is not a bitch. Third, the paws and muzzle would be made into a braise, similar to the one I ate. Fourth, the ribs would be steamed, cut in thick slices, sandwiched with slices of ham and black mushrooms and served hot in their own juices. Exactly the same would apply if you had a whole muntjac, or barking deer, a protected species that is suitable for serving in an up-market eating establishment.)

When the patron joined us for a moment I asked him if the dog we were eating was farmed. He laughed at my foolishness, and Mr Tong explained that no one (except peasants on state farms in mainland China) raises dog for the table – 'you can't eat a dog that you have fed'. The old man grinned, revealing his need of a dentist's attentions, and made a pun to the effect that it was a 'hot' dog. He belongs to a buying syndicate with the other dog meat restaurants, and when one of them has a request, it is passed on to the supplier, who supplies the original requester with his few kilos and sells the surplus to the other members. Thus the restaurant owners all have clean hands, and it is no use for the police to interfere, though they know every bite of dog served in Macao is stolen.

The breed of preference is the black tongue chow. Straight-haired 'Chinese' dogs are always eaten in preference to curly-haired 'foreign' dogs. And only puppies are used for the pot.

'We do serve cat, as well,' the owner of the restaurant explained, 'but you did not give sufficient notice.' 'Dog must be young,' Tong explained, 'but old cat is better. Old cat is lazy and has some fat on it, like young dog.' Cat is scarce and expensive, as it's not easy to separate an older cat from its rightful owner. (In Hong Kong and southern China 'wild civet cat is in fact bred for the table, and with – perfectly legal – snake and chicken, goes to make up the famous dish of "tiger, dragon and phoenix".')

What, you may ask, is classically drunk with dog? It is Sheung Ching Chiu, a fiery double-distilled rice liquor. But because of the lingering influence of Portugal in Macao, we were served Mateus rosé wine from the former mother country. There were crates of it on the floor of the restaurant. By Cantonese standards, it had been a successful meal and, we were told, should in theory provide us with a benefit we hadn't expected. Cantonese believe dog and cat – and all 'funny food' – are aphrodisiacs. While I cannot report any increase in libido following my dog dinner, I think I can explain its alleged aphrodisiac effect. It was so indigestible that I lay awake most of the night. Presumably Chinese couples experience the same effect, and find there's little else to do in those sleepless hours.

Solving the monkey puzzle

The southern Chinese, as any northerner will tell you with distaste, will eat almost anything. I have heard southerners themselves tell the story about the Indian and the Cantonese confronted by a creature from outer space: the Indian falls to his knees and begins to worship it, while the Chinese searches his memory for a suitable recipe.

Naturally, there are a lot of famous Chinese gastronomic atrocity stories. The most famous one features live monkey brains, and I have been told it fifty times – but always at second hand, by someone whose friend, husband or mother has absolutely, definitely witnessed it. It is claimed that decadent Chinese gourmands give banquets at which little boys are employed to shove shaven-headed monkeys up through a table with a hole in the centre, following which the host slices off the top of the animal's head with a machete, and the diners eat the still warm brains with long silver spoons.

I first began to think this might be monkey business only when an American traveller told me that *he* had a friend who had been present at such a feast where unwanted girl babies were substituted for the simians. That was what made me class the tale with those of the disappearing hitch-hiker and the Swiss couple who ended up eating their own ginger and bamboo-shoot garnished poodle in a Hong Kong restaurant. (The truth of this last was sworn by a man sitting next to me at lunch one day at my Oxford college. He assured me that he had not only witnessed it, but was the author of the first newspaper report of this event of, I seem to remember, the summer of 1970.)

In fact, in *The Listener* for 1 March 1984, Derek Cooper gave an account of how Arthur Helliwell, a 'campaigning' journalist, was the original victim of the monkey brain hoax, a jape invented in Singapore in March 1952 by other British journalists seeking to deflate his pomposity. Arthur Helliwell reported the story, and his paper, *The People*, was promptly and successfully sued for defamation by the only Chinese millionaire living in Singapore's Queen Astrid Park. (The hapless Helliwell had begun his gastronomic horror story by writing, 'In his Arabian Nights palace out at Queen Astrid Park tonight, one of Singapore's many Chinese multimillionaires is giving a party to celebrate the birth of a son.') Cooper added that the table with the hole in it, which clinched the hoax for Helliwell, is used to hold the chafing dish or wok for *ke-tze* or steamboat, the local variation on hot-pot, in which the diners cook their own food in boiling broth heated by a flame placed beneath the table.

Thirty years later, Fred Thomas, controller of the Hong Kong RSPCA, claimed (in the Asian *Wall Street Journal* for 23 May 1983) that RSPCA personnel, four years earlier, rescued 'a monkey that escaped from a Kowloon restaurant, its body shaved in preparation for the table'. And that, a year before that, they had found, in a Kowloon dustbin, the carcass of a monkey with pate and brains removed. While this does not amount to an eye-witness account of live monkey brains actually being eaten (or rule out the possibility of the first primate escaping from a veterinary surgery), it is always possible that the currency of the story has led some people to imitate art. There are rumours amongst Hong Kong's large gastronomic community that someone had staged a monkey brain feast for a Japanese film crew, and the film *Mondo Cane* is often cited in this connection.

Willy Mark, the professional Hong Kong gastronome, assured me that he would have no compunction about telling me so if this practice was genuine. He had no experience of the dish, and his aged father, whom he consulted about it on my behalf, had never heard of it either. Neither one of them expressed any horror at being asked the question – to them it was just another query about edible species of animals, of which they can count a great many more than you or I – but they knew nothing of it. It appears that the monkey brain feast is at bottom a *canard*.

Nippon tuck

Everybody knows that Japanese food is the most beautiful and decorative in the world, and that the Japanese diet is a healthy one. But the cuisine of Japan is not as straightforward a subject as this would suggest. While it is true that the presentation of most Japanese dishes is exquisitely pretty, and has greatly influenced the French *nouvelle cuisine* chefs, I personally find the best-known one-pot dish, *sukiyaki*, a distasteful brown mess.

And while it is also true that the Japanese eat a lot of vegetables, relatively little meat and, because they have a high incidence of lactose intolerance, almost no dairy fats, they also consume a vast amount of pickled food. Some doctors think this is what accounts for the extra-ordinarily high incidence of stomach and digestive tract cancers among the Japanese.

Twenty-four hours spent at Narita, the new airport for Tokyo, was perhaps not the best way to begin my study of Japanese food habits and customs. As a token of my earnestness, however, I did manage to eat four meals in the short time I was there.

Dinner at the Narita Prince Hotel was the usual 'soup plus three' formula for an everyday Japanese meal: clear soup or *miso* soup (flavoured and thickened with fermented bean paste), pickles, rice and one meat or fish dish. On this occasion it was *miso* soup with tiny freshwater clams, strong pickled cucumber, the glutinous rice that the Japanese always eat in preference to separate-grained Chinese rice, and *tempura*, lightly battered, deep-fried Pacific prawns and aubergine cut in the shape of fans, with the traditional garnishes of a little pile of green *wasabi*, grated Japanese horseradish that you mix with your little saucer of *shoyu*, Japanese soy sauce, and a tangle of shavings of *daikon*, the giant white radish.

A completely different experience was provided when I opted for Japanese breakfast: rice plus a small, whole dried fish, *miso* soup with clams again, and a small dish of strangely complicated pickle. The contrast with dinner was provided by the canned music. At first I thought it was merely, if incongruously for breakfast-time, Western palm court music. But then: ta tum, ta tum tum tum tum, tah tum, ta tum ta tum ta tum, I recognised Schubert's 'Trout Quintet', and realised simultaneously that everyone in the dining-room who was eating Japanese breakfast, myself included, had raised their rice bowls, and were shovelling with chopsticks from bowl to mouth, in time with the music. The music speeded up to a lunatic tempo. Had I inadvertently discovered one of the secrets of Japanese industrial success?

In my mad attempt to give myself a crash course in Japanese food, I couldn't resist the specialised restaurant where a young man sat at the front with a scarily sharp knife, beheading and skinning little eels in a single swoop of the blade. So for elevenses, I wandered into the town, took off my shoes, struggled up on to the *tatami*-matted platform, sat uncomfortably on my knees, and ate 'high class broiled eel with rice', served in red-lacquer boxes, along with tiny, whole dried fish, and 'eel stomach soup'.

Worse, I actually tried to eat lunch. I had the onomatopoeic *shabu-shabu*, which gets its name from the sound of the simmering stock in which are cooked thin slices of raw beef, Chinese cabbage, squares of bean curd and little parasol-type mushrooms. But I did not realise that the kimono-ed and elderly waitress who cooked it at table was going to stay to see that I ate every bite.

When I took up my Japanese food researches later in London, I realised that I had, during my compressed sojourn at Narita, absorbed quite a bit of information. But it took Professor Naomichi Ishige of the National Museum of Ethnology, Osaka, and Mr Tadayoshi Tazaki, my mentors in Japanese eating, to make me understand what I had seen.

Japanese restaurants are more specialised than Western, or even Chinese or Indian, restaurants. There are *sushi* bars, where the fare consists exclusively of expressly prepared raw fish and other ingredients, such as seaweed, thin omelette, pickle or fresh vegetable wrapped around vinegar-flavoured rice. *Sushi* chefs are very well paid, and the people sitting at the bar are not there for fast service, but for the expensive attentions of the chef. And London has both *teppan-yaki* restaurants, serving grills, and some restaurants with *tatami* rooms.

I have only recently mastered the art of ordering from the bewildering menu of even the most ordinary Japanese eatery. As in Chinese, the Japanese word for a meal is the word for cooked rice. The first distinction made by Japanese diners-out (who are almost exclusively male), is that they never drink sake (rice wine) and eat rice at the same time. Thus, though the four tipsy Japanese businessmen I saw at my local Japanese restaurant actually ate a good deal more than we did at our table, they were not technically having a *meal*, but only 'drinking sake' that evening, for they ate no rice.

Sake etiquette is interesting. There should be one small bottle of the hot rice wine for each person. You never fill your own cup. So if you are empty, you replenish the cups of everybody else from your bottle. It is up to one of your companions to notice that you need a refill. And the cup must never be on the table when sake is poured, but held in the hand. The Japanese use whisky as an all-purpose drink, and often drink it in place of sake.

Classical Japanese food, *ryori*, is rarely encountered here. But it is useful to know that the principles on which a meal is organised are not to do with the ingredients, but with the method of cooking used. Thus after some trifling starters, my dinner at the Yamaju restaurant proceeded from pickled (*sunomo*) to raw fish (*sashimi*), to boiled (clear soup of salmon and seaweed in *dashi*, the all-important basic stock of kelp and *kat-suobushi*, shavings of dried *bonito*), to simmered (bean curd, *tofu*, with potato), to grilled (marinated beefsteak), to fried (*tempura*), and, as the Japanese eat few sweets, to fruit (snow pear, salted and sprinkled with parsley).

The reason for the emphasis on cooking methods, rather than ingredients, is historical. Japan is one of the few countries ever to have been officially vegetarian. Before the fourteenth-century mass conversion to vegetarianism, under the influence of Zen Buddhism, monks as well as ordinary people ate both meat and fish raw, as many of the peoples of South-east Asia still do; and as the Chinese, who now eat nothing raw, once did. The consequence was that, when the meat-eating Portuguese Jesuits reached Japan in the sixteenth century, there were no recipes and no technology for cooking meat. (The meat of mammals was not widely eaten in Japan until the latter half of the nineteenth century.)

In food as in so many other matters, the Japanese are a borrowing culture. They borrowed the grill from Korea, and from the Portuguese they learnt to fry (*tempura* is a word of Portuguese origin).

Seasonability and freshness are the two qualities most prized by the Japanese. Raw fish is the one indispensable ingredient in a formal Japanese meal; and the quality and quantity of the fish is the chief determinant of the cost of the meal. This is true even in London, where it is possible for one Japanese businessman eating *sushi* to consume £40 to £50 worth of raw fish at a sitting; and where Tadayoshi Tazaki and his associates are building an amazing business empire on a foundation of importing absolutely fresh fish from all over the world.

In my four-month-long exploration of London's Japanese restaurants, I have eaten an entire aquarium's-worth of raw fish, and discovered that you really do get what you pay for. The best and freshest raw fish I've had was Mr Tazaki's *sushi* at his restaurant Azami and the raw squid and whitefish *sashimi* at Yamaju. At less expensive places I have several times been given raw fish that Professor Ishige would have left on the plate or plank of wood on which it was served.

Japanese restaurants are expensive – they have never pretended to be cheap. However, every one I visited had a fixed menu, which represented excellent value. My advice is always to stick to it, and avoid raw fish unless you are paying quite a lot for it, or are with a Japanese-speaker.

———————

India diary

22 January, 1985   I had forgotten that the chief thing about India is the waiting. One waits constantly and for everybody, sometimes for hours on end. This time, we have been waiting for the chefs from France and Europe, whose gastronomic tour of the sub-continent is our excuse for being here at all.

The chefs finally appeared – one and a half *days* late – except for Pierre Troisgros and his wife Olympe, who, because they had come, dottily enough, via Hawaii, did not encounter any delays. Those who did arrive today are all in a distinctly bad state of mind. Their plane left Paris late, because of fog, and couldn't land at Delhi, because of fog. It was diverted to Bombay, but the distinguished passengers weren't allowed to leave the airport, because their visas, arranged unorthodoxly and personally by the Foreign Minister himself, were at Delhi.

The French chefs are Jean-André Charial, who has taken over the cooking at Baumanière from his grandfather, Raymond Thuillier; Jean Lameloise, who has three Michelin stars of his own at Chagny; Michel Rostang, whose eponymous Paris restaurant has two stars, and Alain Dutournier, who had two stars for his Paris establishment, Au Trou Gascon, and has now moved to a smart new location. The 'foreigners' with three Michelin stars each, are Eckart Witzigmann of Munich and Pierre Romeyer of Brussels. (Their merits are always calculated, for PR purposes, in Michelin stars: on the more accurate Gault-Millau scale, the differences among them are as apparent as their similarities.) With them travel a coach-load of French journalists – some of real distinction, and Yannou Collart, the Paris PR who nannies, inspires and leads them by the collective nose.

Back to the waiting: Fay Maschler (food editor of the London *Standard*), Gael Greene (restaurant critic for *New York* magazine, better known here and in Britain as an 'erotic novelist' – remember *Blue Sky, No Candy*?), Camellia Panjabi, Vice-President for Marketing of the entire Taj Hotel Group and the organiser of this huge *dal-Fest*, several photographers and the odd television crew are all waiting on the steps of the Taj Palace Hotel in Delhi. We have the occasional diversion. Two elephants have been standing patiently for hours. One of them turns out to be a bull. I don't think any of us have ever seen an elephant with an erection before, and it causes more than a slight stir.

The coaches arrive. A seven-man orchestra plays songs of welcome; the marble steps of the hotel are occupied by beautiful girls, six of whom are dressed as brides of various regions, wearing their gold dowries as nose chains, collars, head ornaments and necklaces. There are also fourteen girls with *mala*, garlands made of flower petals, eight Indian chiefs in their whites, all the hotel managers we have met in the last two days, and Pierre Troisgros, who is planning his shopping list for the dinner the European chefs are going to cook the next day. (Is sorrel available? No, but there are several kinds of spinach. Caviar? *Oui, mais très cher*.)

The *luxe* of the welcome is having its effect. They are definitely becoming a little more gruntled, and agree to be led off to the garden, rather than going first to their rooms. What they see restores their spirits totally. An entire village fête has been created – the stairs leading up to the garden are decorated with flower petal patterns, while overhead is festooned with garlands. There are seven or eight little stands making and distributing food. There are the Bombay beach and road-side snacks, *bhel-puri*; the mixture of puffed rice, lentil-flour vermicelli; miniature puffed fried breads; onions; green chillies; raw mangoes and fresh coriander tossed in chutney; and *pao kheema*, the delicious minced lamb dish served with curious Western breadrolls. There's a specially erected brick and clay *choolah*, charcoal fired, cooking the handkerchief-thin *roomali roti*, griddle bread, the more familiar *paratha* and also a mutton *biryani*. Another stand is frying *samosas, pakoras,* vegetable fritters and *aloo tikki*, a vegetable filled potato 'cutlet', that is browned on a *tawa* griddle. From a cart in the middle of the lawn, a man dispenses Delhi's favourite snacks, with the chant, '*Channa jor Garam, Le lo Babu, Channa jor Garam*; roasted chick peas, dear sir, buy my roasted chick peas.'

The entertainments include two terribly frightening men dressed and made-up as monkeys, with stiff tails they put up the women's skirts, and a troupe of Rajasthani dancers. Yannou's spirits have lifted so much that she dances with the two turbaned little boys (one who looks to be six and the other three) and their veiled mother. A highly decorated fortune-telling cow (who has the gift because she was born with a rather disgusting 'third eye') lopes round in a circle, and accurately stops at Fay Maschler, when asked, 'Who has moved house?' I am inspired with a new ambition when, in response to the question, 'Who wants to make a movie?' she stops and nuzzles me. An elaborate Rajasthani puppet show, like a Punch and Judy performance even to the use of the razzer, has been mounted, involving three musicians and dozens of puppets. The puppet-master's artistry is impressive: but the conjuror steals his audience away easily, by levitating over five feet above the ground, with his head showing through a slit in a dirty old rug. Quite a welcome. The chefs are greatly mollified.

By the evening we have got a sense of how extravagant this visit is going to be, and, naturally, have begun to wonder about the motives of the sponsors, Air India and the Taj group. Part of the motives are almost disinterested: the Taj group wants to convince the chefs and journalists (who are at least the equals in fame of the chefs, our doyen being Craig Claiborne of the *New York Times*) that Indian is the world's third-greatest cuisine.

Not only is the Festival of India soon to be mounted in Paris and New York but, following the success of the Bombay Brasserie in London, Camellia Panjabi is about to open a Taj restaurant in Paris. Astrologers and builders permitting, the Île de Kashmir will open on a barge in the Seine in mid-April, 1985. It will be only the third Indian restaurant in Paris, and probably the first authentic one. They have decided to special-ise in the mild and accessible Kashmiri cuisine in the hope that the Frenchman will find it possible to drink wine with this type of Indian food. So they are serving a sample menu to us tonight. The *badam* soup of almonds and cream is a knock-out, and so is the *murg* pistachio, chicken with yoghurt and pistachio nuts. Also very good is the *poryal* dish of French beans with cashews. But the rest satisfies neither the French nor the Indians – too spicy for the former, and not brilliantly cooked by the exacting standards of the latter. Still, there is a great deal of time to get it right before April.

23 January   We are taken, early in the morning and half-unconscious, to several markets. The first was too crowded to move at all. The second wasn't much better. I was run down by a rickshaw, and made to feel only slightly better by our impromptu breakfast of *puri* with chick peas. We felt *daring* eating in the market, and were emboldened to negotiate to buy a smaller quantity of the Cape gooseberies, *physalis*, than the wholesale five kilos for 50 rupees on offer. They have a short season, are stunningly delicious, and are perversely called raspberries by the Indians.

The chefs are cooking tonight. If they had arrived on time, they would have had three or four Indian meals first. As it is, they remain almost innocent of any acquaintance with Indian food. So they plan a menu that requires familiar and therefore hard-to-get ingredients. We journalists pop in and out of the kitchens of the Taj Mahal hotel's Casa Medici restaurant, pretending an interest we do not feel. Pierre Troisgros appears to be in charge. He seems happy enough, with at least two French-speaking Indian chefs. There is harmony in the kitchen, but it *smells* foreign to me, un-Indian and unpleasant.

Later the same evening champagne flows in the roof-top reception room. It is slightly lifeless, as though it has had some bubbles knocked out of it by its long journey from France. I pop into the kitchen, and Pierre Troisgros *tips* me, like a schoolboy, with a teaspoon of caviar, the principal ingredient of one of the three *amuse-gueules*. The others are squid rings, and tiny quiches made ingeniously from *paneer*, the Indian curd cheese.

In the dining-room, it is immediately apparent that something's wrong. There are two empty tables. (Later, the hilarious reasons become clear. We are in the middle of a spy scandal involving Rajiv Ghandi's Cabinet Secretary and the French. When the invitations went out last week, a large number of members of the Government accepted – even Rajiv himself, rumour says. The French Ambassador also accepted. Neither party could be sure that the other would absent itself, so both caught diplomatic colds and sent last-minute regrets.) The Government is represented by K. P. Singh Deo, who has three portfolios. He is Minister for Administrative Reform, for Personnel and for Culture. He is seated with his wife, Savitri Devi, a member of one of the royal families. I am given the honour of being seated on his right, while Fay Maschler is seated next to Ajit Kerker, the President and Managing Director of the Taj Group. This makes us feel *very* superior to our French and American colleagues.

The menu itself seems to me an international misunderstanding on the scale of what happened to Miss Quested in the Marabar caves. The first dish of prawns with *julienne* of ginger was delicious, but suffered from not being hot enough. My fillet of pomfret in saffron sauce was over-cooked, but others reported that it was magnificent. Then came the masterstroke, a dish that could have been specifically designed to give the maximum outrage to the orthodox vegetarian Hindu sensibility: two kilos of chicken blood were used for the sauce of the *civet de poulet*. I very much liked the fresh *paneer* in vinaigrette with herbs, a really interesting cheese course. But I could have done without the dessert of *îles flottantes* with praline. There were not only no vegetarian dishes, there were no vegetables. Though the vegetables and fruits were really the only things of interest in the markets this morning, they failed to catch the attention of our two- and three-star chefs. Yannou, ever the show-biz type, made a speech in Hindi (which she had learned an hour earlier). Pierre Troisgros led the chefs in dancing the cancan.

24 January My extremely predictable hang-over seems to have been cured by drinking two Indian prairie oysters: egg yolk, fresh lime juice, chilli, an awful lot of Worcestershire sauce, and, of course, secret spices. I drank these in the *chowk*, the village market that had been set up for us in the Taj Mahal hotel grounds, where we were all interviewed by the local press and fed wonderful food, such as the onomatopoeic *tak tak*, a mixture of sheep's offal, including brains and testicles, cooked on the *tawa*, and minced, *tak, tak, tak*, with two choppers.

By evening we've lost Craig Claiborne, who hasn't been well for the entire trip, and is planning to leave tonight for home. The rest of the English-speaking journalists and Malavika Sanghvi, a beautiful and clever Indian free-lance journalist who is covering the trip, decide to buy a meal at the Taj chain's rival, the Bokhara restaurant in the Sheraton Maurya hotel. I've been before, and the others have heard a rumour that it's the most popular restaurant in Delhi. Its limited *tandoori* menu is very good indeed, but I feel I've over-dosed on protein, with only raw onion and cucumber, one dish of *dal* and another of *raita*, a single veg – fried cauliflower, and wonderful breads to relieve the platters of barbecued meat, fish and chicken. The others are delighted, but Gael doesn't like the food arriving all at once. It's an easy way to appreciate Indian food; but the restaurant is designed for very fast turn-over. Even the seats are made too uncomfortable for you to linger at table. Early to bed, as we must be up at 5.45 for an early start to Agra.

25 January Western buffet breakfast. Disgusting. I had forgotten how revolting Indian bacon and sausage can be. We suffered in vain, of course. The plane is still on the tarmac at 9.30 – fog, for a change.

The fog lifts, the plane takes off, the Taj Mahal is still there. Unfortunately I'm too tired to appreciate it as much as I should. But my spirits soar when I see the restored Fatehpur Sikri, the Emperor Akhbar's ruined city. We gasp, rapturously, and munch monkey nuts.

We are whisked off by coach to a bird sanctuary. There, on a jetty on the edge of the marshes, they have set up an elaborate picnic lunch. Uniformed waiters serve us heavenly food in celestial surroundings, as though we had just returned from a divine shooting-party. Malavika says the food is the best we've had: home-made, like what she serves at her own house. The servants have packing cases full of goodies stashed behind a makeshift screen at the edge of the reeds. Even so, I am astonished when they produce, in response to a demand for white wine, a drinkable '83 Chablis, the first wine in really good condition I have tasted in India. The four-hour coach trip back to Delhi was tiring and terrifying, as our driver was both adventurous and in a hurry.

In the evening we go to a private party given by the Daryani family, in their modern painter-turned-architect designed house in Delhi. The food is Sindi, abundant and good. The garden has been covered in flower petals, and all the trees are garlanded with *mala*. Our jet-setting, elegant hostess arrives a little late, from Madras, where she had gone to fulfil a religious vow. The evening reinforces my growing suspicion that Indian food, like Italian, is essentially domestic, and does not benefit from being served in restaurants.

26 *January*   The Republic Day parade, which we watch from the VIP enclosure, opposite the President and bulletproof-vested Prime Minister. The security arrangements are so thorough that they have dampened the crowd's ardour. Instead of the day of national rejoicing (for surviving Mrs Ghandi's assassination, the sectarian riots, the Bhopal disaster and new elections) that the politicians were expecting, we witnessed a brilliantly co-ordinated parade. This is surely the only event in India that ever happens with precision and on time.

A private plane takes us to Jaipur. We are greeted at the gates of the Rambagh Palace hotel by two horse-drawn carriages, twelve elephants with mahouts and howdahs to carry us to the hotel, twelve mounted lancers in uniform and twelve camels, each with a boy musician. There are the usual troupes of dancers and beautiful girls with garlands. We would be in danger of becoming blasé, except that the huge Pierre Romeyer (the French tease him and call him Grosmeyer) breaks the ladder as he climbs on to the elephant. The French television man shouts in triumph – he has recorded the whole scene.

We are invited to dine in the evening at the City Palace by the Maharajah and Maharani of Jaipur. We start by trekking to the upper terrace for a fireworks display. 'Bubbles' Jaipur is by no means just a Rent-a-Maharajah; he is the most socially skilled human being alive. He not only talks to every single person in the party ('Yes, I would be quite interested in the possibilities of elephant polo . . .'), he even convinces me that he remembers that we have met before.

The meal is served formally, sitting on cushions on the floor along the four walls of the vast dining-room. Silver *thalis* are brought, first to the Maharani, who, as are her many ladies, is dressed in yellow to celebrate the first day of spring. Rajasthan is mostly desert, as you can see from the plane, and the food is almost entirely composed of pulses and cereals. About the only green comes from *methi*, fenugreek leaves, which grow in the terribly short wet season, and are dried for use the rest of the year. I like it. I am in a minority of one.

We had been allowed in the ladies' quarters, the *zenana*, earlier, and saw the exquisitely costumed women. Sitting next to us at dinner is a young girl of nineteen. She speaks American. On investigation we find out that she *is*, more or less, American. She hadn't been back to India since birth, before her marriage was arranged and her baby born last year. Her father is an academic at Cornell and she was a perfectly normal American schoolgirl. Now she wears masses of jewellery, lovely clothes, is a member of the Maharani's Court – and she says she is perfectly happy.

27 January   It's incredible. Our hosts seem to have set out to recreate the whole of the Raj for us. Following a morning's sightseeing, we have come back to the Rambagh Palace to find, on the lawn, two dancing bears, a pair of trained monkeys, a snake charmer with a cobra, a python and a mongoose, and a band of musicians to escort us to the swimming pool area. There they have set up a *shikar* lunch, refreshments for an old-fashioned shooting party, with special delicacies that include barbecued smoked fish, special breads (very like Southern American hush puppies) cooked over cow dung, chicken cooked in layers of *poppadoms*, rice cooked in clay containers that are then smashed to reveal the contents, whole kids and kebabs and quails. It is somehow obvious that this delicious food is now as obsolete as the *shikar* itself, and that great effort has gone, not only into preparing it, but into *remembering* what was served on these occasions and researching the recipes. The French take great pleasure in eating with their fingers off stitched-leaf plates; but they don't really take in the occasion or appreciate the food. And they certainly haven't understood that the people dressed in hunting uniform are the staff of the hotel, and include the manager, who is the most powerful man after the Maharajah in still-feudal Rajasthan.

Later in the day we fly to Ahmedabad, to have dinner with the Sarabhai family. They are famous textile manufacturers and are Jains, members of a vegetarian sect, some of whom – though not the Sarabhais – are so radical that they won't eat root vegetables for fear of harming earthworms and wear gauze masks to avoid inhaling insects. The state of Gujerat, because it was the birthplace of Mahatma Gandhi, is still dry, so the Sarabhais will serve no alcohol at their home. And what a home. It was designed by Le Corbusier, who came and lived with the family in the '50s, when he was building Chandigarh. Manorama Sarabhai, the vivacious elderly matriarch, is also a great collector and patron of the arts. The house is hung with Hodgkins, Stellas, Mirós, Rauschenbergs, Richard Smiths and Saul Steinbergs – a very catholic collection. The food is the most handsomely presented we've encountered in India – even the *puris*, the puffed fried breads, have been made with spinach and beetroot so that they come in attractive colours. We have a special *bajri rotla*, a bread made from millet. It is served with white butter and *jaggery*, palm tree sugar. In fact, all the food is slightly sweet. I'm told this is a Gujerat characteristic. As there are no cocktails, we started with *panoo*, a sweet and sour soup served in glasses. Its ingredients were turmeric, red chilli, tamarind, mustard seeds, asafoetida, curry leaves – and *jaggery*.

Asher Sarabhai, Mrs Sarabhai's daughter-in-law, is an old friend of mine, and we were meeting for the first time in several years. There was scarcely time to gossip, and Asher was really slightly cross that we had come on such a mad expedition, so that we had to leave to catch our chartered plane to Bombay as soon as we had eaten. Asher was much in demand that evening, as she is equally at home in the English and French languages. Her two children are enchanting, and she remains one of the most beautiful women I have ever seen.

28 January Not surprisingly, we are mostly wiped out today, as we didn't get to our beds at the Bombay Taj Mahal much before 3.30. Most of us stay in them. Some of us attempt a little shopping, but it's fairly hopeless.

They've laid on a Parsi dinner for us at the hotel. The menu is that for a wedding or for the Parsi equivalent of a *bar mitzvah*, and they've employed the caterer who usually does such affairs for the hotel. I note that Parsis are extremely fond of eggs; we must have consumed four each. I loved the fish coated in green chutney and wrapped in a banana leaf, *patra-ni-machi*, which is served also at the Bombay Brasserie, and I liked the scrambled egg with 'dried fruit'. As dried fruits are mostly nuts, it was a savoury dish. We ate with fingers off banana leaves, and sat at only one side of the long tables, so we could be served formally from the other side. Today's aeroplanes brought *The Observer* containing my half-page onslaught on the Michelin guide (the French nodded their heads in agreement as they read it – they don't like the implied devaluation of their own stars that they see the British guide perpetrating), and the *Tatler* containing Elizabeth David's half-page onslaught on me. I wanted to consult an astrologer retroactively.

29 January   None too soon, we leave for Goa and sun and sand. That night, Prem Kumar, the chef of the Fort Aguada Beach Resort, who speaks French because of his year working in Paris and has accompanied us on the whole of the trip, returns the chefs' compliment, and cooks a dinner of local ingredients, but served, *à la nouvelle cuisine*, on the plate. The first course, *petit pomfret farci, bouillon des épices à l'indienne*, is a wonderful bit of poached fish served with two mussels in a pool of spicy, clear broth. I found the *langoustine* and *crevettes* of the next course overcooked, as they invariably are. Perhaps these warm water *crustacea* require less cooking than their northern brethren. The *poulet au cafreal d'Aguada* was chicken all right. What else it was defies translation and must remain a mystery. But it was certainly more welcome to me than the *civet* had been. Prem's cheese course was terrific: it was a fresh cheese with green and black peppercorns, and though made of the milk of the sacred cow, it had the zing and zip of a fresh *chèvre*. The carefully thought-out pudding was a coconut ice cream, with *chikoo* (the fragrant, grainy tropical fruit that, unpeeled, looks like a potato) and a sauce of *caju feni*, the local marc-like hooch distilled from the fruit that grows above the cashew nut.

30 January   With all sorts of aching muscles from unaccustomed exercise, I readily agree to follow Jean-André Charial as a patient of the beach (as opposed to the hotel) masseur. This unofficial therapist has a magic touch for 'freeing nerves'. He is quite certain that, with his bottle of coconut oil and grubby towel, he can relieve several chronic injuries, especially to my neck and lower back, and improve my digestion. The sand sticks on the oil-coated skin to form a crust. It all seems to be part of the treatment. I especially relish the last bit of the massage, where he caresses my head, getting me to relax so completely that I am taken by surprise when, with an incredible scrunching noise, he rotates my head 180 degrees. I agree to return at 8.30 a.m. tomorrow.

And a good thing I did. For I acquired a hangover of historical dimensions that night. I suppose it all started with Pablo Bartholomew, India's most famous photographer, who has been with us from the beginning. I knew Pablo's work from his exhibition at the Museum of Modern Art at Oxford. What I did not know is that he's so well known in India that the local Goa papers reported the chefs' visit under the headline 'Ace Clicker in Town'. Well, there we were on the beach at St Anthony's Bar, the hot spot in Goa, where the Taj cooks had set up another little barbecue. I don't know if it was Pablo who plied me with, among other things, Mumm's (sweet) *Cordon Vert* ('the *only* champagne,' stressed the chefs, 'that no Frenchman will drink'), or whether it was the film-star gate-crashers, who included Karim Kapoor, the stunning son of Sashi Kapoor and Jennifer Kendal, and the even more stunning Madeleine Potter (of *The Bostonians*). The next day, some people unkindly suggested that my new friends had only spent the evening with me under the impression that I was Peter Ustinov. I can't remember, honestly. But there was dancing, and there was singing, and sand, sea and champagne, of a kind.

31 January   Cured of hangover by my sandy massage, it's time to begin work. We leave early tomorrow morning, so I must ask the four chefs who have lasted the course (the others had to leave early) whether they have been impressed and affected by what they have tasted and learnt. Pierre Romeyer has ordered a couple of *tandoori* ovens to be sent to Brussels. Charial is interested by the possibilities of yoghurt. 'Doubtless there are historical, and even medical reasons for the combinations of the spices, the *masalas*,' goes the majority opinion. 'But it is not relevant to the French palate. Indeed, it is the kind of confusion we are always striving to avoid – it is the denial of the maxim *faites simple*. It is all wonderful in its place; but its place is India.'

I had hoped, before we came, that the Europeans would be flexible. But even the Austrian Witzigmann and Belgian Romeyer have a culinary sensibility that is fundamentally French. The flavours, it is fair to say, were not easily distinguishable. It was not really possible, say, to get hooked on cumin or develop a passion for fenugreek. And, Indians apart, I was the only one in the entire party with a taste for Indian sweets, though others were able to share my enthusiasm for the variety of breads, *roti*, and for the breakfast dishes of South India, the *dosas, idlis* and *uttappams*. Gael Greene now probably knows as much about Indian food as any American journalist, and Fay Maschler and I have had our love for it enhanced.

But Michel Rostang had the last word. He arranged for the entire French party to have lunch at his restaurant after their arrival in Paris on the first of February. He telephoned the menu through to his wife: steak, salad and cheese.

Ceylon and salmonella

What though the spicy breezes
Blow soft o'er Ceylon's isle;
Though every prospect pleases
And only man is vile:
In vain with lavish kindness
The gifts of God are strown.

So wrote the hymnist. He might have added that the food is not much to write home about either.

My fortnight in Sri Lanka was the generous prize given me by Corning Ltd in its 'Food Writer of the Year' competition in 1980. My own experiences confirmed the accuracy of Bishop Heber's observations – though he was wrong about the cause of the degradation of this lovely island. He blamed religion; the fault lies with tourism.

It is my fellow tourists – American, British and especially German – who are not only corrupting the morals of this gentle island people, but destroying their culinary traditions as well.

Bishop Heber's Ceylonese 'heathen in his blindness' who 'bows down to wood and stone' is a Buddhist and more or less a vegetarian. The Europeans who demand meat twice a day in the dining-rooms of their big hotels will not eat the delicious but unfamiliar 'rice and curry' of the natives.

In a coconut and rice economy, where there is little refrigeration, where the cow is sacred to the Tamil minority and rarely eaten by the Sinhalese Buddhists, where pork is eaten only by Christians and 'mutton' chiefly by Muslims, the foolish tourists who demand meat are served up beef that is cooked the day it is slaughtered, usually even before rigor mortis has set in. It is nasty.

The appetising alternative is masses of rice with mildly curried potato, sweet peppers, and *alakola dalu*, the 'tender leaves' of the wild yam from which poi is made in Hawaii and Polynesia. There are also fried cured sprats, poppadoms and a *mallum* of finely shredded tree leaves cooked with grated coconut, turmeric and onion. Jak fruit is served in a 'white curry', with cardamom, onions, turmeric, fenugreek, cinnamon, green chillies, coconut milk and 'Maldive fish', powdered dried tuna.

This, the best meal we had in Ceylon, was a lunch at a village house outside Pussellawa, near Kandy. The guest of honour was Mrs Bandaranaike, the former Prime Minister of Sri Lanka, and her son, Anura, was also present. (It was also, I have no doubt, the occasion on which I contracted the rare *Salmonella oslo*, a bug so infrequently encountered that, by the time it was finally diagnosed at the School of Tropical Medicine and Hygiene, nature had done her stuff and effected her own cure.)

As usual, at this lunch one was supposed to eat a large quantity of rice (the native rice is delicious and streaked with pink) and use the curries as flavouring for the rice. Fish, I noticed, seemed to be accounted a vegetable. There were a few other dishes I could not identify and, for afters, a chew of areca nut with lime paste wrapped in betel leaf.

Before following Mrs Bandaranaike to a Buddhist ceremony of blessing and on to a giant open-air rally, my wife took advantage of the circumstances, and Mrs B's polite enquiry about how we enjoyed our lunch, to complain about the 'European' food served in Sri Lankan hotels. She did not succeed in extracting a firm commitment from the former head of government; but I can assure those who, like us, have suffered gastronomic injury from the Sri Lankan tourist industry, that the matter received a sympathetic hearing in the highest quarters.

As a developing country, Sri Lanka has its share of economic problems connected with food, not the least of which is the inflation that has recently doubled the price of sugar, put up the price of bananas (the delicious tiny variety) from ½p to nearly 2p, and of mature Jak fruit from 5p to 17½p.

In such circumstances the cookery writer can sometimes take on the social importance of the technological innovator in the West. For example, we several times drove past farms with a sign saying 'Winged Bean Experiment'. Once in a market I saw some green leguminous things that I instantly identified as 'winged beans'. The Government has hit on these beans, the *dambala*, as the solution to the nation's nutritional problems, and is subsidising research into this latest food fad. But there is one serious problem: no one is quite sure how to cook them.

At four inches long, as I saw them in the market, they are too tough and fibrous to eat as green vegetables. In any case, the maximum protein value would be got by treating their mature seeds as pulses.

But, to quote Dr W. R. C. Paul in the *Ceylon Daily News* of 13 February, 1980, '*Dambala* seed is so hard that it cannot be cooked by ordinary methods; and so, no one will take to cooking it, even if the mature seed is available in the market.'

I have disappointing news for Dr Paul. As I suspected, and as I was able to confirm in conversation with a leading food writer, Mrs Chandra Dissanayake, *dambala* – or the winged bean – is the larger cousin of a plant we grow at home.

Its scarlet flower is so pretty that we often grow it in the flower beds. And its fruits are a great delicacy if picked when extremely young and less than an inch long. It takes hundreds of them, though, to make a first course, lightly boiled and served with melted butter.

Some readers will recognise from these remarks that the Government of Sri Lanka has sadly pinned its agricultural hopes on a variety of that most delicious, but luxuriously exotic of all vegetables, the asparagus pea.

Yak, yuck

Without a doubt the worst food I have ever eaten was in Nepal. I remember trying to eat *mo-mos* (like Chinese pan-fried dumplings, filled with minced meat, ginger and garlic) so doughy that they were impossible to swallow, even though they were being served in the most sublime lunch-time setting in the world: on a sunny terrace from which you could see Everest. Another Nepalese meal was cooked by tribeswomen, involved black magic and was served in the dark, which was just as well. It was deeply inedible.

I now know what I was eating – or rather, not eating – thanks to Alan Davidson's zany publishing firm, Prospect Books, who have brought out an entire book on the culinary first cousin of Nepal – Tibet. Rinjing Dorje's *Food in Tibetan Life* is absolutely definitive. Mr Dorje, whose name means 'flat-headed thunderbolt' (most Tibetans sport nick-names 'except some high lamas and officials, who are usually treated more formally'), puts food and drink into a global context. He does so with great charm.

For instance, it is important to realise that some offensive food smells, such as the famous rancid butter (of *dri*, not yak – the yak is the male of the species), would go quite unnoticed, because 'bathing is not very common in Tibet, especially during the colder parts of the year. A person might just take one bath in a whole year. Some people do not bathe at all, and older people sometimes say that taking a bath washes away all the good-fortune *yang*. Everyone washes his hair at least once a month, though.'

Now that tourists have been banned from the sky-burials, in which vultures pick clean the dismembered bones of the dead, one obstacle to good foreign relations has been removed. But Tibetan table manners still pose some difficulties to the traveller. 'Sometimes,' Mr Dorje admonishes the reader, 'a guest should nicely lick off the plate or bowl he ate from and wipe it out before getting up. If he can he should belch out loud. This is considered a sign of appreciation for the meal.'

What about the meal itself? Well, there are problems. Many Tibetans don't eat meat, being Lamaistic Buddhists. On the other hand, 'not many kinds of fruit or vegetable can grow in Tibet'. If it's anything like Nepal, I can vouch for the accuracy of this – though a Russian called Boris has introduced a strain of giant cauliflowers that seem to flourish around Kathmandu.

A lot of *yoe*, popped or toasted dried grains, are eaten. They are not terrifically nice. On the other hand, the Tibetan diet contains masses of butterfat, which doesn't seem to do them any harm. They float it on the surface of their tea, and rub the surplus into their noses or behind their ears to keep the skin from drying out. When they do eat meat, they don't leave any bits over. So this book contains very clear recipes for stuffed lung (take 'one complete sheep or goat's lung with windpipe still on . . .'), sheep's head, and blood sausage, a very nice-sounding blood-pudding (take 'one complete set lamb or goat's intestines . . .'). The consolations are small. There is beer (*chang*), and *arag* distilled from it. They have exact analogues in Nepal. I cannot recommend them. But they are not devoid of culinary interest. To make *chang*, you need *pap*, Tibetan yeast. Mr Dorje says, 'There are legends about how yeast was made for the first time, and some people today say yeast ought to be made the same way. But that would require ingredients such as eagle shit, the dried blood from a *drong* (wild yak), the tail of a jackal, and similarly inaccessible things. They really do not seem to be necessary after all.'

With Rinjing Dorje's own drawings, an endorsement and preface by the Dalai Lama, and good-natured and humorous chapters on everything to do with food and drink, I am willing to overlook the recipes. In fact, I can think of a dozen people for whom this would make a wonderful present. And the section on *kyurtse* or *gundru*, pickled vegetable greens, has given me a very thrifty idea for using up radish tops.

Imagine, tagine

The cuisine of Morocco depends for its effects on the combinations and permutations of a few ingredients. It is not a question of overcoming the limitation of a small variety of seasonings – think of what Chinese food would be like without soy sauce, garlic or ginger – but of making do with a relatively small quantity of foodstuffs. Geography, after all, is a powerful force in creating a cuisine. Though blessed with a coastline so long that it makes Tangier both a Mediterranean and an Atlantic city, the interior of Morocco consists of fishless desert and railroadless mountains. In the south, all but the lushest oases are too arid to graze cattle. Pigs are forbidden by the Islamic religion.

That leaves goats, sheep, chickens, pigeons, rabbits and, above all, hen's eggs as the non-vegetable sources of high-grade protein for most of the population. The desert folk are said to relish camel meat, and Tangerines have one of the most varied and copious fish and shellfish markets I have ever seen. But south of Marrakesh, the building blocks of the diet are few and soon grow monotonous. Add to this the fuel shortage endemic to mountainous regions and deserts, which means there are very few methods of cooking. Ovens are communal – usually the baker's –

seldom domestic. Cooking is done over glowing embers, for the most part, and is therefore limited to what can be simmered in earthenware vessels or grilled on skewers. Given all this, the alert traveller will not be surprised to be offered a version of a single dish at each of the day's principal meals. It is called *tagine*, which is the name of the flat dish of *terre cuite*, with its attractive conical lid, in which the ubiquitous stew is cooked.

Necessity is the mother of many recipes. It is not possible to brown meat or poultry in a terra cotta dish over a fire of coals, so the Moroccan *tagine* is almost always made without browning. The finished dish is therefore often pale in colour, or coloured a striking yellow by the turmeric or saffron that are generally included among the spices. These last are the true glory of Moroccan cooking. Not surprisingly, when ingredients are limited and cooking methods restricted, seasoning is the chief means of culinary expression. Every spice merchant in every souk in every medina has his own *ras el hanout*, or general spice mixture. It is not uncommon for the *mélange* to include twenty-four separate and distinct items, of which some will be pungent, some piquant, some perfumed, and, almost always, one or two that are said to be included for their aphrodisiac properties. Cumin is the chief constituent of all these mixtures, and the principal flavouring agent of most Moroccan food. Indeed, it is quite often to be found as a table condiment, along with the salt in a two-bowl cruet. If you like it, and the flavours of garlic, ginger, onions and fresh coriander, you will like Moroccan food.

It is the seasoning above all that gives Moroccan food its high standing in the Middle East. Among the states of the Maghreb, the French-influenced, Berber-populated states of North Africa, Morocco is famous for its *haute cuisine*. This is not altogether surprising when you realise that Tunisians have been known to spread their breakfast bread with *harissa*, the fiery red pepper paste that is the basis of all North African *sauce piquante*. What Moroccan cookery lacks in variety, it makes up for in subtlety. From classical Persian cooking it has taken the fruit and meat combinations so characteristic of the Fassi (Fez) dishes that are supposed to be the best Morocco has to offer.

Even the casual visitor will need to know something of Moroccan table manners, for often *tagine* is the only dish on offer, and it is frequently brought to table in the way Moroccans eat it themselves – in the dish in which it has been cooked. No matter how many of you are dining, you are all expected to eat from the common dish, with your fingers. You use only the thumb and first two fingers of the right hand (as is so often the case, the left hand is reserved for another, complementary, purpose). But there is always plenty of flat, round Moroccan bread on the table, and this easily takes the place of fork or spoon: it pushes and it absorbs. Before and after eating you rinse your hand under the tap that is to be found even in the meanest café and, to signal you are done eating, you lick your fingers.

So far, we have covered only the most common Moroccan dishes, the *tagine* and *brochettes* (kebabs). The great dishes, some or all of which you would get at a *diffa* or banquet (and don't worry about the Gargantuan portions – you are not expected to eat them all: there is an army of the cooks' friends and relations waiting in the kitchen for the left-overs), include the national dish of *couscous*. It is always served on a platter, the pale yellow grains of steamed semolina surmounted by the meat, fish or vegetable stew over which the starchy pellets have been cooked. It comes with a spicy sauce composed of the cooking liquid stirred into some *harissa*.

Couscous can be cooked in earthenware over embers, though it seldom is any more. The other great Moroccan dish requires an oven, and is therefore a dish served by the grander sort of host. *Bisteeya* (as it is spelled by Paula Wolfert, whose *Couscous and Other Good Food from Morocco* is the American authority) or *bstilla* (as it is spelled by Claudia Roden in her definitive *A New Book of Middle Eastern Food*), often listed on Moroccan menus (in misleading French) as *pastilla*, is the famous huge layered pie of stretched pastry, pigeon, scrambled egg and almond paste, always served topped with sugar and cinnamon. No traveller in Morocco should omit to taste it; and, if its ingredients sound bizarre, think for a minute about its close culinary relations, Christmas pudding and mince pie.

Another grand dish is *mechoui*, a whole roast sheep cooked in such a fashion that the skin is crisp but the meat falls off the bones. Sprinkled with cumin, it is the ultimate barbecue treat – if you're keen on fat. It is rare nowadays for the head of the animal to be served with the *mechoui*, so you don't have to worry about what to do if the host offers you the eyes.

Of the *tagines*, the best is *djej emshmel* (or *meshmel* or *emsharmel*), chicken with olives and brine-preserved lemons. *Kefta*, minced meat, is always reliable and can turn up grilled on a skewer, or stewed in a *tagine*, often with added eggs, poached at the last minute. Eggs abound, and are used in large quantities – a problem for the cholesterol-conscious tourist.

But just as omelette is universally on the menu, so is soup, of which my favourite is the chick pea-laden, egg-thickened *harira*, the dish with which the pious traditionally break the fast each night of Ramadan. Most street vendors have a version. You can tell by the stacks of decorated bowls; it is not they that are for sale, but soup. Moroccan salads are usually fairly finely chopped combinations of tomato and other vegetables such as onion and sweet pepper, often flavoured with cumin and sometimes green coriander.

Where do you find Moroccan food? There's the rub, for there are virtually *no* outstanding restaurants. The once-famous Maison Arabe in the medina of Marrakesh is no longer so celebrated for its food. As in Italy, and many other countries come to that, the only really good cooking is to be found in private homes. Fortunately, Moroccans are very hospitable, as are the many American and European expatriates one bumps into in the major cities. On the whole, Moroccan food is best sampled in hotels, such as the poolside luncheon buffet of the Mamounia in Marrakesh; or the specialities you order in advance at La Gazelle D'Or or Hotel Palais Salam at Taroudant, or in the *table d'hôte* (there is seldom any choice in Moroccan menus and it is unknown for any but the grandest establishments to take orders *à la carte*) of hotel dining-rooms like that of the Hotel Tinsouline at Zagora, whose couscous has much to commend it. Occasionally you come across basically French restaurants, but with a good selection of Moroccan dishes such as Au Sanglier qui Fume at Ouirgane, or the Rotisserie du Café de la Paix, Rue Yougoslavie, Marrakesh, or the amusing Chez Dmitri at Ouazarzate, a relic of the former presence of the Foreign Legion.

Outside the bigger cities of the south, incidentally, it can be difficult to obtain beer or wine with your meals. Again, resort to the hotels – at least one tourist hotel is licensed in every town, often the local outpost of the government-owned PLM chain.

Spanish fly

Spanish fly – cantharides – has been universally regarded as an aphrodisiac since antiquity. There is a reference to it in English dating back to 1398, and the Oxford English Dictionary even allows its use as a verb, 'to cantharadize', adding '(esp. as an aphrodisiac)'. When I was a teenager in Kentucky, my friends and I had heard smutty tales of its powers to cause sexual excitement (though we thought it only worked on girls), and our hearsay theory that it stimulated desire by causing a sort of itching was basically correct.

Cantharis, which is the same in Latin and Greek, is a blister fly or beetle, *Lytta vesicatoria*. Its bright blue or green wing covers (elytra) when crushed yield cantharadin, a substance that can cause the skin to blister, and is used medicinally as a skin irritant in plasters and as a diuretic. These uses are better documented than its aphrodisiac properties. One other thing is certain: the substance is highly poisonous. The lethal dosage for human beings is .03 grams.

I was a bit surprised to learn this myself, as I have eaten cantharides several times and am even guilty of having fed it to my family and to guests – though without any ill effects. We are fond of Moroccan food and were once given a packet of mixed Moroccan whole spices called *ras el hanout*. Some of the ingredients, such as orrisroot, earth almonds (*Cyperus esculentus*), and something else I couldn't identify, but which looked very much like a chunk of glass, you had to smash with a hammer before grinding. It was quite easy to recognise the brilliant blue Spanish fly; one just popped it whole into the spice mill. A generous friend had brought us this particular assortment (which contained about twenty ingredients in all) from Fez.

In the standard book on Moroccan cuisine, *Couscous and Other Good Food from Morocco*, Paula Wolfert lists cantharides amongst the usual ingredients of the *ras el hanout* mélange. Indeed, she says 'the aphrodisiacs (Spanish fly, ash berries and monk's pepper) that appear in most formulae seem to be the reason why the mere mention of this mixture will put a gleam into a Moroccan cook's eye'.

Moroccans tend to giggle at the mention of cantharides. On a visit to southern Morocco in the winter of 1986, I found that when I tried to buy the stuff the spice merchant or medicine man would titter, or even howl with laughter. None of them ever believed I required it only for purposes of research, and not for my personal use. Moreover, I was accompanied on several occasions by my wife, and it is used as a specific for impotence and female frigidity. It took us several shopping expeditions to realise that we were making ourselves into figures of fun.

Our first and successful attempt to buy it was in the medina of the lovely town of Taroudant. We were picked up by one of the ubiquitous

French-speaking young men who frighten away the younger boys that otherwise plague the obvious tourist, and who ask only for a tip – they scurry around afterwards and collect their commission from any shop-keeper to whom they have guided you. Our cicerone took us to a stall belonging to his friend Mohammed, who, like him, appeared to be in his twenties. There we easily bought 20 cantharides for a dirham (a little more than fifteen pence, each. We also bought a sixteen-ingredient *ras el hanout* costing about ten pounds all together. He obviously did *not* regard the *cantharides* as a constituent of the mixture.

There were some other surprises. The first is that it is not called 'Spanish', but 'Indian fly', *dbana India* in Arabic. Mohammed, though he leered at my wife and me a bit, and made some fairly indecent gestures as he assured us that he had tried the *dbana* himself to good effect, did immediately warn us against its use by pregnant women. He recommended taking it as a decoction: pound the flies finely and boil furiously for five minutes with dried mint flowers; simmer until reduced by one half; add sugar to taste; cool; strain through a very fine nylon mesh and drink. How many flies was the dose? I asked. 'Ten to twelve for a Moroccan,' Mohammed replied, 'but at least twenty for Europeans, who need more help.' He and our guide were by then helpless with laughter. Mohammed said nothing about it being toxic, and again denied that he knew of any culinary uses.

We bought it again in the souk at Marrakesh, this time for only two dirhams per gram; there were sixteen flies in two grams, so the price was only 25 per cent of what it was in Taroudant. At first, the eighteen-year-old boy who sold it to us said it was for impotence. Then, chuckling to himself at what he imagined to be our discomfiture, he admitted that it was also lust-provoking or pleasure-enhancing. 'Grind them into powder,' he said, 'and put them into a glass of whisky or milk' – a very un-Islamic prescription – 'then watch out!'

In a spirit of experimentation, I also ate some *majoun*, a sort of fudge that is reputed to contain hashish. This was in a private house in Marrakesh. I don't think it had any effect; and later I learnt that *majoun* invariably contains some Spanish fly.

My biggest adventure in the cantharides trade came in the desert town of Zagora. There I finally got someone to take my research seriously. Another French-speaker called Mohammed took me to call on the local holy man, 'Le Haj Ali'. We made our way to a mud hut. In a white-washed room with one naked electric light bulb and two mattresses covered with carpets, we found the Imam at prayer. When Haj Ali finished his devotions, he uttered some words ('A spell,' Mohammed whispered) and cast some incense on to a charcoal brazier in the middle of the room. Haj Ali's young-looking face (he is thirty-five) was half covered by a black shawl. From under his voluminous white robe there peeped bright pink longjohns.

Mohammed had prepared a list of questions in French and translated them into Arabic. Again, the holy man denied that there were any culinary uses for cantharides. He said, after consulting some printed pamphlets, that it was an 'antidote to certain love charms given to men by women, and a specific against some kinds of worms' that are intestinal parasites.

Having consulted another pamphlet whose subject was evidently gynaecology, the Haj then said there was a substance called *lachoub*, which contains forty-four plants and one-quarter of a fly, in a medium of pure honey. Reaching into a reticule, he produced a worn plastic bag, into which he lunged with the fingers of his right hand. He exhibited some goo, which he then popped into his mouth, and scraped against his teeth. He noisily licked his fingers, and invited Mohammed and me to help ourselves. *Lachoub*, he explained, cures female frigidity and is good for impotence. It should be taken before breakfast.

I asked the Haj, as I had my other informants, where the *dbana* came from. They had all thought India; he thought it came from 'the desert of Saudi Arabia' where he had last bought it, on the occasion of the pilgrimage to Mecca that conferred his title 'Haj' upon him. The attribution to India came about, he thought, 'because it is gaily coloured, like Indian clothing. But it's from Saudi – the biggest fly that lives around there.' You must not, he said, infuse the fly, for 'the goodness goes with the steam'. I asked about its effects. He told his rosary and spoke in a hush. 'Purely psychological,' he replied. 'It's the lack of *chaleur humaine* that causes impotence.' 'Women,' he reflected, can tolerate a higher dosage than men, and 'have ninety-nine times more pleasure than men in sex, after taking *dbana*.'

There then arose an awkwardness. How was I to pay this holy man for his time? A way out suggested itself. Would I like him to prepare a talisman for me? He could do an enormously powerful charm, which would protect me, ensure happiness and material success, and confound my enemies. I agreed with alacrity.

First, I shut my eyes, said *Bismallah*, the magical invocation of God's name for a blessing, and pointed a finger on the page of a book. I got a *carré*, the intersection of four boxes. Haj Ali then proceeded to tell my fortune, in frighteningly specific and accurate detail. This was to allow him to prescribe the Koranic texts that he would write with a bamboo splinter on the parchment that made up the talisman. He asked my mother's and father's names and was delighted that my father's name ('Chaim' in Hebrew, and also in the French we were actually speaking via Mohammed) was an auspicious Arabic name – 'Hakim'. The paper was folded many times. It enclosed some herbs and spices, and was passed over the incense fumes from the brazier. I was told to get it sewn up in a leather cover, and to wear it on a string around my neck or right arm, but only when 'clean'. It was all right to wear it after the bath, but not in the *hammam* (the communal bath) or when having sexual relations or even sharing a bed – no one else must ever touch it. It was *very* potent. I paid 150 dirhams for my talisman, having been told politely that the 100 I offered was not enough for a charm of such power.

While waiting for the leather craftsman to make the cover for my talisman, I tried to buy some Spanish fly from an old man in the medina of Zagora. He told me a great deal of *dbana* lore, but his brow clouded over when I asked to buy some. 'I have none for sale,' he patently lied. Mohammed later discovered that the old man was afraid I might misuse it – or abuse it – and that the law would blame him for selling it to an ignorant foreigner.

I had meant to end by reporting the effects upon myself of swallowing a decoction of the twenty flies. Now that I have discovered the toxicity of such a small amount of this terrifying beetle, I am certain the reader will excuse me from the experiment. And I must remember to warn the friend to whom I gave some as a 51st birthday present.

Granny food

Everybody told me that the food in the Soviet Union would be filthy. But I am a romantic about Russian food, and in the end my culinary package-tour pilgrimage to Moscow and Leningrad was justified by two dishes that finely echoed the tastes of Grandmother's cooking.

In Moscow I found vast barrels of brine-cured pickled cucumber, almost innocent of vinegar, tasting chiefly of dill and garlic, crisp when new, and though soggy when older, full of matured flavours. And for breakfast in our Leningrad hotel we were served blini like Grandmother's, a thin crêpe enveloping a soft curd cheese filling, served with soured cream and jam.

The Russian–Jewish equivalent of madeleine and lime-flower tea, I suppose. At least in retrospect it made sense of the comedy of my first trip to Russia, in the company of two friends who shared my interest in eating out and shopping for food.

Breakfast on our first morning in Moscow started with superb buttermilk and went on with a basket of boiled eggs, some soft, some hard, and some medium – but with absolutely no way of telling which was which. There was a platter of cheese on the table, one of the two basic types of Soviet cheese: semi-hard, and looking and tasting like Tilsit. There were sweet rolls, good white bread and the wonderful coarse black sourdough bread (without which, I suspect, the entire population of the Soviet Union would be constipated), also EEC butter, a bowl of fruit preserve, coffee of a sort and deliciously scented Georgian tea.

After the ballet we dined at the foreign currency restaurant on the fourth floor of the Metropol Hotel. Luckily we arrived before 10.30 when last orders are taken. All restaurant kitchens shut promptly at 11.

We drank vodka, which is always sold by the 100 cl, and is very cheap. (In no time at all, I'm afraid, we discovered that the three of us always drank exactly half a litre at a sitting.) We particularly liked the flavoured vodkas, especially Zubrovka (buffalo grass) and Starka (port, brandy and tea).

We ate buckwheat blini, pancakes the size of the diameter of an orange, with melted butter, soured cream and 'soft' (black) caviar; translucently creamy, rose-tinged slices of smoked sturgeon with black bread and butter and sturgeon *à la Moscou*, hot with potato, onion, mushroom and soured cream. This really scrumptious late-night nosh-up cost £17.82.

Our great adventures began Monday at noon, when we met up with an English friend. For lunch she and her husband took us to a typical Soviet cafeteria, the Café Arfa, on Stoleshnikov Pereulok, a poky, Lower Depths of a place, only a few streets away from the wide main drag of Moscow, Gorky Street.

It is a paradox that Russian service of food is the exact opposite of service *à la russe*. All food in the Soviet Union is, in principle, hot when it is served – but it is served whether or not there is anyone present to eat it. One could understand this in the tourist hotels, where between 500 and

1500 meals could be – and sometimes were – dished up at a single sitting, but it seemed odd that the 'hot' food should be dispensed this way in a self-service establishment.

The Arfa was modest and not unpleasant; it was clean and comfortable enough. The only strikingly unusual thing about the Arfa was that there were no knives at all.

We had a good selection of the dishes, which represented the lunch of the average Muscovite. There was *smitane* (sour cream, eaten with a spoon), *kefir* (buttermilk, which is drunk), *studen* (a meat brawn eaten with mustard), and a salad of julienne of turnip or some other white root vegetable with sour cream. These were the *zakuski*, the starters.

The hot dishes included *tabaka*, a Georgian recipe for chicken, which is flattened, marinated and grilled; *kotleti*, a thick, sausage-shaped object made of minced meat, breaded and fried; and *zapekanka tvorozhnaya*, a savoury cake of *tvorog*, which is the soft variety of Soviet cheese.

With tea, this efficiently served meal cost about one pound each.

After lunch my friend's husband took us to Petrovka Street, to a *kvass* bar. Beer and wine could be bought to take away, but most of the customers drank, standing up, *kvass*, the national drink, which is made from fermented black bread. I liked it. It is far less sticky and cloying than Coca-Cola, and reminded me of old-fashioned American root beer.

A visit to the main market in the south of Moscow, Cheryomeenskee, revealed that the quality of the food there was better than we had seen in shops, but it was some distance from the centre. The hundred-odd stalls of the market (not all were occupied the day we were there) are run by peasants, selling the surplus produced by their communal farms, or their own personal produce. The few fresh vegetables available had come, like the extraordinarily expensive flowers (tulips one rouble each), from Georgia.

We moved among (and photographed) the rows of *babushkas* selling salted (pickled in brine) cabbage, cucumbers and green tomatoes, tasting this one's proffered cabbage and that one's cucumbers. It was at this point that we were arrested. A plainclothesman tapped my Russian-speaking friend on the shoulder: 'You must come with me.' My friend asked, 'Are you a policeman?' and the chap looked daggers at her. She said we'd happily accompany him if he would prove he was a policeman, and tell us what we were doing wrong. He melted away into the pickle barrels, and our friend translated the conversation for us. We were breathless at her bravery.

But he was, in fact, replaced by a uniformed cop, and we had no choice but to accompany this one up a flight of stairs to a well-heated room containing a fur-hatted man behind a desk. 'You have been taking photographs in the market,' he accused, with perfect accuracy. 'Is it a crime?' asked my brazen friend. 'No,' said fur hat, 'but it requires the permission of the Director of the Market.' My friend decided to try a new approach, contrition: 'I am sorry we have unwittingly breached the regulations.' The man behind the desk relaxed: '*I* am the Director of the Market; *you* have permission to take photographs.'

The *babushkas* now seemed happier to pose for us with their dried mushrooms strung with the smallest on the top and the biggest on the bottom, like elongated cones, and their pink pickled garlics. We felt obliged to take a few token photographs. My knees felt weak as I pressed the shutter, and we took ourselves off to the bus stop as quickly as we felt we could without loss of face.

Like every Soviet restaurant we saw, the entrance to the Slavyansky Bazaar, a restaurant famous for its typically Russian food, was grotty in the extreme, but we were cheered considerably by the sight of the purpose-built restaurant interior, with its bright colours.

We ate three platters of *zakuski* – fish, meat (including a particularly exotic smoked *fat* with only a tiny streak of meat running through it) and egg and meat salad with sour cream – with special bread that included a white sourdough roll, shaped like a bagel.

As we got to our next course, blini with soured cream, a remarkable sociological fact struck us: the other tables were segregated by sex. But by the time our over-cooked fillet steak with potato, onion and soured cream came, the Soviet soldiers at the table near us were beginning to flirt openly with the four heavily made-up, fur-hatted girls at the next table.

When the (good) Soviet ice-cream on macaroon, topped with cream Chantilly and the ubiquitous blackcurrant preserve, appeared, one of the boys actually had the nerve to ask one of the girls to dance, and the whole place exploded into heterosexual behaviour.

We took the day train from Moscow to Leningrad. The food in the dining car was delicious, from the tea in a glass with blackcurrant jam to the *selyanka*, soup with fish or meat, olives and lemon slices.

The food at the Hotel Leningrad was almost uniformly good, especially the breakfasts. The one snag was Leningrad water, in which thrives an amoeba to which, I'm told, four per cent of the population is not immune. There are two sorts of Leningrad mineral water, one of which allegedly tastes of rusty pipes. We had the other sort, which tastes of fish. Consequently we drank a good deal of Georgian wine, and I can recommend two whites, Gurdjani and Tsinandali.

Our grand restaurant meal was at the Baku, an Azerbaijani restaurant, and cost 78 roubles (about £60) for four people. The remarkable *zakuski* that were produced in exchange for my *Observer* credentials (a tip proved helpful, but not definitive) included thick slabs of smoked sturgeon, cold chicken bits in a nutty sauce, and ewe cheese 'with our national grasses', which were fresh dill and coriander, plus superb mild-cured pickled chilli peppers, along with whole white loaves of flattish bread.

The main course was shashlik, of which lamb was the best, though sturgeon was good and chicken not bad, and a pilau with raisins, dried apricots and slabs of ham fat.

At the Hotel Leningrad I was separated from the rest of the large party my friends and I were travelling with, and given a particularly nice room, with a spectacular view of the *Aurora*, moored in the river, just outside my window. It was *so* nice that seven or eight of us met there every night for a dormitory feast of smoked sturgeon sandwiches, sweet Georgian bubbly and flavoured vodka. We discussed nothing but food. The Thompson Tour organisers later told us that it was one of the 'surveillance' rooms: its amenities included a full bugging system. We laughed, as poor Boris or Ivan must have thought our conversation either lunatic or very cleverly coded.

It wasn't so funny when immigration and customs officials at Leningrad airport turned my luggage inside out as we were leaving. I got angry when they threatened to open my 500 gram tin of caviar, though I had tolerated their flinging my papers all over the floor. Suddenly the man holding my passport spoke up, and the rough stuff stopped at once – caviar still undisturbed. The reason? As the tour organisers had known all along, there was a man called Lewis on our flight, who was distributing YMCA pamphlets. 'Lewis' and 'Levy' differ very little when written in Cyrillic characters. I wonder if they thought I had hidden a Bible in the Beluga? Lewis, in the meantime, had boarded the plane, unmolested. I hope he sometimes thinks of me when saying grace.

Eat when you're Hungary

Sunday's lunch was almost ready; the fish kettle was simmering nicely. But as I unwrapped the fish I had removed from the freezer the night before, I discovered it was not a salmon trout but a pike-perch that a diplomat Foodie friend had brought me from Russia.

Fortunately I knew what to do with it. I had been to Hungary this summer, and in that land-locked country pike-perch and carp are almost the only species of fish available. (It is doubtful that my specimen was genuine *Lucioperca sandra*, the famous *fogas* of Lake Balaton; mine was more likely *Stizostedion lucioperca* (Linnaeus), which André Simon dismisses sniffily in his *Concise Encyclopedia of Gastronomy*.

Using the recipe in Károly Gundel's *Hungarian Cookery Book*, I filleted the fish, steamed it, used the bones and trimmings to make stock, and made a sauce of minced onion sweated in a little butter with sweet paprika, topped up with the stock and thickened slightly with soured cream.

It was rather better than the meal I had at the most famous restaurant in Budapest which bears Károly Gundel's name. In fact, it was at least as good as anything I had to eat in Hungary. Hungarian food used to be celebrated for its excellence, and four different friends of mine have spoken to me with nostalgia for the flavours of their Hungarian childhoods. It is sad that one of them who has returned most recently agrees with my impression that the quality of the food has degenerated considerably.

My week in Hungary was spent as the guest of Colmans of Norwich; they had taken me there to learn about Hungarian wine, as they held the concession from Monimpex, the state organisation responsible for wine. They list several lesser-known Hungarian wines that will be of interest to wine buffs, as the grape varieties appear to be indigenous to Hungary, and radically unlike the vines grown in western Europe. They include Hárslevelü, the 'limeleaf' grape, Kéknyelü, the 'blue-stalk' grape, and wonderful grape varieties that bear names that are hilariously and misleadingly like other European *cépages*, such as Médoc Noir, Kabernet Franc, Burgundi and Oporto.

Even the best-known wine of Hungary, Tokay, is confusing. In the first place, Tokay Essence (or to give it its correct name, Tokay Aszú Essencia), the liquor that is supposed to revive the dying, isn't really wine at all. It has so much sugar that it never ferments fully and after twenty years is often no more than one per cent alcohol – it is more akin to jam than to wine.

The Tokay that we know and admire is a good deal more alcoholic. It is a Botrytis wine, made from grapes shrivelled with the fungus known as the 'noble rot', and picked late – starting about 28th October and sometimes continuing into December. Botrytis-infected berries are called *aszú*, and the sweetness of the final wine is measured by the number of *puttonyos* or tubs of these special grapes that are added to the must or new base wine before fermentation. Three, four or five is the normal number. I was astonished to learn that the wine is then oxidised on purpose – placed in casks and exposed to air so that it becomes slightly brown and takes on a taste that we normally associate with white wine that has been kept too long. I suppose that the extreme sweetness of the higher grades of Tokay masks the oxidised taste somewhat, and makes it unobjectionable.

These often strong and sometimes strange-tasting wines are the best possible accompaniment, I think, to the forceful flavours of Hungarian food. I am sure I am not the first traveller to Hungary to find the food monotonous, with its ubiquitous seasoning of paprika. Surprisingly enough, the use of this condiment in Hungarian cookery is only a century old. According to Károly Gundel, 'in the Hungarian cookery-books of the first half of the 19th century we find scarcely any mention of paprika, to say nothing of the fact that it was completely unknown in books dating from the 18th century'.

Prepared from the fruit of *Capsicum frutescens, var. tetragonum*, paprika comes in five distinct grades, of which we normally see only two, one of which is sweet and mild, and the other hot, but less so than cayenne. The pungent quality, André Simon informs us, comes from a substance called *capsaicin*, and paprika is a valuable source of vitamins A and C.

We do have quite a lot of misapprehensions about Hungarian food. A study done by Louis Szathmary for Alan Davidson's Oxford symposium on food showed that the Hungarian dishes we think of as typical and demand in restaurants – such as 'goulash' – are in fact party dishes that are served only on special occasions in Hungary itself. Not only can I confirm the truth of this, but I can now point out that what we English speakers call 'goulash' is really *pörkölt*, 'a stew in which finely chopped onions have a much greater importance than they do in *gulyás*', as Gundel points out. Moreover, *pörkölt* 'is braised rather than boiled and has a thickened sauce', whereas '*gulyás* is something like a soup or a kind of meat stew'.

I've been told that the Hungarian tourist authorities are conscious that the quality of food available in hotels and restaurants has declined, and that they are anxious to make improvements. They blame their troubles on the huge increases in tourism, especially from East Germany, which have resulted in a dearth of chefs. Certainly there were no shortages of good things to eat in the markets I saw, except that there were almost no salad stuffs and relatively few fresh vegetables. Their attempt to recover the historic greatness of their cuisine is noble; I hope they succeed.

S.S. *Mein Kind*

It's been twenty-four years since I visited Israel, and my memory of what I ate on that visit makes me certain that the standard of food available has to have improved in the interval. It is impossible for it to have got any worse.

Evelyn Rose, the distinguished cookery editor of *The Jewish Chronicle*, has compiled *The Israel Good Food Guide* (Robson Books), a genuine candidate for the title of 'shortest book ever published'. In her introductory matter, Mrs Rose tacitly acknowledges that France and China are in no immediate danger of losing their gastronomic laurels to Israel. And she confirms my memory that the best food in Israel is the indigenous fare of the Middle East. Unfortunately, I was not allowed to sample a great deal of it, as my hosts in that benighted time obviously did not consider Arab food suitable nourishment for a nice Jewish boy.

What I did encounter often, and came to enjoy, was the 'kibbutz breakfast', that enormous dairy collation that Mrs Rose tactfully calls Israel's 'main contribution to international cuisine'. In fact, she offers the precautionary advice that 'the wise visitor also considers it as a main meal'. In other words, taking it seriously and eating enough 'kibbutz breakfast' can save you from requiring another meal that is likely to be disappointing.

Life can be perverse, and it is a paradox that it is the very awfulness of Israel's catering industry that makes Mrs Rose's book so necessary. The tourist to Israel needs not only culinary guidance, but protection. The reasons are simple, but profound and sad. The *haimishe* Jewish food of Eastern Europe is not suitable for serving in restaurants, as most of it is made by long cooking processes. Stewing, simmering and roasting do not produce the kind of dishes the modern diner-out is looking for; and the use of the deep-fryer is not healthy, or even appealing in a hot country. The Arabs understand the use and the pleasures of the grill, and their cuisine is accordingly more suited to the climate.

Perhaps only a Jew can say this, but the laws of *kashruth* are not very helpful to those who are engaged in producing food for sale to the public. For example, I had to laugh at the entry under Eilat for the Pagoda kosher Chinese restaurant. Now, the Chinese eat no dairy produce at all (lactose intolerance is very common among Han Chinese), so that's one problem out of the way. But the Chinese have very few recipes for lamb or beef, as most ethnic Chinese dislike these meats. This trying to make Chinese food without the use of pork or shellfish is very like what Dr Johnson said about women preaching and dogs walking on their hinder legs: the wonder is not that it's done well, but that anybody wants to do it at all.

Far better, when in Israel, to try to dine as the long-time inhabitants always have done: shun Chinese restaurants, French bistros, and 'kosher Italian dairy' restaurants (even ones like the Mamma Mia in Jerusalem, with its charming-sounding waiter 'wearing a yarmulke and a single earring'). The Maharajah kosher Indian restaurant is another one I'd give a miss, along with all Sheraton and Hilton hotels. Tel Aviv's South African-inspired Safari Steakhouse and cutely named Seafari fill me with gastronomic apprehension, and I'd walk several miles out of my way to avoid Jerusalem's Mishkenot Sha'ananim, where the chef's French specialities include 'mixed hot hors d'oeuvre Kissinger'. I think I'd also be prepared to miss the delights of the various Hungarian restaurants listed by Mrs Rose, and the coffee house that has 'faint echoes of a Konditorei in Vienna'.

In Jerusalem, I'd head straight for the many restaurants listed in Machane Yehuda market, where I'd gobble up *kibbeh* and hummus at Hashelosha, Kurdistan food at the six-tables Menagen, felafel balls at Rama and eat meat only at the Yemeni Barbecue. I expect I'd be happy, full and exceedingly grateful to Evelyn Rose for directing me there.

I hear America eating

On this side of the Ocean, we tend to think that my American countrymen subsist on a diet of Kentucky Fried and Big Macs. Those who know a little more about American eating habits are equally convinced that all 250,000,000 of them breakfast exclusively on Sugar Pops, waffles with maple syrup, or synthetic cream-filled chocolate cupcakes called Twinkies; lunch on hot dogs with garishly turmeric-coloured French's mustard in doughy buns or overstuffed roast-beef sandwiches from Arbie's or quarter-pound hamburgers from any one of a thousand fast-food chains; and dine on pizza or take-away tacos.

Wrong. In urban centres (and I don't just mean New York and Los Angeles, but Philadelphia, Chicago, Kansas City, Washington, Louisville, Atlanta, Detroit and Cincinnati, to mention but a few), what you *see* is the giant hamburgers and hot dogs picked out by the fast food emporia's neon lights. But what people are actually eating is little bits of raw fish laid out decoratively on a plate, goat-cheese pizzas, stuffed vine leaves, buckwheat blini with native gold caviar, Pacific oysters, New York State *foie gras* and Minnesota huckleberry tarts. They're washing it all down with so much imported French white burgundy that there is actually a shortage in the rest of the world.

What they are *not* eating is whole menus such as this exquisite one from a recent issue of *Gourmet*: artichokes *gribiches*, eggplant *rollatini* with three cheeses, *rugola* salad, prosciutto bread, and ginger poached pears.

The reason they're not eating the above is that it all actually has to be *cooked*, and urban Americans no longer eat at home at all. A celebrated British cookery writer, who had just returned from a book-promotion tour of the East, told me that, 'Though I was in the company exclusively of Foodies, not one of the sixty or so meals I ate in a fortnight was taken in a private house. Though I was staying with friends who talked and thought about nothing but food, *nobody* ever cooked. Many of our meals were eaten in somebody's car.'

This is not an isolated report. More and more, we hear that Americans no longer have structured meals at all. Breakfast, dinner, lunch and tea the American frame no longer requires. Instead, sophisticated Americans now nourish themselves by a process they call 'grazing'. This is what accounts for my friend's experiences in the back of the car. This is no longer the venue for teen-age sex; instead it has become a mobile dining-room for grazing.

The grazer, feeling hunger pangs, drives to the Chinese restaurant and orders a couple of dozen *jiaozi*, either of the pan-fried pot-sticker variety or, with the same minced pork, ginger and garlic filling enclosed in noodle dough, poached in chicken stock. This is consumed in the car, using the chopsticks that are permanently kept in the glove box for the purpose.

Hunger may strike at any hour. American restaurants obligingly expect to serve food all day – and most of the night. Peckish at the office? Grazers pop into the local sushi bar for a couple of bites.

Nobody, of course, ever eats at the lunch or dinner hours any more. But if you happen to need re-fuelling any time before 4 a.m., you can always drive to the neighbourhood gourmet pizzeria and order some mussel-stuffed *calzone*, with a side-order of *arugula* or *rugola* (rocket) salad dressed with hazelnut oil. O brave new world, that has such things to eat in it.

THE INNER MAN

Après nouvelle, le déluge

Since the mid-Eighties, journalists have been predicting, announcing and hoping for the death of the *nouvelle cuisine*. This is only just, as the expression itself, if not the culinary movement, was the creation of journalists.

Henri Gault and Christian Millau, the two Parisians who produce the guidebook and monthly gastronomic magazine *Gault–Millau*, coined the term in the October 1973 issue. They only baptised the phenomenon; it was actually discovered, though not named, by Raymond Sokolov, then of *The New York Times*, in 1972. It described the sort of cooking being done by the followers of Fernand Point (who died in 1955), the famous chef of La Pyramide at Vienne. His disciples, who included the celebrated French *chefs patrons* Raymond Thuiller, Paul Bocuse, the Troisgros brothers, François Bise and Louis Outhier, practised a new lighter style of French cookery. They threw out the old flour-thickened sauces, which had occasionally masked the taste in pre-freezer days, and replaced them with airy concoctions based on reductions of cooking juices. To avoid disguising the ingredients, which were always fresh and of the highest quality, they always placed these sauces *under*, never over, the food. Serving yesterday's fish had become a thing of the past. It follows that the arrangements of the plate became the duty (and pleasure) of the cook, not the waiter – and food as art was born. Silver service died, as chefs everywhere made pictures on plates.

What food was on the plates? A very small portion of something terribly expensive. Well, this was the popular journalist's-eye view of the *nouvelle cuisine*. What had actually happened is that what began as a movement to reform classic French cooking gave way to the excesses of Romanticism.

The pioneers of *nouvelle cuisine* stressed the freshness of the ingredients. Second-rate imitators stressed their expense. NC was concerned with health – avoiding refined flour, reducing fats and shunning fried food. The band-wagon jumpers-on lowered calories by making portions minute. NC chefs liked to experiment with new ingredients and techniques. Their sedulous apers valued novelty above all else. Alain Senderens invented lobster with vanilla (pointing out that we think of vanilla's place as being puddings simply because we always associate it with sugar). In lesser hands this became lobster with strawberries and raspberry vinegar with everything. Kiwi fruit replaced parsley.

Even the furniture of the table changed. A new sauce-spoon was invented, which made it perfectly polite to lick up the last drop of exquisite and expensive sauce. Plates grew – they got bigger and bigger so what was on them became increasingly miniaturised. Round plates gave way to chic, plain white, octagonal plates. White plates then became black ones, against which microscopic bits of food looked like clusters of jewels.

It was bound to happen. Once chefs started taking themselves seriously, once they had convinced themselves that they were artists, they were bound to fall prey to Romanticism, and emphasise the preciousness of the ingredients and the novelty of their preparation. Imagination took over from the hard-won skills of the classically trained cook, and strong passions became a substitute for thinking. The odd combination replaced the balanced composition on the plates of diners all over the affluent world.

Let's be quite clear about it – this is not what *nouvelle cuisine* became as practised by an Alain Chapel or a Michael Guérard in France, or by Anton Mosimann, Pierre Koffman or Raymond Blanc in England. But not long ago, in London's best-known and most expensive basement restaurant, I was served sliced breast of poached chicken in a cream sauce with shredded fresh basil on a bed of fresh noodles. It incorporated chunks of skinned, de-pipped tomatoes, and what I would swear were fresh lychees. The perpetrator of this yuck is thought by many to be one of Britain's best chefs.

A reaction, you might think, was long over-due. It has come. Not surprisingly it has all the hallmarks of Neo-Classicism – restraint where there was excess, and the replacement of unnatural marriages of food by the refinement of traditional dishes. Self-expression has yielded to sober reflection on the regional roots that most French chefs still know from experience. Before the war, French domestic cookery was dominated by regionalism and produced by women cooks, using the tried and true recipes of their mothers, which they followed rigorously. Granny ruled and it was OK. Restaurant cooking was rule-bound – Escoffier had laid down the law and every chef of classic French cuisine obeyed it. Things began to ease up a bit in the Fifties, as Dior bent the rules of fashion and Point rebelled against Escoffier. The *nouvelle cuisine* and the New Look were being cooked up at the same time.

The Sixties were a typical Romantic time. Individualism took over in fashion, architecture, the fine and decorative arts – and, naturally, in food. There were no rules any more. We all got interested in foreign food, and the Chinese and Indian restaurants appeared in every High Street. French restaurants with good cooks served Mediterranean delicacies; restaurants with bad cooks served pineapple rings with the pork chops. Culinary freedom was a by-word – until the late Seventies, when, in the wrong hands, it became licence, and untalented, untrained so-called *nouvelle cuisine* chefs began making messes.

Now, of course, the whole world has gone conservative. The counter-revolution has followed its normal historical path, and we are all fed up with the little purées, sorbets and luke-warm salads of the Romantic day-before-yesterday.

But Victorian values won't dictate a return to Victorian puddings. We are too health-conscious now to tolerate suet and custard. Fogies may long for the return of *sauce béchamel*, but Foodies thank God that in the recurring historical cycles from Classicism to Neo-Classicism, the reforms of Romanticism remain behind. The baby is not thrown out with the bathwater, but the sauces are utterly changed. Thus Granny's food has been lightened and refined by the salubrious aspects of the *nouvelle cuisine*, until it is now worthy to take its rightful place on the restaurant table.

In 1985, a trip to Paris for purposes of gastronomic research very much confirmed these impressions. Funnily enough, though I am using the analogy with Neo-Classicism very much tongue-in-palate, another parallel also emerged. There was a definite Orientalism in evidence in the best restaurants of Paris. What's more, the rococo Chinese and Japanese elements such as the lacquered *poulet de Bresse* we had at Guy Savoy, (28 rue Duret, 16e, which had just received its well-deserved second Michelin star) have mostly given way to Neo-Classical Middle Eastern touches, such as the *pastilla* served us by Alain Dutournier at the Trou Gascon (still at the unfashionable 40 rue Taine, 12e, though Dutournier himself is now at the Carré des Feuillantes, 14 rue de Castiglione, 1er). The same chef has invented an Indian-inspired rabbit dish, *cul de lapereau, 'retour des Indes'*, marinated in yoghurt and flavoured with cardamom. Napoleonic Egyptiennerie cannot be far behind: watch out for *foul medames* on smart menus.

But it is *French* regionalism that really counts, and here Dutournier scored mightily with his pigeon with broad beans and his whole leg of milk lamb, studded with anchovies, cooked *en croûte*, and served, with reactionary generosity, for one person. *Agneau de lait* was also on the menu at Michel Rostang (20 rue Rennequin, 17e), but in a *navarin*, served with lots of pasta. Rostang has reverted so thoroughly to *his* grand-mother's style that he gave us *amuse-gueules* of *fried bread* surrounding a quail's egg. And my main course was an up-to-date version of *boeuf à la ficelle*: rare fillet steak, poached in strong beef consommé, with a sauce made of the reduced stock with a bit of horseradish stirred in, and blanched cabbage as the veg.

After the triumph of the *nouvelle cuisine*, certain implements of the culinary *ancien régime* were hidden away as carefully as American Leftists hid their volumes of Marx and Lenin during the McCarthy era. So I could not dissemble my surprise when Michel Rostang wheeled out a duck press – the symbol of the old days of *haute cuisine*. Sure enough, the waiter lifted the *magrets* off a Barbary duck, and pressed the bloody carcase. The result was a civet-ish sauce, served with *nouvell*-ish rare slices of the breast.

Of course, Claude Terrail's Tour d'Argent, 15–17 quai de la Tournelle, 5e, never stopped using its duck presses, and it is good to say that the world's most dramatic restaurant is now back in the mainstream with its famous duck served in two courses. The menu has been slimmed to a more manageable size; and the young chef, Dominique Bouchet, has added a few lighter dishes, such as jellied compote of oxtail that was the alternative starter to a perfectly delicious old-fashioned *quenelle de brochet* perfumed with pistachios. Except on Sunday, M. Terrail offers an affordable 195 francs lunch menu, with a supplementary charge if you have, as we did, the (overcooked) breast of duck with sauce from the press, followed by its legs crisply grilled and served with a salad. Several bottles are offered at around 100 francs, making this an unexpectedly accessible treat.

Granny food really is everywhere in Paris. Even the dreadfully pretty Beauvilliers (52 rue Lamarck, 18e), the epitome of self-conscious culinary chic, tried (but failed), with a *blanquette de veau*.

Without doubt the best meal I ate in 1985 was at Joël Robuchon, 32 rue de Longchamp, 16e. M. Robuchon was the darling of Gault-Millau, who discovered him years before Michelin gave him his three stars, and who, that year, give him 19.5 points out of 20 ('only *le bon Dieu* achieves perfection, and he does not spend much time at the stove'). M. Robuchon regards his own cooking as classic, though its delicacy and refinement owe everything to the *nouvelle cuisine*, and nothing to anybody's grandmother.

Yet there was something faintly shocking about the glorious lunch he gave us. The first-course ravioli of langoustine came with a heap of robust shredded cabbage in a light brown sauce redolent of truffles. My lobster *civet* was roundels of lobster meat wrapped in blanched spinach in a richly concentrated fish *fumet* and reduced red wine sauce. The main courses were three generous lamb cutlets, pink against a background of a brown truffley sauce, on a plate strewn with red and green salad made of all the herbs of the garden. The contrast with the meat was magic. I had a dish that wouldn't have amused my Jewish grandmother – *tête de cochon*, morsels of pig's cheek and all the other edible bits, with florets of broccoli, minuscule French beans, tiny broad beans and more truffles.

The shock was the *purée de pomme de terre* that the waiters handed around to everyone having lunch that day. Mind you, this wasn't ordinary mash: it was so light and fluffy it almost floated off the plate, cloud-like. After the 15 years of hegemony of the *nouvelle cuisine*, simple mashed potato strikes exactly the right note of rebellion. My grandmother would have applauded M. Robuchon's *chutzpah*.

Another feature of the *nouvelle cuisine* is sadly doomed. The day of the *chef patron*, the cook who owns his own restaurant, is almost certainly coming to an end. In France the tax on business entertaining has made deep inroads into the lunch trade. But more ominously, the already small profit margin for serious restaurants is shrinking everywhere in the world. Without the prospect of big profits, it is getting more and more difficult for a talented young chef to find financial backing – and it costs an awful lot these days just to buy napery and cutlery.

More and more, the culinary world belongs to those chefs such as Jacques Maximin, of the Chantecler restaurant at the Hotel Negresco in Nice, or Anton Mosimann at the Dorchester, who have the profits from rooms and banqueting of a big hotel behind them. It is chefs like them who have the time and money to experiment. London has a tradition of great cooks in grand hotels, stemming from the time of the unfortunate Escoffier and the Ritz. Paris has no such tradition and, until recently, no such chefs. But now, the *grand luxe* hotels have ambitions for their restaurants. Just look at the Crillon, Le Bristol and the Nova Park. Chefs who can find the backing to strike out on their own, such as Raymond Blanc of the Manoir aux Quat' Saisons, Great Milford, Oxford, are dependent on their new establishments having rooms. Nico Ladenis of

Chez Nico has joined their number. The only apparent exception to this rule is Alain Senderens, who has left his tiny Archestrate for the huge splendour of Lucas-Carton, 9 place de la Madeleine, 8e. But he was already in business for himself.

The last word on *l'après-nouvelle* belongs, I feel, to Anton Mosimann. His *Cuisine Naturelle* has seemed to some, because of his highly decorated plates, the ultimate extension of the *nouvelle cuisine*. Others have mistaken it for another version of Michel Guérard's slimming *Cuisine Minceur*. Important though it is to distinguish NC from CM Mosimann's is neither the one nor the other. It is the application of the refinement of the *nouvelle cuisine* and sound nutritional principles to very old-fashioned dishes. Just think of his boiled beef with raw vegetables, his poached chicken, his tongue with lentils. Neo-Classical, like Granny would have made – if she had been a good cook.

Great sandwiches of the world

Pastrami

Pastrami is chic. It cashes in on the continuing stylishness of everything that comes from Manhattan, but it has always had a certain cachet that the quite similar salt beef lacks. Even when I was a child in the autochthonous culinary region of a land-locked Southern American state, where Jewish food was as rare and mysterious as the subtle spices of the Orient, we knew of pastrami; though few there were who had tasted it.

Corned beef (for that is what Americans call salt beef) was always worth a detour to any Jewish inhabitant of small-town America. But the more sophisticated pastrami was the goal of gastronomic pilgrimages whose extent would have amazed the French. In my family, ninety miles – the distance to the nearest city – was not considered excessive to drive for hot pastrami on rye. And most excuses would do for a 600-mile excursion to New York, of whose denizens my parents did *not* approve, but where the fleshly pleasures available at the Stage Delicatessen were known to include the juiciest and spiciest pastrami imaginable.

As London is discovering, and Edinburgh, Dublin and Cardiff will no doubt soon know, pastrami is cured and smoked brisket of beef. It is heavily spiced (garlic being mandatory, though the other usual condiments are optional) and can be eaten hot or cold. Pastrami *must* be pink and moist, and not dried out; for it is usually thinly sliced, and taken between slices of fresh rye bread, with benefit only of mustard, as butter would violate the prohibitions connected with its presumably kosher origins. Its correct garnish is a pickled cucumber.

I always like to know the etymology of what is on my plate. In the case of pastrami this would have been difficult before 1982. But then the third volume of the supplement to the Oxford English Dictionary was published, covering the letters O–Scz. We now know definitively that 'pastrami' is Yiddish, derived from Rumanian *pastramă*, from *păstra*, to preserve. (This information had been available for many years from the American Webster's Dictionary. But I could not bring myself to trust it wholeheartedly, because it confidence-shakingly speculated that there must be a missing Vulgar Latin link, *parsitare*, to spare.)

The OED has found the first reference to a hot pastrami sandwich on rye to date from 1941; and a gastronomically less orthodox mention of 'a plate of pastrami and eggs' occurred in 1945. But the pleasant news is that the absolutely first citation of pastrami in English literature is to be found in a letter written in 1940, by Groucho Marx: 'The catering was delegated to Levitoff, the demon pastrami prince.'

I have always believed that pastrami, like its name, was Rumanian in origin. Though I have none but the etymological evidence for this I have recently engaged upon a quest for pastrami, inspired by the discovery that my local Rosslyn Delicatessen has *two* sorts. There is the round-ish, natural-shape pastrami, coated in coarsely ground black peppercorns; and there is a perfectly rectangular pastrami, that has obviously been moulded in a press, and dusted with rosy paprika.

I am an enthusiast for the first, which I found moister and spicier even than the pastrami of childhood memory. M. Bellier, the deli's French proprietor, is a partisan of the second, which is made for him by Orlik's of Albany Street, NW1.

Thus did I come to inspect what, in America, would be called a pastrami-factory. Gerry Orlik, a third generation Austro-Hungarian master butcher and sausage-maker, explained to me the processes by which pastrami is called into being.

First (and this has contributed a great deal to its current popularity), the brisket must be lean, which means that it must come from the shoulder of a steer or young animal if it is not to be tough. This in turn means that pastrami, not being so fat as salt beef, appears to the animal-fat-shunning consumer to be the healthier meat – which it is.

The brisket is pickled in the traditional pickling spice and garlic brine that contains saltpetre (potassium nitrate), which contributes its preserved taste and pink colour. Formerly this was done in machines like tumble dryers, that battered the beef into absorbing some liquid into its tissues. But Mr Orlik's family discovered the technique of injecting brine directly into the meat. This reduces the pickling time (and thus the expense) considerably; though the modern brisket still spends a few days after treatment in the pickling vat. The brine recipe is the principal trade secret.

It is then smoked for twelve to fourteen hours over wood, which, of course, cooks it. Pressed pastrami, which has the advantage of slicing very evenly, and without waste, is smoked in its spring-loaded mould. Mr Orlik conceded that it might be a tiny bit less juicy than the free-form pastrami, as a little – but very little – liquid is lost under the pressure.

Pastrami *au naturel*, the unmoulded, black peppercorn-covered type, is the New York variety. British pastrami makers prefer the more regularly shaped, rectangular, paprika-coated and slightly less spicy sort. As the origins of pastrami are definitely eastern European, I wonder whether this difference might not reflect other differences in taste between Ashkenazi Jews. There is a preponderance, I believe, of Jews of Polish origin in Britain, as there is of Russian origin in America. Could this account for the general liking for sweetness found in British Jewish food, which is absent in its American counterpart?

In her *All-American Cookbook*, Martha Lomask gives a recipe for 'Pastrami – or something very like it' for domestic cooks. As she confesses, you can't make the real thing at home unless you have a smoker. Mrs Lomask marinates silverside of beef, with slivers of garlic inserted, in allspice, sea salt, black pepper, sugar and saltpetre in the fridge for a week; simmers it with onion, carrot, bayleaf, ginger and cloves; covers it with cracked pepper and puts it back in the fridge under a heavy weight.

A hot pastrami sandwich is ideally made by warming an entire piece of pastrami over steam, then slicing it thinly, and using a generous amount, say $\frac{1}{8}$ to $\frac{1}{4}$ lb, for each sandwich. But as its price is above pearls, who can afford to cut up a whole piece of pastrami?

The great American sandwich

This year Americans celebrated the 110th anniversary of their independence from Britain. Most of them – including me and a lot of other expatriates – had an alfresco meal, for it is traditional to have a picnic on the 4th of July. Most often festivities involve a barbecue, though on the East Coast this is sometimes altered to a clambake. When I was a child, though, our July 4th picnic fodder was usually either cold (and home-made) Kentucky fried chicken or else a sandwich. Indeed, the American sandwich is one of the happiest results of the break with the British.

By one of those grand coincidences, the eponymous Englishman was alive during the American War of Independence; indeed, by 1776 he was probably busy making improvements to his original invention. According to the OED, the bready article is 'said to be named after John Montagu, 4th Earl of Sandwich (1718–1792) who once spent twenty-four hours at the gaming-table without other refreshment than some slices of cold beef placed between slices of toast'.

This alone proves that the noble lord knew a trick or two that most of his compatriots seem to have forgotten. He used toast to make the original sandwich, and I am sure that even if sliced white bread had been available, Lord Sandwich would have had none of it. There is no secret to making the great American sandwich, merely a few golden rules.

First, use good bread. This eliminates most of the well-known brands available from the supermarkets and corner shops, but flat pitta is increasingly available, as are French loaves, rye breads, onion or poppy-seed rolls, bagels, wholemeal loaves and a lot of other floury concoctions that offer some resistance to the teeth and are actually worth eating.

Second, bread should be buttered. This is partly to keep it fresher, and partly to keep the sandwich from getting soggy. In any case, though it adds to the calories (and if you're counting those there is not much point in continuing to read this piece), it tastes better.

Third, be generous with the main ingredient. Following this rule alone will distinguish your creation from a mingy British sandwich, and result in an immediate up-grading of the product. When you think you have piled the buttered bread high enough, add another slice of rare beef, pastrami, roast pork, smoked salmon, turkey, salami, cheese, ham, or another anchovy, sardine, prawn or egg. The only constraints you should acknowledge when stuffing the great American sandwich are those of engineering.

Fourth, pay attention to the textures of the sandwich, and be sure that there is sufficient contrast between or among the ingredients. This implies, correctly, that a genuine American sandwich usually has more than one element in its filling. Smoked salmon, for instance, is usually served with a wodge of Philadelphia cream cheese, and sometimes even with a slice of raw onion. (North American salmon is far coarser than Scotch or Norwegian, and can stand up to this brutal treatment.) Lettuce is the best conveyor of crunch – at least, American Iceberg lettuce or Webb's Wonder do this job. Ordinary cabbage-type lettuce is hopelessly crunchless. Firm, ripe tomato is a good addition to most sandwiches; and we can now buy the American beef varieties in most supermarkets and greengrocers. But strips of raw pepper, pickled cucumber or even bean sprouts will add interest.

Fifth, provide some lubrication. Americans use mayonnaise on almost everything. (They do not, thank heavens, eat or even know the recipe for the abomination called salad cream.) Home-made 'mayo' or imported American Hellman's actually is good with many sandwich fillings. But so is soured cream or strained Greek yoghurt – and don't forget the essential flavourings such as mustard.

The American sandwich – the greatest American sandwich, I think – that best exemplifies these rules is the famous 'BLT', bacon, lettuce and tomato. American bacon is cured differently, and gets much crisper than ours; but that is not absolutely essential. Indeed, I have known American BLT connoisseurs who *prefer* this classic sandwich made with English or Danish back bacon. But streaky would be more orthodox.

Toasted bread, however, is *de rigueur*, as are good lettuce and mayonnaise; and the tomatoes must be ripe, and salted and peppered. Pile the ingredients high; a proper BLT is at least two inches thick. It can be eaten as a picnic sandwich, provided you have remembered to butter the toast. But it's best scoffed at once, with warm toast and bacon providing a toothsome contrast with the crisp green of the lettuce and cool ripeness of the tomato.

Le sandwich au bord de la mer

Several readers felt moved to write to me about my piece on the Great American Sandwich. Their letters have made me reflect on the subject a bit – and convinced me that I ought to give the French their due.

The Great French Sandwich is not, of course, the normal mingy bit of *jambon* or *saucisson* between a foot-long length of *baguette* sliced in half (which gives me a chance to thank Dr Stanley Freedman, of East Finchley, for reminding me of the lines from Alan Sherman: 'Do not make a stingy sandwich; / Pile the cold-cuts high; / Customers should see salami / Coming through the rye').

No, the GFS is generous, as are all great sandwiches. Besides bread, it has at least five ingredients to chew or crunch as well as one or two just for flavour and quantities of olive oil for lubrication.

My researches have unearthed eight recipes for *pan bagna* (or *pan bagnat* or *pan bania*). We used to take *pan bagna* for lunch on the beach at Pampelonne or for a picnic in the hills near the ruins of a Roman bridge, when I was younger and able to stand the exertions of a summer holiday in the south of France.

The name of this sandwich is a mystery to me. It is Provençal, rather than French, as it comes from the area around Nice. 'Pan', of course, comes from the Latin for bread, as does French *pain*. Perhaps, like the English 'bagnio', *bagna* comes from the Latin for bath, and refers to the bath-like aspect of the bread as a container. I rather hope it does, as I have always mentally translated it for myself as bathing-beach sandwich, and my first taste of one was on the shingle beach at Nice.

The eight recipes I've found have nothing in common to all of them but bread, and three different sorts of that are mentioned: the long *baguette*, the round *pain de campagne*, and a soft bread roll that I remember, resembling a bap.

Jean Noël Escudier, in *La véritable cuisine Provençale et Niçoise*, specifies a filling of green peppers cut in strips, onion rings, tomato slices, stoned black olives and fillets of anchovies, between the two halves of a round loaf. You anoint the cut side of the bread with a great deal of olive oil, put the whole thing together and cut it into pie-shaped wedges. But, unlike the recipes given by Claudia Roden (in *Picnic,*) and three of the five given by Elizabeth David (in *Mediterranean Food* and *Summer Cooking*), Escudier does not make the sandwich in advance (as much as the day before) and press it under a heavy weight. In fact, he recommends eating it straight away, for breakfast.

Mrs Roden adds a sprinkling of wine vinegar to the foregoing, and advocates (correctly, to my way of thinking) the addition of garlic. I would not crush it, as she does, but mince it finely and scatter it – and I should use a clove per person. If using one of those big loaves the French call *restaurant*, or a thick round loaf, I always hollow out most of the actual crumb and discard it, leaving the two halves of the crust as a shell to be filled more generously than is possible if you retain all the bread. I prefer the crusty version to the squidgy one.

Arabella Boxer's recipe in the *Mediterranean Cookbook* is for the bap-like snack you can buy on the beach at St Tropez or Nice. She says it was 'originally a sort of salad with bread, rather like the first version of gazpacho, but later developed into a sort of sandwich composed of a simple *salade Niçoise* in a soft roll, moistened with olive oil'.

She also mentions the Arab *fattoush*. Her version is the only one to add hard-boiled egg, radish and celery to the list of ingredients. Delicious – but remember to be lavish with the filling; the ones you can buy are almost entirely bread, and disappointing.

Elizabeth David gives five variations of the recipe for *pan bagna* (and two of the spelling). Her first omits the anchovy, but adds sweet red pepper, raw young broad beans and garlic. Her second has anchovy, but no tomato, onion or pepper, and adds gherkins, sliced artichoke hearts and lettuce. A third has optional vinegar, but requires peppers, onion, garlic, capers and gherkins.

Mrs David's fourth variation on this edible theme is made with anchovy, onion, black olives, celery, artichoke hearts and mushrooms *à la Grecque*. A peculiarity of this recipe, which she attributes to *Recettes et Paysages Sud-Est et Méditerranée*, is that the halves of the *baguette* are soaked in salted water as well as olive oil.

For her final, triumphant *pan bagna*, Mrs David uses round bread, peppers, tomato, lettuce, green and black olives and salt herring fillets.

As if this wasn't enough, the bountiful Mrs David gives us another dish, *patafla*, in which the crumb of the *baguette* is removed, mixed with a combination of peppers, onions, black and green olives, tomato, capers and gherkins, bound with oil, replaced, weighted in the fridge, and sliced and served the next day as hors d'oeuvres.

Pan bagna is an amazingly versatile food. As you may have guessed from several of the recipes, substituting boiled potato for the bread, and adding canned tuna fish, lightly cooked French beans and wedges of hard-boiled egg to the basic tomato, peppers, onion and anchovy fillets, results in a *salade Niçoise* that needs only to be dressed with a garlicky vinaigrette to provide a one-course lunch.

Chill the wine – even if it's red – and *pan bagna* or *salade Niçoise* makes the perfect hot-weather meal. It always reminds me of the south of France – without the bother of actually getting there.

Sizzling digits

When I saw lesson twenty-five of the Observer French Cookery School, I was filled with emotion. There they were, those recipes for puff pastry, *pâte feuilletée*, the pinnacle of the pastrycook's art.

There, too, were photographs of that noble creation, the *Gâteau Pithiviers*, with its toothsome but not sickly-sweet filling of almond cream; those golden spin-offs from puff pastry, *Palmiers* and *Sacristans*; and those savoury, bronzed coffers, the *feuilletées* filled with Anne Willan's seafood and spinach mixture.

My feelings when confronted with puff pastry, with *successful* puff pastry, with dough that someone has managed to give precisely six turns, with that miracle substance that incorporates about a pound of butter with the same quantity of flour, in exactly 729 layers – my emotions are then ambivalent.

I feel both admiration and despair. I have to admit to myself that I *know* that should I ever so much as attempt to make puff pastry again, the certain failure will give me a bad case of nerves, and make me be rude to my wife and unpleasant to dinner guests.

But I also cannot help rejoicing that *somebody* has once again succeeded in taming nature, in creating the most artificial and extraordinary of edibles, *le feuilletage*, which, Paul Bocuse assures us, chefs have known how to make since the thirteenth century, though the art was only brought 'to a high level of pefection' during the eighteenth and nineteenth centuries.

It was 1959 or 1960 when I first tried to make puff pastry (the second half of the twentieth century) – and I have not been able to achieve even a low level of perfection. In fact, in spite of being able to buy the best French unsalted butter, that with the lowest water content, despite having caused a marble slab to be mounted at waist-height near a window in my kitchen, and though I must have acquired every gadget ever invented to combine flour and butter without touching either, all I have ever succeeded in making is a sticky mess.

How many other people, I wonder, have had motives like my own for learning to cook in the first place? I am an auto-didact. With the exception of those vital *tours de main*, those physical skills such as folding (not stirring) whisked egg whites into some other substance, which every cook has to be *shown* (not told) how to do by another cook, I learned everything about cookery from books.

I decided to learn to feed myself – and to feed myself well – because I had experienced one of the most powerful sentiments of all: chagrin.

When I was an undergraduate, living in digs and on breakfast cereals and fried food, I was shaken from my adolescent sloth and acne'd torpor by a girl friend who, in proposing to prepare dinner for me, inadvertently revealed to me the mystery of the gas oven, which I had assumed was broken beyond repair. It was necessary, I learnt from her, to *light it with a match*.

I take no pride in this confession of the depths of my practical ignorance. But I am rather proud of how I set about remedying my inability to nourish myself. I asked the best cook I knew for the name of a book that would teach me to cook properly; by which I meant that I was prepared to add to my university course in philosophy the extra burden of training as a cook.

In the end my friend the good cook produced a book whose title I have forgotten, though I shall always remember that its author was Louis Diat, and that, by following it through its many pages, with thoroughness, and near-religious concentration, I acquired the rudiments of a chef's training. I began, I remember, by learning how to buy a knife.

By my own efforts, with a little help and occasional proficiency examinations from my friend, I learned to do most of the jobs that are done in the restaurant kitchen. I taught myself: to mince, to bone, to sauté, to clarify; to make sauces, white and brown; soufflés, sweet and savoury; grills and roasts; marinades; timbales and terrines; pâtés and puddings. All with success and increasing ease.

Then I came to the chapter on pâtisserie, which, though it did not excite my interest as greatly as some others had done, held no particular terrors for me. After all, I hadn't known how to poach an egg until I taught myself to do it by doing it.

I began, as we all must, with short crust pastry: flour, salt, water and fat. What could be simpler? I followed the instructions. The result was a ball of dough. I approached it with the rolling pin, flattening it as prescribed with a sharp tap. It shattered.

I tried again. This time, I suppose, the pastry must have been *too* short. It would not roll out. So I took the perfectly malleable pieces and tried to poke them with my fingers into a shape that would line the flan dish. But at every push a hole appeared, and at every pull the dough was rent. It resembled a sponge.

Puff pastry? I kneaded as little as possible. The butter was the right temperature, and the dough was not too hard. I spread the butter and gave it the first turn; I folded the dough and turned it again. I let the dough rest and cool. Turns three and four. Rest and cool. Fifth and sixth turns – the dough should be ready to use.

But, wait a mo. What size should the dough package be? It's smaller than it was and it feels like leather. I bake it anyway. The result shows that I have not learned the technique for making puff pastry, though I may just have stumbled on the secret of shrinking heads.

So it continued. The next batch was obviously wrong; it was tacky and oozing butter. I've rarely tried since to make the stuff from scratch. Though I've bought frozen puff pastry and vol-au-vent shells, something always goes violently wrong when I handle the dough.

Other people's unbaked pastry cases, standing firm and four-square, have been known to collapse at my approach. An elegant concoction that would have become a proud tower of flour, butter and air detumesced in my presence, though I swear I did no more than glance at it from a distance.

Those readers who are more adept than I at the witchcraft that produces pastry have already guessed the secret of my disability: sizzling digits. My hot but dry fingertips are anathema to all dough, except that containing yeast or otherwise requiring the warmth of my hands.

The world's greatest pickle

I am not a connoisseur of Jewish food. Even so, there is one important item of the traditional Jewish cuisine concerning which I claim a good deal of knowledge and experience. I make the best pickled cucumbers in Great Britain.

Aware as I am that this is no great boast – anyone who has ever eaten Jewish food in New York or even Miami would respond to that claim with less than astonishment – it is no mean accomplishment to have tracked down the recipe.

What I am about to divulge is the best recipe in the world – I write this without conscious hyperbole – for one of the classic dishes. And if anyone should object that a pickled cucumber does not, in itself, constitute a 'dish', I shall simply have to quibble.

It is true that man cannot live by pickled cucumbers alone, or even make a complete meal of them without accompaniment. But it is equally true that there are some noble gustatory experiences that would not merely be incomplete, but almost unthinkable, without their pickled cucumber garnish.

The dreaded salt beef sandwich, of course. But what about coarse *terrine, pâté de campagne, rillettes d'oie* and *de porc*, and all kosher products of the charcutier's art?

My recipe for pickled cucumber is not only suitable for putting up the *cornichon* that is indispensable to the enjoyment of the above, but it produces a superior gherkin to any you can buy. For mine is pickled in brine, and has very little vinegar. Of course, the recipe is not, strictly speaking, mine, although I tracked it down.

The search for the perfect pickled cucumber was a relentless one. It took me to Manhattan more times than I would care to recount. In the service of the quest I ordered and consumed incredible, sick-making quantities not only of salt beef, but of (much nicer) pastrami.

My researches took me to the further reaches of Florida, where I should not care to return. And to neighbourhood delicatessens in Chicago. I combed the East End, not for a perfect pickled cucumber, merely for a *good* one. Even some well-known establishments not a million miles from Baker Street could not satisfy my questing palate.

In the end, I found the recipe in my own backyard. It belonged to the mother of my best friend from childhood. This tale may seem unbelievable to those who cannot credit the existence of a large colony of people of Russian-Jewish descent in Lexington, Kentucky, where I was born.

Yet truth will out. One day, down there on a visit, Ada Gail, the mother of my friend, a renowned cook and a good painter, gave me a pickled cucumber. And I instantly knew that *that* was the pickled cucumber of my youth, the taste I was seeking to recapture. (And, incidentally, it was so literally. For my own mother told me that Ada's pickled cucumbers had been among the most precious of gifts, frequently bestowed in my infancy and youth.)

You can plant dill and even cucumbers – though seed for the sort used in America and Russia is difficult to get here, and you would be well advised to buy a case of the short, stubby Israeli or Cypriot cucumbers if you ever see them at your greengrocer.

In each large sterilised storage jar (Kilner or Le Parfait) place sprigs of fresh dill; three peeled cloves of garlic; one chilli; six black peppercorns; a pinch of mixed pickling spices; and, to keep the pickle crisp, a pinch of alum (obtainable from the chemist).

Fill the jar with scrubbed *cornichons* or gherkins about three to four inches long, and pour *hot* brine, made by boiling 10.5 litres (14½ pints) of water with 340 g. (12 oz.) coarse salt and 120 ml (4 fl. oz.) cider vinegar. Place a vine leaf, if available, over the contents of each jar and seal. Wait for the brine to ferment, after two or three days, and top up with boiling brine that you have reserved for this purpose. You can start eating the pickle four or five days after fermentation has ceased.

In the same sugarless brine, following the same procedure, you can pickle almost anything. But do try French beans, shallots, tiny cobs of sweetcorn, small sweet peppers and, especially, green tomatoes.

Cheese

B or C?

Cheese is an interesting and complicated subject – as interesting and as complicated as wine, another natural substance with whose manufacture it has much in common. Though the world teems with Grapies, who drop the names of Châteaux as others sprinkle their conversation with the names of peers or pop-stars, cheese has not yet acquired its groupies. (Though cheese does have its social implications: American Foodies speak sneeringly of the 'Brie and white wine set'.)

Perhaps this is because there's no cheese equivalent of Blue Nun, to start the inexperienced climbing the gastronomic ladder that leads from mousetrap to Maroilles. Or perhaps it is because, like the last-named example, cheese – even at its greatest (or *particularly* at its greatest) is a smelly business. Maybe cheese is essentially – not, as philosophers used to say, accidentally – a suitable source of schoolboy jokes.

After all, cheese is (like wine) made by a process that takes advantage of the tendency of food to spoilage and corruption. Just as fermentation *could* merely render the grape inedible and useless, the turning of milk into separate curds and whey *could* be merely destructive. Instead, it is the first step in the manufacture of one of man's oldest and yet most sophisticated foods.

The analogy with wine is even stronger than this. Both are agricultural products of the utmost simplicity, but requiring to be produced under conditions of scrupulous cleanliness if the bacteria and yeasts that 'turn' them are to be harnessed and put to good use. Both are strongly regional, so that the same material can produce a different result if it is from a grape grown on a sunnier slope or milk from a cow pastured in a lusher field. Conditions of ageing and storage are crucial in both cases. And though the mature wine or the perfectly ripened cheese may appeal to many different sorts of people, to appreciate its finest virtues requires a degree of connoisseurship.

The complexities of wine are commonplace, every tyro knows better than to chance his drinking arm (or palate) against the experts – and knows better than to take them on in objectively evaluatable blind tastings. But cheese? Can cheese be a field for expertise and gastronomic exhibitionism? The answer, *cher collègue* Foodie, is yes.

As a very junior specialist writer on a national newspaper, I came close to losing my first job six months after I had begun it, when I wrote – incautiously, imprecisely, but not incorrectly – that Brie and Camembert were close relations, 'identical except for the shape of the mould'.

One of the paper's most senior journalists then fired off a Munster of a stinker to the Editor. 'How,' he demanded, 'can you employ someone to write about food who can't tell the difference between Brie and Camembert?' I had to eat humble quiche (but remain defiant at the same time). Of course, I had not meant to say that the *taste* of Brie and Camembert was the same, only that 'their manufacture is identical, except for the moulds used'.

Brie is the older. The fifteenth-century Charles d'Orléans, the father of Louis XII, gave New Year gifts of Brie to his friends, and there is even a report in one of the chronicles that Charlemagne tasted Brie in 774. At a dinner at the Congress of Vienna, given in the hopes of obtaining a little light relief after Waterloo, Talleyrand proposed a mock resolution, which was unanimously adopted, that Brie be proclaimed the king of cheeses.

Both Brie and Camembert are soft-curd (*pâtes molles*) types of cheese, and both are designed to ripen or mature. Up to the point where the mould is introduced, the manufacture of these cheeses is the same as for any cheese: raw or pasteurised milk is treated, usually with rennet, to separate the curds and whey. The whey is drained off (and usually discarded, though it is sometimes used to make other cheeses). The curd is cut up – this step is important, as it determines the final consistency of the cheese – and put into moulds. When sufficient moisture has been drawn off, the pressed curd is either washed or salted to discourage mould, or, as in the case of Brie and Camembert, infected.

Authorities disagree about the flavouring agent. It is either *Penicillium candidum* (Androuët) or *P. album* (André Simon). Confusingly, it is not *P. camemberti*, which is the mould used for Livarot and Pont-l'Evêque, not for Brie and Camembert and the related cheeses of Coulommiers, Chevru and Fougerus.

The surface mould proceeds, under correct conditions of storage, to ripen the cheese by the action of enzymes working inwards – which is why you sometimes get a Camembert (less often a Brie) in which there is one hard spot in the centre where the enzymes have not yet reached. This enzyme diffusion, of course, is the answer to the big question of why Brie and Camembert differ so much in taste though they have everything except their shapes in common. When it comes to ripeness, thickness is all.

Unless you like slightly chalky Brie or Camembert (and lots of Frenchmen do), don't buy one that is not of the same consistency all over. It will ripen unevenly or not at all, and the tell-tale spot in the middle is unlikely to yield much until the rest of the cheese starts to ooze out of the rind. It is at this point that the ammonia smell of stale Brie and Camembert become distastefully evident.

André Simon says that Camembert and Brie undergo two 'fermentations'. In the first the penicillin mould 'disposes of every trace of lactic acid present in the curd'. The second 'results in the decomposition of the casein', at which point the cheese is at its best and must be consumed rapidly, before further decomposition produces the ammonia smell.

It follows from this that Brie and Camembert in their prime are not completely gooey. It should be possible to cut off the rind and be left with something more resilient and substantial than a mere puddle on your plate. *Do* cut off the rind: the cheesemaker never intended you to eat it.

The shelf life of a soft cheese, from when it leaves the farm or factory until it reaches you, is ten days to three weeks. Brie and Camembert, under proper conditions, require about ten days to go from having a chalky inside to full creaminess. But the proper conditions for ripening are difficult to achieve, and should be the responsibility of the *affiveur* or the retailer. I do not recomend buying Camembert or Brie much more than one day before you mean to use it, as you can then buy it in the condition in which you intend to eat it. Also, both cheeses begin to alter from the moment they are cut and lose the protection against oxygen provided by the rind.

If you must attempt to ripen your own cheese, place it in its box in the vegetable drawer of the refrigerator, and check it every day: it can take ten days to mature. Far better to choose a ripe one in the shop. Start by pressing the cheese with your thumb, to see that it has the same consistency and elasticity everywhere, and don't forget to check the circumference.

Often in French chain stores, and almost always in British and American shops, Brie and Camembert are kept too cold and in conditions of too little humidity. At home, store cheese loosely wrapped in the vegetable drawer (with some vegetables to provide humidity), and always take it out at least one hour before serving, so that it reaches room temperature.

More than 2000 brands of Camembert are made in France. The best still come from Normandy, from the Auge region between Touques and Dive, says Androuët. The best Brie is still made in the Île-de-France.

Most Camembert and Brie are at their best from May to September, during the three cycles of the meadows where the cows graze: the first flush of grass, the flowering of the grasses, and the second growth of the grass. These distinctions tend to be effaced when pasteurised milk is used, as it is in any cheese marked *Brie Laitier*. Seasonal differences are much more pronounced in Brie de Meaux Fermier (though shipping it can be difficult in hot summer weather), Brie de Melun Affiné (as opposed to the rindless, non-maturing Brie de Melun Frais and the Brie de Melun Bleu), the rare Brie de Montereau and the (Androuët says) extinct Brie de Nangis. Brie de Coulommier, on the other hand, is less good in summer. At 26 cm (10 inches), it is smaller than Brie de Meaux, which is normally 33 cm (13 inches) to 54 cm (22 inches) in diameter.

Choosing Brie can be difficult – the more desirable varieties look very like the others, and the consumer simply has to memorise their names. Camembert, on the other hand, is easy to choose. Look for one that says *Fermier*, and always choose an unpasteurised one *au lait cru* in preference to the less characterful pasteurised product.

Cheese made from pasteurised milk has been robbed of all nuance. As Evan Jones says of Camembert (in *The Book of Cheese*), 'It is the fresh milk of Norman cattle that gives the distinctive flavour to the region's unpasteurised cheeses, and of course it is the grass nurtured by salt air and long days of rain that flavours the milk.' This is as close as anyone has ever got even to hinting at the taste of Camembert (or Brie, for that matter). It is a pity to allow pasteurisation to undo the effects of both nature and art.

Blue Cheese

Blue cheese is a subject that makes people emotional. Most blue cheeses are of respectable parentage and ancient lineage. The odd bastard, such as the newly invented Lymeswold, though it strikes most observers as a particularly unhappy and vicious child, is really quite exceptional. Its German and French cousins, blue-veined variations on Brie and Bleu de Bresse, have all settled down to untroubled adolescence. Most of the disquiet has to do with disputes over the pedigrees of the aristocratic ancestors of the English branch of the family.

About Roquefort, the French forbear, there is no disagreement. It, a Corsican brother and one or two others (some British) are the only blues made from ewe's milk. This venerable cheese was mentioned by Pliny the Elder and it was Charlemagne's favourite. The *appellation contrôlée* legislation of 26 July 1925 and the international confirmation of it in the Stresa convention of 1951, merely spell out the details of the charter granted by Charles VI in April, 1411. This gave the denizens of Roquefort-sur-Soulzon the monopoly of curing the cheese, made exclusively from whole sheep's milk, in the humid natural caves in the mountains of Combalou in the ancient province of Aquitaine. The *Penicillium roqueforti* is encouraged to do its stuff by being propagated on breadcrumbs, as it always has been, though the process can now be controlled. The resulting powdery culture is put between layers of curd, which, as it solidifies, is punctured with needle-holes to facilitate the spreading of the spores. The caves of Combalou are kept at a constant temperature by the presence of deep underground fissures, and the cheeses take three to six months to mature. It must be stressed that the essential thing about Roquefort is where it matures. Nowadays, it is made all year around (from frozen milk), not just in lambing season (though it is best after the end of winter), wherever there is sheep's milk – in Corsica, in Quercy, in the Pyrenees or in Provence; but it is all aged in the limestone caves of

Combalou. Androuët says that the best Roqueforts come from milk from sheep grazed near the caves on the limestone plateau of Larzac, in the department of the Aveyron.

Roquefort is one of the few unpasteurised cheeses allowed to be imported into the USA; Americans have a strong taste for it, and make an excellent salad dressing from it. A cheesemaker with a sense of humour told John Ardagh that the reason Roquefort can't be pasteurised is that: 'Before the milk is churned, the ewe pees into it. *That* is what gives the special flavour . . . If we pasturised the pee, there'd be no taste left.' One other word of warning: there are several other towns called Roquefort in France. Shopkeepers are quite used to Mugginses like my wife and me turning up and demanding to buy the stuff at Roquefort-de-Landes, but that doesn't make you feel any less foolish.

There's no problem about this in the case of the other noble blue cheese. Stilton has never been made at Stilton. It got its name because it was sold at the Bell Inn, at Stilton in Huntingdonshire, in the early eighteenth century. It was probably made earlier, at Quenby Hall, near Leicester, where, says Patrick Rance, it was made to a recipe called 'Lady Beaumont's Cheese'. Certainly, though, it existed by Daniel Defoe's 1722 *Tour through the Whole Island of Great Britain*, where he reported that the cheese is 'called our English Parmesan and brought to the table with the mites and maggots round it so thick, that they bring a spoon for you to eat the mites with, as you do the cheese'.

It surprises most people to learn that there is virtually no farmhouse Stilton. It is nearly all made industrially in dairies, and has been since the end of the First World War. Worse still, there is only one Stilton made from non-pasteurised milk, that made at Colston Bassett Dairy in Notts. I personally do not think it worth bothering to eat any other Stilton. Once you have tasted the creamy, smooth unpasteurised Colston Bassett, you will probably agree with me. Fortunately, you can buy it the year around at Major Rance's Wells Stores at Streatley, Berkshire, as well as from the Neal's Yard Dairy, London WC2, and from time to time at Harrods.

Major Rance recommends that you eat Stilton with an 'uncracked, tough, hard crust', when 'the interior is cream coloured to yellow, not white, and its veins reveal a well-spread greeny blue rather than a blue-black or cindery aspect'. Rance thinks the texture of Stilton is a matter of taste, and says he has many customers who prefer a crumbly one to a smooth one. Not me. I think a proper Stilton should be creamy, like Colston Bassett.

There are actually several English blue cheeses – most made from cow's milk, of course – such as Blue Cheshire, Blue Wensleydale, Shropshire Blue and Beenleigh Blue. But in the popular imagination, apart from Stilton, there is only one other – Blue Vinney. And in the popular imagination, Blue Vinney is the matter of legend, and it is extinct. Well, it is not clear whether it was ever true that this Dorset skimmed-milk cheese was 'blued' by drawing a mouldy harness through the milk; but it is true that someone has been prosecuted (by the Berkshire Trading Standards Department, in March 1982) for passing off second-grade Long Clawson Stiltons as Blue Vinney.

And yet, all is not lost. Just when Patrick Rance, who, as you would imagine, was leading the team of sleuths searching for a fossil cheese, had given up hope, he learned in April 1981 that 'there is one farm between Dorchester and Puddletown which has never stopped making'. Their identity is secret, and they only supply 'family and friends'. But the recipe is known (and reprinted in Rance's *The Great British Cheese Book*), and some Blue Vinney has been available commercially since 1983. If you do run into a piece of Blue Vinney, remember it is made from skimmed milk and is not intended to be yellow and creamy like Stilton.

The problem with all strong blue cheeses is not how to eat them, but what to drink with them. They are all salty, and, in my view, benefit from being associated on the palate with a sweet wine. Thus the Sauternes that the French take with their Roquefort is ideal, and so is the English habit of drinking Port with Stilton. But if the Stilton itself is any good, only a senseless barbarian would pour the Port *into* the Stilton. And it's no use bringing out the best claret for the cheese course if you're having a blue cheese – to my mind, it is a marriage made in hell. I've never yet encountered a fine claret, Burgundy or Rhône that could stand up to the assault of a blue cheese. Save them for the Brie.

The great white truffle hoax

Black diamonds that are normally bought and sold on the black market, truffles are surrounded by large quantities of mud and folklore. The white truffle, *Tuber magnata*, appears to be even scarcer than the black or Perigord truffle, *T. melanosporum*. The prices of both are high, but in northern Italy, where the best white ones are found, the number of noughts necessary to express their cost in lire makes them seem dizzyingly dear.

Truffles are a kind of fungus that grows under the ground. It is probably this aspect that invests them with mystery and makes them so potent a subject for the folklorist. In fact, they grow nearly everywhere. The black and white truffles appear to flourish only in certain lucky corners of Europe. But British mushroom authority Roger Phillips had a summer truffle, *T. aestivum*, which he assured me was as perfumed and delicious as both the white and black examples which I brought back for him to compare with his own. His find was discovered in mid-October, in Burnham Beeches. (And an *Observer*-sponsored truffle hunt has since turned up pounds and pounds of *T. aestivum* in Scotland.)

Jane and Geoffrey Grigson and I went to learn about the white truffle at Alba, the capital of the Langhe district, not far from Turin. Alba depends on truffles for a living. There are economic activities not connected with the smelly nuggets, but it is truffles that put Alba on the map. Even the tourist trade is enhanced by the presence of truffles under Alba's earth; and each year at the Fair of St Martin, calculated by the lunar calendar so as to coincide with the beginning of the truffle season in mid-October, more than 100,000 people come to pay homage to the tuberous fungus with the nut-like consistency and the pungent smell that some people find sexy and others irreverently describe as strongly reminiscent of wet old socks.

Peasants and truffle-hounds had been laid on for our visit in early November, the very best time to look for truffles. But the very heavens freaked at our enterprise: it snowed.

Some of the truffles grubbed up by the dogs ('they must be of bastard race', explained a helpful interpreter) that day must surely have been planted by their eager-to-please peasant handlers. They were too big, too quickly located, and too near the verge of the road to have been placed there by nature. (But our photographer had little doubt that the finds made in front of his camera were genuine – he had chosen the spot himself.)

The truffle-hunters explained to us that truffles are created by lightning: thunderstorms in August and September augur well for the autumn. They *always* appear in exactly the same spot, growing on or between the roots of oak, poplar, willow or nut trees, at *exactly* the same day every year in the lunar calendar. That is why they are hunted after dark by a solitary man and his dog: their location minuted carefully and kept secret from the competition.

Folklore and its attendant falsehood are not accidental, but essential components of the truffle industry. This is also true in France where, though everybody knows black truffles have long been cultivated success-fully, the peasants of the Haut Var sell their *caches* from the boots of their cars in a furtive, near-parody of typical black market activity. In France, what is not cultivated is considered windfall – game falls into this category as well as truffles – and is not subject to VAT.

Truffles are VAT-able in Italy – at the stiff rate of 38 per cent. And every person, peasant, dealer or restaurateur, known to traffic in the precious mushrooms, is obliged to produce the odd invoice showing that VAT has been paid – at least on part of his truffle turnover. Of course, VATman is not in a position to say how many truffles anyone has bought or sold in any particular year, and the existence of the profitable black market depends on this, which in turn depends on the fact that truffles are windfall. As they can't be cultivated, say the Italians who make their living from them, the authorities cannot systematically tax those who deal in this buried treasure.

This was evidently why my line of questioning so upset the Truffle King of Alba, Signor Morra (who was, incidentally, the proprietor of the Hotel Savona, where our party was staying). I'm afraid I caused some embar-rassment by asking mildly informed questions about the (spurious) distinctions between male and female truffles, and by being sceptical about the every-year-in-the-same-place claim. But the real trouble was caused by asking questions that implied that it might be possible to cultivate the white truffle.

Signor Morra is the local chamber of commerce's truffle 'expert'. He also has a perfectly legal monopoly (though not monopoly in law) on dealings in white truffles. Signor Morra's father founded the truffle fair in 1928 and was said to possess the secret of preserving the texture of the white truffle in tins. When he sold the business to the canning giant Urbani, he kept the secret of the brine, which he delivers to them for a percentage of the turnover. Signor Morra pays VAT; and it is from him alone that peasant and restaurateur alike must obtain their invoices to satisfy the VAT inspector that at least some of their business is kosher. Naturally, Signor Morra determines the price of the commodity (which ranged from 39,000 to 60,000 lire per *etto* – 100 grams – at Tartufi Ponzio Alba, the biggest shop dealing in truffles).

This is done when the finder presents his booty to Signor Morra, who offers the peasant a price; he can accept on the spot, and get the coveted invoice. Or he can take his chances at Alba's Saturday truffle market, and perhaps get a better price for his valuable wares.

I think Signor Morra may have been cross at my questions – small wonder. Because the following evening our hosts, all of them firm believers in every item of truffle folk wisdom, nevertheless produced a pair of eminent scientists for Jane and Geoffrey Grigson and me to question.

Giusto Giovannetti is professor of Mycology at the University of Turin. He was accompanied by Francesco Tagliaferro, whose Turin firm special-ises in mycorrhising the root of young trees – infecting them with truffle spores that will give rise to mycellium when the tree is planted, and, within about five years, the actual fruiting body of the truffle.

Was this being done on a large scale? we asked Prof. Giovannetti. 'Certainly,' he replied. Signor Tagliaferro had collected some black truffles only that morning. Could it be done on an economic scale? 'Yes,' replied our modest-looking academic, 'the production of the black truffle is 100 kilograms per hectare. Quite satisfactory.'

And, we asked, is it possible to cultivate the *white* truffle, the particular pride of Alba? 'Absolutely,' replied our charming interlocutor, dropping a bombshell whose effect, I fear, future visitors to Alba cannot fail to notice.

Designer pasta

Pasta asciutta was the Enemy, thought the artist Marinetti. All Italians were pasta-junkies, making themselves unfit for Futurism. Poor Marinetti would be appalled by the spread of the pasta habit. Now every upwardly mobile neighbourhood in London and New York has a shop called Fasta Pasta or Greener Pasta or Pasta Pasta Please.

Designer pasta just had to be on the cards. It is only surprising that it wasn't Armani or Versace (or Ralph Lauren or Calvin Klein) that got in on the act first. No, the first designer macaroni was produced by an industrial designer, who worked on cars and sewing machines before he got interested in eats. Giorgetto Giugiaro won a competition, and now his *marille* is manufactured commercially by the Italian firm Voiello.

It is not easy to describe; it is more easily explained – and grasped – by drawings showing it in cross-section and elevation, than by words. But, here goes. A *marille* looks like two tubes of hollow pasta stuck together – macaroni Siamese twins, but with a lip protruding from under the near-side member of the pair. Or, to put it another way, a *marille* looks like a furled tongue of flat pasta supporting a length of conventional macaroni. It's possible, I suppose, to envision the *marille* as a Moebius strip gone wrong.

But you *can* see at a glance what the designer's problems were: how to make a shape that would capture sauce and bits of goodies in its folds and holes, while taking the same time to cook the entire shape to the same degree of doneness. The trick is, obviously, for the whole *marille* to have a uniform thickness – to put the problem into layman's language, perspective and a nutshell.

As the late Tom Stobart put it, in one of the best-humoured entries in his wonderful *The Cook's Encyclopaedia* (Papermac), considerations to be taken into account when inventing a new pasta ('apart from tradition, which should be respected unless there is good reason to depart from it') are that:

First, pasta for very liquid soups should be small, because long strands need a fork, and it would be silly to eat such a dish with both a fork and a spoon.

Second, thick soups such as minestrone should have pasta of the same size as the vegetable ingredients, because smaller pasta would 'fill the spaces in between and make the soup stodgy'.

Third, thick hollow pasta stands up better than thin, 'which tends to get squashed flat'.

But Stobart's most important norm is the 'surface-to-volume ratio': 'it takes less sauce to cover a piece of dough shaped into a ball than to cover the same piece rolled out into a large sheet, which has the same volume but a bigger surface area.' Even more sauce, he points out, is necessary if the sheet is made into strips.

Judged by these criteria, we can see that Signor Giugiaro's new pasta looks like being a winner. It appears to be of uniform thickness, so it obeys Levy's *al dente* Law. It is obviously not meant for soup, thick or thin, so it escapes two of Stobart's Strictures. It is thick- rather than thin-walled, so the *marille* satisfies Stobart's third criterion. It is when it comes to surface-to-volume ratio that Giugiaro's genius is really apparent: he has succeeded in *minimising* the sauce needed. This is a triumph, not only of engineering, but of economics.

So here we have it at last, pasta for intellectuals. Eat your heart out, Marinetti.

And do pass the sauce, please. *Marille* (is the plural *marilles* or is it already in the plural?) seems to be the perfect pasta for the self-consciously chic who inhabit the pasta belts of Manhattan and Mayfair. Its edges and ledges are just right for supporting shavings of truffle, and its tubes seem made for enveloping grains of caviar. Any but the tiniest of peas would be out of place, and *cozze* would be coarse.

Thus is the Designer Ideal truly realised. Just as designer jeans only really look good when worn by the rich, so Signor Giugiaro's pasta achieves the ultimate. It *looks* best on plutocratic plates, adorned very simply and very expensively, with large oysters or small slivers of *foie gras*. Bella Belons! Bravo Beluga! *Grazie*, Giorgetto Giugiaro!

Striking oil

Olive oil, as every good cook knows, is the best vegetable oil for almost every use in the kitchen. Whether used for salad dressings or for cooking, it has the best flavour of any oil, save some of the nut oils. It also has one of the highest critical points (210° C) – butter burns at 110° C – and is very suitable for frying. Except that it is too expensive for most people even to consider using it for that purpose.

All olive oil comes from the ripe, black olive, not the green sort. This may seem surprising, because the gold colour of the oil usually has a green tinge. But the percentage of fat that is added by the ripening of the olive is so great that it is not worth any grower's while to press the immature fruit. Picking is difficult, expensive, and mostly done by hand, as otherwise the ripe fruit would bruise and spoil. The oil is extracted within three days after the olives have been harvested, which can be from November to March, depending on the region. Rapid extraction of the oil is important to prevent fermentation, which would raise the oil's acidity. As the acidity is inversely proportional to the quality of the oil, everything possible is done to keep it low.

It is a perfectly natural food, unlike almost all other vegetable oils, which must be refined – or at least heated – for extraction of the fat content. As its producers never tire of pointing out, it is one of the few fats to which absolutely nothing has been done. That is why almost all the olive oil consumed in Britain, France and America is called 'virgin': it is the result of a single pressing. What remains of the olive paste after this initial pressing can be used to make oil, but it must be refined, as it is too acid, too highly coloured and too strong in smell and taste. Some of it will be blended with virgin oil and sold under the confusing label 'pure olive oil', which is what you will find on most supermarket shelves.

Like the French, English-speaking Foodies turn their noses up at anything but the 'virgin' stuff. But there are even better grades. Though, you might ask, as did my mother-in-law, how can there be such a thing as 'extra-virgin' olive oil. Isn't that like being 'more dead'? In the Tweedledum-world of olive oil, the words 'extra', 'fine', 'ordinary' and 'semi-fine' (you are not likely to see the last two in Britain or America) refer to the oleic acid content of the oil, with extra-virgin being the lowest. As for the words 'cold pressing' on the label, ignore them. All unrefined olive oil is cold pressed.

Spanish olive oil is gutsy and good, as is Greek. Most olive oil bores prefer the oil of Tuscany – the current snob favourite being that from the estate of Mrs Leslie Zyw at Poggio Lamentano. Niçoise oil is very elegant, though it is chic to prefer that of Nyons, in the Drôme. My current favourite is headily scented and fruity and comes from Les Baux, in Provence. But apart from the measurable differences of oleic acid content, the differences in virgin olive oils are wholly questions of taste.

Table olives are another matter. The Spanish have a virtual monopoly of the highest quality table olives. The manzanilla olive – and the best *gordo*, or extra fat olives – grow only in a tiny area around Seville, whatever the California Chamber of Commerce would have you think. Green table olives (all olives are botanically the same, the fruit of the cultivated olive tree, *Olea europaea sativa* Hoffsgg, Link) are harvested from the end of August to the beginning of November. Black olives are picked, as for oil, from then on. Table olives are horrid and inedible (as you can discover by eating one from a tree) until they have been fermented in brine; but they are delicious as soon as the process is finished, with no further treatment. Some black olives are matured artificially, though, by a process of oxidation. They are then packed in brine, like all other olives.

It is entertaining to visit an olive 'factory', for there is a wildly funny side to the manufacture of stuffed green olives. In Spain, anchovy and almond stuffing is still done by hand, which is why these varieties are so dear. Pimento-paste is the stuffing usually used, though; and this task is – more or less – mechanised. Wonderful Heath Robinson machines attempt to remove the stone, and replace it, in a flash, with a bit cut off a continuous length of tasteless paste made up of crushed-up sweet red peppers. They fail, about 50 per cent of the time, necessitating a high quality control force in the olive-stuffing production line. The failures can be glorious – olives stuffed sideways on instead of lengthways, olives stuffed twice instead of once, and so on, to the limits of solid geometry and the imagination. Fortunately, there is a large market for broken olives among the world's delicatessens and pizza parlours.

What's your grouse?

The rich man may dine when he will, but not on grouse. For that, even he is obliged to wait until after the Twelfth of August. Though grouse must be the most seasonal of all foods, my own game merchant, Richards of the Covered Market in Oxford, almost always has grouse for sale on the Glorious Twelfth. This is because they have prudentially taken some of last year's hoard from the freezer in time to thaw on the date. It freezes superbly.

Grouse is interesting in many respects, including the etymological. 'Of unknown origin,' says the OED, but admonishes the philological seeker after truth thus: 'The suggestion that *grouse* is a spurious singular evolved to match the supposed plural *grice* appears to be inadmissible.' (The word has nothing to do with its cognate, which 'has a curious resemblance to Norman Fr. dial. *groucer*' and means 'to grumble'.)

It is the most British of birds. Until fairly recently the red grouse was thought to be the only species of bird that was unique to these islands, and was mis-called *Lagopus scoticus*. Now admitted to have cousins on the continent among the willow grouse, our own are today known as *Lagopus lagopus*. But the birds offered me in 1980 for £20 each at a chic restaurant at Barbizon, and pronounced 'groose' by the waiter, were definitely delicious British red grouse.

Similarly, the so-called grouse of America, the rugged grouse, the prairie chicken and the sage grouse, for example, are not even of the genus

Lagopus. Though related to European game birds with feathered feet, such as the capercaillie, they have about as much to do with our red grouse as does the American 'robin' with a genuine one.

As Terence and Caroline Conran say in *The Cook Book*, much the richest source of information about game birds in my library, grouse 'tastes deliciously of game at its gamiest'. This may well be because of their 'clean' diet of tips of the heather, plus berries and small insects. The Conrans warn that there are no easy consumer clues for telling young grouse, which are best eaten plainly roasted, from old grouse that need to be casseroled. Buy them from a purveyor whom you trust to tell you the truth is the Conrans' good advice.

It would require the analytic powers of Karl Marx to explain why so few shops sell grouse – and so expensively. (I have more than once paid £10 a brace for young birds of the last year's vintage.)

But it is not unrelated to the fact that Debrett's *Etiquette and Modern Manners* has a paragraph that begins: 'Considered by many to be the premier form of shooting, grouse shooting has some peculiarities of its own.' It is very exciting, as the driven grouse 'fly fast and low, following the contour of the moor and appearing suddenly for a few fleeting moments. The sport is . . . more dangerous than pheasant shooting as the target presents itself at head height.'

This, parenthetically, is why the brown trilby, which is the hat 'most acceptable for pheasant shooting', is displaced by 'something with a lower profile' if your game is grouse. So expensive is the paraphernalia of the grouse shoot that the 'guns' (those who do the shooting, as well as what they do it with) only get two brace each at the end of the day, no matter the size of the bag.

The remainder of the bag is sold to pay the wages of the keepers, beaters, loaders and others who make possible the slaughter undertaken by the gentlemen for their sport. I don't know how to assess the surplus value of a brace of grouse, but Marx would doubtless have something to say about the fact that estate agents value sporting properties at a capital value of so many thousand pounds per brace of grouse (and other, lesser, game as well) taken the previous season.

I don't know how to answer the vexed question of whether it is proper or gastronomically correct to eat grouse that hasn't been hung. Every year we witness the silly season spectacle of grouse being expressed to London to be eaten on the Twelfth itself. Surely this is unseemly haste, and may, for all I know, be caddish.

But it is certain that a young grouse – i.e., one born that season – is not too tough to suffer this fate; though all Scots of my acquaintance say that it is even more certain to have no flavour. The delicious 'gamey' flavour is the result of hanging by the neck, in a cool and airy place, unplucked and undrawn, for at least two to three days, if not for a week or more.

The Conrans advocate roasting young grouse for ten minutes at 220°C/425°F/gas mark 7, and then reducing the oven temperature to 180°C/350°F/gas mark 4, for a further ten to fifteen minutes. This is absolutely correct, for grouse must be eaten 'pink and juicy'. It is criminal to cook a young grouse to the dried-out, well-done state. If you are rich enough to have young ones, wrap them in fat bacon, put a lump of butter, a sprig of lovage (the traditional herb with grouse) and salt and pepper in the cavity, and baste three or four times during the cooking.

In *English Food*, Jane Grigson suggests wrapping each roasting bird in a vine leaf, then in bacon or pork fat, and filling the inside with wild raspberries or cranberries. I've done this recently, substituting blanched raspberry leaves for the vine leaves, and tucking a quartered orange in with some cultivated raspberries.

To braise grouse, brown first in butter with diced bacon, before adding aromatic vegetables – onion, celery and carrots – in dice. At this point it is normal to remove the bird, pour off any extra fat, and de-glaze the pan. It is possible to use Scotch whisky for this purpose, but try using raspberry vinegar. And I have made a casserole of grouse using an infusion of heather flowers as the cooking liquid, which I added after browning the bird.

If you like you can marinate the birds for a day or two in red wine with sliced onion and carrot, and use the marinade as the braising liquor. It is very good, especially with the addition of a little redcurrant or rowan-berry jelly.

Lovage is my favourite flavouring. I grow it in the garden chiefly for the few times each year when we can afford to have it with grouse. Thyme, juniper berries and bay go well with all game. But why not flavour grouse with the very thing that implants its exquisite taste, and add a few sprigs of heather near the end of the cooking time?

Out of this world

The second question most people ask about life in space is how astronauts eat.

I was inspired to learn the answer, and to do some further research into astronautical gastronomy, by an exhibition at Sotheby's called 'Living in Space'. On 20 July 1981 Sotheby's intended to sell, as a single lot, the space archive of Raymond Loewy, the designer who not only gave us the living spaces of Skylab and the Space Shuttle, but also the Coke bottle, the Heinz soup labels and the 1951 Studebaker.

Food in space is a slightly disgusting subject. It was positively revolting before Loewy made his contribution, as NASA's 'Habitability Consultant'.

This was only natural, as, when the manned-flight programme began in the late 1950s, the initial requirement was thought to be to keep a man in space for one day at most. So the food in the old Mercury programme was adapted from survival food, such as the rations provided for the crews of downed aeroplanes.

Everybody who has ever watched a late night World War Two movie on the television knows about the horrors of these emergency rations, whose purpose was to sustain life, not to make it more enjoyable.

According to Dr David Baker, the Space Consultant who helped me with my research, the early space programme had no objective beyond the moon landing for which planning began in 1961. The only gastronomic goal was to develop the minimum technology to feed men long enough to get them to the moon and back. The solution was again found in aircraft design, this time from the Strategic Air Command big bombers, which often remain airborne for two days at a time. There seemed no real need to keep men in space for more than a week.

Culinary considerations did not loom large in the minds of the planners, and the conventions civilisation has developed with respect to the eating of meals played no part at all in their thinking. In conditions of zero gravity, after all, there was not much point in a sit-down dinner: the ceiling, floor, or any of the four walls would do as well as a table.

To quote from 'NASA Facts': 'Meal components must be eaten directly from a sealed container, because the condition of relative weightlessness during space flight makes it impossible to keep solid foods on a plate or liquids in an open cup. .,. These foods consisted of puréed meats, vegetables and fruits, packaged in collapsible aluminium tubes.

'During space flights, when the space suit was not pressurised, the face plate was opened to allow the food to be squeezed directly from the container into the mouth.' So much for table manners.

But the gorge also rises, and part of Loewy's 'food management' brief from NASA was 'control of errant food debris and surfaces that were flush and easy to clean to prevent the accumulation of matter ejected through space sickness'.

Future astronauts (and present readers) had reason to be grateful that Raymond Loewy decided that the most important thing about food in space was that it be familiar, and eaten in familiar conditions.

Under his influence, space catering moved away from food in tubes and the sort of meal consisting of survival rations plus a hot water tap (a tragic spin-off of which is today's loathsome meal-in-a-pot that is turned into noodle goop when hot water is added) to pre-packaged foods.

The two essential factors for the storage of food on early space flights were its weight and its volume; Loewy realised that good packaging could result in more normal food – and better astronautical morale.

The most recent space menus are still not examples of high living: I'd hate to be invited to a typical Space Shuttle lunch of thermostabilised frankfurters, rehydratable turkey Tetrazzini, irradiated bread, freeze-dried bananas, almond crunch bar and apple drink.

But I'd prefer it to a dinner with the crew of Apollo II, who constructed their meals to the following recipe: 'After water has been injected into a food bag, it is kneaded for about three minutes. The bag neck is then cut off and the food squeezed into the crewman's mouth. After a meal, germicide pills attached to the outside of the food bags are placed in the bags to prevent fermentation and gas formation. The bags are then rolled and stowed in waste disposal compartments.'

It is a measure of Loewy's genius that he realised that most of us – even astronauts – would prefer to do the washing-up. In fact, David Baker told me, 'Loewy's primary contribution came with Skylab when he designed the galley and laid out the table and its equipment.' (Incidentally, Dr Baker said, 'He chose a triangular shape to bring all three crewmen into equal position with respect to each other.')

The papers and drawings in Sotheby's archive show how Loewy's designs made it possible for NASA to boast that for the more than seventy food items provided in Skylab, 'the food is a familiar kind; the food portions are processed to be prepared, served and eaten in a familiar manner; and the prepared food is satisfactory with regard to taste, aroma, shape, colour, texture and temperature'.

If Raymond Loewy could only design a galley that would persuade the commercial airlines of the world to adopt the same criteria for the food served on ordinary aeroplanes, mankind would truly be in his debt.

D'Artagnan and Armagnac

Armagnac is not a subject about which I knew a great deal – except that it seems to have become the chic *digestif*. When after-dinner tipples are offered, it is very common nowadays to hear Armagnac accepted with more enthusiasm even than Cognac. It is a prejudice I share; and now I think I know why.

Armagnac used to be a province of south-western France, in the romantic region of Gascony. It is now in the department of the Gers, but the people still think of themselves as Gascons, as were Dumas *fils*' Three Musketeers and Rostand's Cyrano.

I now know rather a lot about Armagnac, and have met enough real-life Gascons to verify the accuracy of Dumas' and Rostand's fictional portraits, for I was the guest of André Daguin, the *chef patron* of the Hôtel de France at Auch.

From our midnight-arrival supper of soup of broad beans with *confit* of duck and pork, served in a plate the size of an upturned shield, to our farewell dinner that ended exactly twenty-four hours later with a slightly less large plate containing half-a-dozen chocolate desserts, we were made aware of the macho quality of Gascon cooking. In his preface to André Daguin's *Le Nouveau Cuisinier Gascon*, the French cookery writer Robert Courtine makes the valid point that Daguin's Hôtel de France has become a conservation area *du folklore gourmand*.

As Courtine says, too, if d'Artagnan was alive today, he would play rugby. And Daguin is the undisputed captain of the rugby *équipe*, chef of the kitchen *brigade* and d'Artagnan of the modern-day *mousquetaires*: 'il a ses Porthos, ses Aramis, ses Athos, le bougre!' His food is of the post-scrum variety, too. Based on the extensive use of the goose and the duck,

Daguin's book gives twenty-four recipes for *foie gras* alone, enough to cause teeth-gnashing in vegetarian circles and to spread despair amongst slimmers.

When not eating, we were drinking Armagnac. Well, *some* of us drank it. I was careful, after sloshing it around the mouth, to spit it into the receptacle provided for the purpose. Indeed, I was interested to learn from the very young François de Ganay, of the even younger house of de Montal, that profesional tasters of Armagnac do taste it in the mouth, and do not judge it on 'nose' alone, as is done with some other spirits. 'I nose it first, and if the bouquet pleases me, I take it into the mouth. Armagnac has three characteristic scents – plum, wood and violets – and sometimes a fourth, peach. If I detect one of these aromas, I go on to taste. If not, I don't bother.'

M. de Ganay told me that his firm has achieved a great success in its two or three years of existence, by blending their Armagnac from a wide spread of *eaux-de-vie* from all three areas of Armagnac. 'The areas are Bas-Armagnac, Haut-Armagnac and Ténarèze. We use at least eight sources from among the three areas in each blend.' This produces different sorts of Armagnac of widely varying character – strong and gutsy, with traces of tannin for the macho French market, smooth and silky for the effete American market. Other houses, such as the larger and better known Janneau blend from a smaller spread; the result is smooth and consistent, but to my taste, a bit bland. Bas-Armagnac is thought to produce the best brandy; if it is all from that region, or from one of the others, the label will say so. If the label reads only 'Armagnac', then the bottle contains a blend of two or more areas.

The colourless *eaux-de-vie* that are aged in oak to produce Armagnac are produced by a single distillation from white wine made from grape varieties that include Piquepoul or Folle Blanche, Ugni Blanc, Colombard, and a few others. It is new oak that produces the colour and the tannin, say the producers of Armagnac. But mostly, we saw rows and rows of the ancient oak barrels in which the drink is aged, and which really cease to have any effect after thirty years, though at one house we saw a cask whose contents dated from 1908. The only real effect of this seems to be to lower the alcohol from the usual fifty-ish degrees to forty, and to put up the price of the barrel to £15,000.

We had ample opportunity to sample the stuff in more sociable settings. First, at the Château de Marsan, where we were the guests of the Duc de Montesquiou, who gave us *pousses rapières*, delicious aperitifs made from one part of orange-flavoured Armagnac liqueur to six parts of local sparkler, such as the *vin sauvage* called Brut Monluc.

Lunch was given us by Alain de Taillac, at his ravishing Château de Luxeube, and the home-made *pâté de campagne* and *boudin* first course was followed by succulent roast baby turkey and the local speciality dessert, *croustade*, apple tart with the strudel pastry that is made only in the south-west. This made a very nice foundation for the Armagnac that followed.

Dinner was Daguin's turn, and he surpassed himself (not easy, considering his two Michelin stars and more important three Gault-Millau *toques* and 17/20 points). But it was only after dinner that we learnt of the conspiracy.

The French gentlemen arose and left the table. They came back with a glass of Armagnac that was for me alone. It was 54 degrees, and merely smelling it had an anaesthetic effect on me. Drugged with pleasure, I realised something was afoot.

It seems that the duke is the descendant of the *real* d'Artagnan, Charles de Batz-Castelmore, and M. de Taillac is the direct descendant of Porthos. The musketeers are no longer part of the French military, so these two aristocrats have revived it as a sort of private army of Armagnac boosters.

Their purpose that evening was to initiate me as a member of their band. While M. de Montesquiou made a very pretty speech that not only praised my virtues but proved that he reads *The Observer*, M. de Taillac slipped a beautiful blue sash weighted with a heavy enamelled medal over my head and shoulders, and I became the twenty-fifth musketeer in Britain. I suppose I must not reveal the oath I took (I was so surprised at the proceedings that I swore in all the wrong places); but it had something to do with Armagnac.

Coq au plonk?

There is really only one question about cooking with wine. Does it make any difference if you use plonk in the *coq au vin*, when the recipe calls for Chambertin?

It seems to me logical that if the wine makes any contribution to the taste of the finished dish, then you must not cook with wine you would not drink. On the other hand, if the wine cannot be tasted, even when transformed by the evaporation of its alcohol (as it always is when heated), then you might as well save your money and leave it out altogether.

Following this dictum presents little problem at my house, where the standard cost of the bottle on the table is, at present, just over £2.

There are, of course, instances where one uses wine in cooking without expecting it to impart its taste to what is being cooked. Some marinades, for example, use wine in conjunction with much stronger flavours, such as garlic, herbs and spices, and even such toughies as ginger root and chillis. The wine is included in the recipe for a chemical or physical reaction, which has little to do with its taste – for example, as a tenderising agent.

When wine is used to tenderise meat or game – or even poultry – it is its acid that does the trick. You could get better results by using wine vinegar or lemon juice; though both these, if prominent in the taste of the finished dish, could make it disagreeable to serve with wine. We go in for a lot of grilling at home, as we are watching the *embonpoint* more closely than usual; and, in consequence, have resorted very often to the marinade.

Pigeons are now so cheap that I have often felt able to stretch to the extravagance of using only the breasts, which I marinate in garlic, ginger, onion and fresh lime juice. They can be pan-grilled, served rare and thinly sliced, with a few spoonsful of sauce made by de-glazing the pan, say, with water. When I first made this dish I hovered over the sauté pan with the white wine bottle, and even glanced in the direction of the dry sherry. In the end, I decided that either you could taste the lime juice or you couldn't; and that if you could, you wouldn't be able to taste the wine.

I think I was right about that. However, I wish I'd had the sense to serve the pigeon, which was absolutely delicious, and very tender (though I hadn't a clue as to the age of the birds), with white wine, which would have quarrelled less with the limes than did the red we actually drank.

By contrast, I like cooking fish with red wine. Not only is the colour of the finished dish usually eye-catching, the combination of tannin and fruit in most red wine means that the sauce is never insipid, as is sometimes the case when white wine is used for the same purposes.

Matelote, the fish stew with red wine, always attracts my attention on a menu. But in his Time-Life volume on wine, Richard Olney gives recipes for sole, salmon and even herrings cooked in red wine.

As I like fish cooked as little as possible, we usually steam, poach or grill it in my kitchen. My favourite sauce for turbot (when we can afford it),

salmon trout, salmon, sole, brill or monkfish, is *beurre rouge*. It is made
exactly as *beurre blanc*, except for the substitution of red for white wine,
of which a few tablespoons are reduced with a minced shallot or two (put
them through the garlic press). Then, when just syrupy, add, off the heat,
cubes of unsalted butter, one at a time, stirring and returning to a low heat
from time to time. Stop adding butter when you have sufficient sauce –
very little is needed. Season with salt and cayenne pepper, if you like it
with fish, and a dusting of finely minced parsley or chervil.

You can, of course, use the sauce with meat; but serve it under, not
over, what you are saucing, and remember that it is only served warm, not
hot – too much heat will cause it to separate. And it's not for slimmers.

The principle of cooking with wine is always the same: when heated,
the alcohol evaporates (and so do most of the calories). This is true
whether you are using the wine as a poaching or braising medium, as the
main ingredient of a sauce, or merely to de-glaze the cooking residues in
the saucepan. The only exception is when wine is used uncooked, as it is in
some aspics and jellies, frozen in ices, or as part of the sauce of a fruit
salad. In these latter cases, the wine is unaltered, and *must* be chosen for
the same qualities you look for in a wine you mean to drink.

As for the question asked by would-be culinary alchemists, who hope
by cooking it to turn plonk into potable wine: yes, even plonk probably
contributes some body to a sauce such as a *ragu* for pasta. Still, the sauce
will definitely taste of plonk; and if you don't want to drink it, you won't
like it in the sauce. Concentrated home-made stock will do the job better
and more cheaply. Fortified wines are particularly useful for giving body
to otherwise limp sauces, as are spirits.

The hard conclusion, though, is exactly the same: in American com-
puter jargon, 'garbage in, garbage out' – there can be no such thing as
'cooking wine'. There's certainly little point in boiling off the alcohol
from a great vintage claret. But if it's not good enough to go in your glass,
it's not good enough to go in your casserole.

THE OUTER MAN

Barbara Cartland

Picture Cookery, Barbara Cartland calls the doctrine and school of her book, *The Romance of Food*. Miss Cartland doesn't exactly claim originality: 'The recipes all come from the top, top people in France,' she says disarmingly. She gives the impression, however, of not being absolutely *à la page* with culinary developments across the Channel of the last fifteen years.

Though she (somewhat unfairly) fathers one recipe on the great Jacques Pic, and says of the Roux brothers, 'they're the only people who know how to do' picture cookery in England, the expression *nouvelle cuisine* does not appear to figure in her vocabulary.

In fact, she's clearly *correct*. Her dishes, as both photographs and recipes show, owe very little to the school of Guérard and Bocuse. Their real culinary ancestors are the carrot, pea and mashed potato faces my nursery school teachers constructed on my plate to persuade me to eat up my vegetables.

Originality, though, startles the careful reader. It bounds out at him from the pages of her recipes, disclaim it as she may. Her chef, Nigel Gordon, adapted all the recipes in the book. They come in the first instance 'from Paul Bocuse' or 'from Louis Outhier' (both of whom have three Michelin stars and four Gault-Millau *toques* for their restaurants at, respectively, Collonges-au-Mont-d'Or, near Lyon, and La Napoule, near Cannes), but 'then Nigel says "I do this" or "I do it that way", so it makes people feel that it can be done in England'.

In some cases, the adaptations do, perhaps, stray a bit from the initial intention of the dish. Take 'Flower of the Heart' attributed to Jacques Pic, the original 'flower of salmon purée and caviar' version of which Miss Cartland says she tasted Chez Pic, at Valence, just south of Lyon, 'when I was in France on a gastronomic trip last summer'. To one pound of poached salmon, Nigel Gordon adds half a pint of *béchamel* sauce (the standard white sauce made by adding milk to a flour and butter *roux* and heating till thickened).

When I suggested that Jacques Pic was one of the founding fathers of the *nouvelle cuisine*, a movement whose most characteristic feature was that it banned the use of flour as a thickening agent in sauces, and that it would do Jacques Pic no good at all if his peers thought he was using *sauce béchamel* in his kitchen, Miss Cartland looked me straight in the eye and asked frankly, What *is sauce béchamel*?

It is obviously, and absolutely, out of the question to criticise the powerfully engaging Miss Cartland. Anyway, it is impossible, as she deflects criticism so radically that there is never anything left of the negative question you have put to her. A little surprised at her not having heard of *sauce béchamel*, I asked the author of this and four other cookery books, 'Do you know how to cook yourself?'

'No,' replied Miss Cartland with complete candour.

It would have been churlish to suggest that this could be deduced from her book. She went on to explain: 'I'm like a Victorian hostess. I know *how* it should be done; and I can come back and say to Nigel, "Look, I've found this marvellous dish." This happened once in San Francisco, and I said, "You do this and this is what the result is." It's in the book: tomatoes stuffed with shrimps and cream, and it's a very good dish.'

'San Francisco Tomatoes' is a first-course dish of baked tomatoes stuffed with prawns. The 'cream' is a *sauce béchamel* enriched with mayonnaise and flavoured with garlic, lemon rind and parsley. Miss Cartland writes that she 'found this dish in San Francisco in a French restaurant called Ernie's which advertises itself as being decorated like a bordello'.

Most of our conversation took place around the tea table. Miss Cartland gives an interview every day, and finds that tea is the occasion that interferes least with her writing day. The tea was lavish, and I succumbed to her insistence that I taste a sliver of Nigel's chocolate cake. It *was* good. Miss Cartland fed the slice on her plate to one of the dogs.

She confided in me that it had taken *four whole days* to do *The Romance of Food*, a long time in the working life of someone so prolific as she – it meant that she was not able to keep up with her own record twenty-five books written in 1981. She had no trouble with the recipes – Nigel had been storing them up for ages – or with injecting into the book the vital elements demanded by the publishers: 'love, sex and health'.

Her problems were entirely and only with the original photographs commissioned by the publishers. 'I said, I insist on having picture cookery. They didn't understand.' A fuss ensued, but then the publishers came to her carrying the first set of illustrations, 'and I explained to them what picture cookery was. And I said, "No, I won't pass it." And they were perfectly sweet.'

Thus it came about that, as the copyright page of the book now states,

'All the photographs were taken under the personal supervision of the author at her home in Hertfordshire, using her own backgrounds and ornaments.' Here lies Barbara Cartland's true contribution to food. It has very little to do with eating. But who other than the world's best-known and most senior romantic novelist would have thought of photographing a plate of Chicken Marengo on a cobalt-blue background surrounded by china figures of Napoleon and 'four soldiers that've stood on my dressing table' since they were given her years ago by a journalist?

Miss Cartland is especially proud of the picture of Honeyed Lamb Cutlets. Against a strong yellow background, height and three-dimensionality are given by one sleeping Cupid and one leaping Cupid (Staffordshire?) and a figurine of an Indian deity (could it be Krishna, playing the flute to the milkmaids?). Two lamb cutlets on a bed of rice are flanked by a pair of canned apricot halves, their cavities filled with raisins plumped out in boiling water. The plate is, disconcertingly, garnished with tiny gherkins sliced in fan shapes. Finally, some sprigs of real honeysuckle are tastefully placed to fill out the composition. The caption says: 'Honey is the food of Love. Give the man you love Honeyed Cutlets and with the scent of honeysuckle dream of a honeymoon.'

This picture, and the accompanying recipe, haunt my reveries. You make the sauce for the lamb by pouring some fat from the grill pan into a saucepan. You 'stir in the flour, then blend in the lemon juice, honey and stock, made with . . . water and the stock cube.' Canned apricots, raisins, flour-thickened gravy made with a stock cube? Except for the gherkins and the hint of sex, I shut my eyes, and I am comforted, and transported back in time. I am . . . at nursery school.

Alan Davidson

The man who got out of the stately, twenty-six-year-old Bentley was slight and handsome. His greying hair was tidy, but unusually long for a man in his mid-fifties. It was raining, and he attempted to shield himself from the weather by deploying a regulation black umbrella: this was ineffectual, for one of its spokes had poked through the fabric. When he arrived inside the new building of Saint Antony's College, Oxford, he removed his mackintosh. Under it he was wearing a black tunic, with a black velvet Nehru collar: as he moved, the fly-front of the tunic peeped open to reveal a row of highly polished brass buttons, each bearing the crest of HM The Queen. This gave rise to the suspicion, later confirmed, that this elegant winter suit had been created from diplomatic court dress. Around his neck, suspended from a silver chain, was a medallion bearing in relief the likeness of a Buddhist holy man with a strong resemblance to President Eisenhower. He carried a cloth shopping bag, which contained books, papers, and, in Chinese-box fashion, a wicker reticule, which contained his pipe and a glass ashtray, his spectacles, keys, wallet and change purse. It was obvious that he always wore his necklace and never went anywhere without his reticule.

Later, at the Quat' Saisons restaurant in Oxford, where the young chef prepared several fish dishes especially for him, he refused a glass of really excellent Chablis; he is, for medical reasons, teetotal. The rest of the company was greatly surprised. However, Davidson's abstemiousness did not affect the relish with which he dispatched the hot, feather-light pâté of turbot, or the dish of scallops napped with their silky sauce, or the *quenelles de brochet* that almost had the puffy consistency of a soufflé, and which, the chef told us, were made to a *lyonnais* recipe from locally caught pike.

The perfectly cooked brill served as the main course was delectably fresh and smelled of the sea: it gave Davidson an extra fillip of humour to learn that this chef with a real genius for cooking fish – his name was Raymond Blanc – hailed from the land-locked Franche-Comté. M. Blanc knew the identity of his distinguished guest, and beamed with pleasure at the generous measure of praise bestowed on his creations.

It is distinctly odd that a man whose business is food should have to eschew wine, its natural complement. But alcohol is broken down when heated, so Davidson is able to cook with wine, and it was an important ingredient in the fricassée of ray he cooked one evening in his own kitchen. This was a fascinating meal; it began with a tin of Russian red caviar, a present to Davidson from a famous Soviet scientist, and ended with grilled steaks of opah, *Lampris guttatus*, a fish few people have sampled. Its taste was something between tuna and mackerel, and its consistency more like meat than fish. 'The opah is extremely rare,' said Davidson, 'though it is found in oceans all around the world. Fishermen venerate it, because it is so extraordinarily handsome in appearance: a live opah, or a very recently dead one, is *so* colourful – and has a nice expression on its face. The opah is about three feet long and very deep in the body; the one that provided our steak weighed about 60 pounds.'

But the *pièce de résistance* of this dinner was the thornback ray, *Raja clavata*, which Davidson deftly cut into geometrical pieces – his *batterie de cuisine* could do with upgrading; the knife he used for this purpose had had half its blade snapped off 'while performing major surgery on an opah very early one morning at Billingsgate'. He poached the ray for fifteen minutes in a *court bouillon* with mace and nutmeg. The timing was crucial: 'So few people realise that the crucial factor in cooking fish or meat is its *shape*. The object is to raise the innermost point to the desired temperature: the time necessary for heat to penetrate mass is not directly proportional to the thickness of the mass, but to the *square* of the thickness. Thus the difference between a piece of food one inch thick and a piece two inches thick is that the two-inch piece needs not twice but *four times* the time to cook as the one-inch piece.'

Davidson's sauce for his fricassée used the cooking liquor, several decilitres of dry white wine and a large quantity of cream. It was delicious, but getting the quantities right – the recipe comes from John Farley's cookery book of 1763 – had taken Alan Davidson and his wife Jane many, many attempts.

Davidson particularly likes ray: first because it is an under-fished species, an under-exploited and valuable source of protein; second, because he is fond of the whole family of fish to which the ray belongs, which have no true bones, but cartilage – easier to deal with than small fishy bones, and imparting a special flavour to sauces. And finally because the quality of the flesh is so different from other fish or meat: it is not dense like tuna or meaty like bluefish or delicate like whiting; when cooked, ray forms fleshy strands that slip away easily from the skin and 'bone' at the touch of a fork.

Alan Davidson, cmg, formerly HM Ambassador to Vientiane, Laos, succeeded in shocking some of his more staid colleagues in the British diplomatic service when, at the early age of fifty-one, he abandoned his promising career to become a professional writer. It was a daring move and a particularly risky financial gamble. But it paid off. He resigned from the diplomatic corps six years ago and rapidly became one of the world's most famous writers on fish and fish cookery.

Davidson not only until recently held the prestige-conferring Alistair Horne Research Fellowship of St Antony's College and is a Postulante dell'Accademia Italiana della Cucina, but is also the author of the widely known *Mediterranean Seafood* (a fully revised edition of which has been published by Allen Lane and Penguin), *Seafood of South East Asia* (Macmillan, 1978), and the underground classics *Seafish of Tunisia and the Central Mediterranean* (1963) and *Fish and Fish Dishes of Laos* (1975). These last two titles are so rare that *Tunisia* can scarcely be consulted outside the British Library, though *Laos* is published in America by Charles Tuttle Inc.

Even more difficult to find is Davidson's 'clandestine' novel *Something Quite Big*. The single edition of this Utopian political thriller about the kidnapping of sixteen senior NATO officials bears no author's name, no publisher's imprint, and no date or place of publication. It was printed in a very small edition for Davidson by a Roman Catholic priest somewhere in South East Asia: typographical evidence suggests that the anonymous Father was not normally equipped to publish English-language books. The reasons for this *samizdat* procedure – surely the first case of it for English fiction (and indeed copies of the novel circulate on the Russian *samizdat* circuit) – can be found in *Who's Who*: from 1968 to 1971 Alan Davidson occupied an important post with the British Delegation to NATO. He knows too much – most NATO documents are classified CONFIDENTIAL, SECRET or even TOP SECRET – and the British Foreign Office, to whom Davidson had to apply for permission to publish, made it quite clear that they would rather he didn't. 'They could not claim it gave away any secrets, but they did not like the satire.'

This picture of the conventional British diplomat is difficult to reconcile with Davidson's present career and life-style. He lives in an 1880s house in the World's End district of Chelsea, which has only two rooms on each of its many floors. The basement study where he writes is almost overflowing with cookery books in a dozen tongues. Davidson, though, denies having a gift for languages: 'French is the only language I speak well. And though I can read recipes in the Scandinavian languages, Finnish eludes me. I depend on my wife, Jane, or daughter, Pamela, for Russian: and it took me *ages* to learn to translate recipes in Polish.'

He met his wife during his first posting, which was to Washington. Jane Davidson, who is a working partner in many of her husband's enterprises, was born into an American diplomatic family, resident in London. She was brought up there and in the Near East, before studying Russian and German at Bryn Mawr College in Pennsylvania. Alan Davidson no longer surprises his wife, but he sometimes alarms her, mostly by taking on the responsibility for projects so large that even his prodigious energies seem inadequate.

But no plan is too large or ambitious for Alan Davidson, and no detail of its execution too small for him to worry about. He has finished *North Atlantic Seafood* (Penguin) and has already begun collecting material for the companion book on the Caribbean and the Gulf of Mexico – which means he has only to write four more books in this series to have covered the entire world. Penguin has also comissioned him to write *Science in the Kitchen*, and the Oxford University Press, in collaboration with Penguin, has chosen him to write the *Oxford Companion to Food* – a breathtaking task.

Davidson is a dedicated member of a small band of scholar cooks whose interests in food are not merely practical and culinary, but historical and sometimes scientific. Their doyenne is Elizabeth David, the Englishwoman whose books on the cuisines of France, Italy and the Mediterranean revolutionised British cooking and eating habits after the Second World War. Other members of their circle (who can always be identified by the trouble they take to credit the source of a recipe in a profession where silent 'borrowing' is the norm) include publishers Jill Norman and Caroline Hobhouse, Jane Grigson, Claudia Roden and Richard Olney, the American who has lived in France for thirty years and whose highly readable books on French cooking have made him something of a cult figure in America.

When asked what he thought most characteristic of Davidson, Olney replied without hesitation, 'Alan's deeply genuine eccentricity.' It is undoubtedly relish for Davidson's peculiar combination of eccentricity and efficiency that has caused Olney and the other members of the above-named fraternity of scholar cooks to join with him in the publication of *Petits Propos Culinaires*, a magazine issued, initially, in a limited edition of 500, the profits going to a charity. The first number contained such inspired items of dottiness as an essay by Elizabeth David proving that an obscure but charming seventeenth-century cookery book was *not* written by the Countess of Kent, and another concerned 'the first appearance of recipes for ice cream in English cookery books'.

Davidson began his second career (his first, in the diplomatic service, had begun in 1948, after he had taken a double first in Greats at Oxford), while posted to Tunis as head of chancery and consul between 1962 and 1964. Tunisia was rich in fish, but his wife had difficulty buying it from the local markets. The trouble was that familiar fish bore unfamiliar names, while no one knew how to cook the many exotic fish that lived along the lengthy Tunisian coastline. By 1963 Davidson had produced a mimeographed pamphlet on the subject, and the next year he did a similar job on snakes and scorpions, which reassured diplomatic wives and mothers that the unfamiliar creepies and crawlies that abound in Tunisia were mostly harmless.

The fish book was the germ of *Mediterranean Seafood*. Diplomats are more exposed than most to the problems created by the fact, for example, that the Atlantic mackerel, *Scomber scombrus*, will be called *maquereau, scoumbri, sgombro, caballa, skoumbri* or *uskumru*, depending on whether you are trying to buy it in France, Greece, Italy, Spain, Tunisia or Turkey. Obviously what was needed was a book that gave the scientific name, the vernacular names, a visual illustration and a recipe for cooking the most common fish of the area. Less obviously, diplomats were the best people to supply that information. Davidson found they did so willingly.

Learning to cook, especially to the standard required to test recipes, presented Davidson with difficulties, both diplomatic and domestic. Jane Davidson was, and is, a good cook; but it was essential for Davidson to learn the craft himself. The chief obstacle was always the embassy chef. In Vientiane, for instance, the chef regarded it as outlandish that His Excellency the Ambassador wished to use the stove. 'We solved the problem,' Davidson said, 'by resorting to subterfuge, and sending the chef on invented errands or extended holidays; or by insisting that we wished to occupy the kitchen ourselves in order to prepare a Western-style dinner party. It wasn't easy; but we fully realised – and enjoyed – its comic possibilities.'

Writing, on the other hand, was no problem. Davidson had a talent, and Foreign Office work seems to stimulate people to write. The decision to go to Laos as a last posting, and then to write full-time, was nevertheless a bold one. It was made jointly by a council consisting of himself, his wife and their three daughters. Of these, the youngest, Jennifer, works for the *National Geographic* magazine in Washington; the next, Pamela, teaches Russian at the University of Surrey, and is married to a brilliant Russian Jewish mathematician; and the eldest, Caroline, wrote her first book, *A Woman's Work Is Never Done*, on the history of housework in Britain from 1700 to 1930. Indeed a close look at the names of the partners of the publishing company that produces the magazine leads one to suspect that what Alan Davidson has founded is not so much a new career as a dynasty.

Alan Davidson was my travelling companion in South Asia in 1980. In Bangkok there are still many who know him as a diplomat. That was how we came to be the guests there of an American resettlement official.

Our host arranged for us to visit the camp at Nongkhai, Thailand, on the Mekong River, which is the border with Laos. The eleven Laotians – relatives of a friend of his – Mr Davidson expected to find were, in fact, twenty-odd. He took this in his stride, and we repaired to our prearranged dinner.

Because of Nongkhai's strategic position, a military curfew was in force. When we arrived at the large River Restaurant, which perches on stilts over the Mekong, though it was thirty minutes before sundown, there was scarcely anyone else there.

As foreigners we were exempt from the curfew. So were our host and our Thai driver, who accounted for the third and fourth places at the only table set for dinner. In the restaurant the sole decorations were two framed pages with illustrations of fish. They were photocopies from one of Mr Davidson's most esoteric books, *Fish and Fish Dishes of Laos*.

Alan Davidson had never been to the restaurant before, but he did not seem as astonished as I was to see his own work on the walls. In a flash the explanation came to me: the owners of the restaurant had been besieged by their largely American clientèle with questions about what sort of fish they served. The pages displayed were those in which Alan Davidson dealt with the local fish of the Mekong.

They did not, however, include the most impressive fish of the region, the Giant Catfish of the Mekong, *pa beuk* in the Lao tongue and *pla beuk* in Thai. A large *pa beuk* would have been three metres long and could have weighed 250 to 300 kilograms.

Alan Davidson said the omission may well have been because the catch has diminished so severely, and so little is known about the fish's habits that no one can be sure that the conditions on which its survival depends still obtain in the Mekong.

Alan Davidson had once had a specimen of the fish, which the Lao people consider brings good fortune to those who eat it. This was in 1974, when an American well-wisher in the Agency for International Development telephoned to say that he had bought Mr Davidson the head of a *pa beuk*. It had to be collected at Ban Houei Sai, in the northwest of Laos, a fabled place, where the airport runways, like the streets, are studded with sapphires.

Alan Davidson managed to get a lift from Vientiane aboard a dawn flight, and on arrival found that his benefactor had packed the head in ice on the shady side of his own verandah. It weighed 50 kilos.

With difficulty, Alan Davidson persuaded an agency helicopter pilot to take him and the fish head back to Vientiane. There he interrupted an especially serene performance of the Lao ballet in the garden of the British Embassy, calling for volunteers among the audience to help him stow the head away in the Embassy freezer. British Airways agreed to fly it on from Bangkok to London, where the British Museum was eagerly awaiting the only specimen ever in the Western Hemisphere.

That night, at the Nongkhai restaurant, already on the table when we got there, was a device resembling a Mongolian hot-pot. The central cone contained glowing charcoal, and the outer doughnut-shaped rim was filled with liquid.

We could smell the lemon-grass oil of citronella, which is the chief herb of all South East Asian cookery, and the chilli fumes that stung our eyes even at a distance meant that this was probably a fish soup. Indeed, there were very large pieces of fish swimming in the peppery broth. They had blue-grey, thick, rubbery-looking skin. We huddled over the pot, staring reverently at its contents. *Pla beuk*, announced our furiously grinning Thai driver. And so it was. That is how we became probably the last people of European descent to taste the Giant Catfish of the Mekong – though the amount of chilli pepper in the soup prevented me from forming any clear idea of what the taste *was*.

It occurs to me that, touching though the scene was, it does not prove that the *pa beuk* is not extinct. Certainly, a local fisherman did catch one of the huge creatures some time that week. It's a horrible thought, but it could have been the last one. And, reader, we ate it.

Claudia Roden

Claudia Roden is a sort of culinary Columbus. In 1968, when she published the original version of *A Book of Middle Eastern Food*, the cuisine of the populations of a significant part of the earth's surface was revealed to Europeans and Americans for the first time. It came as a shock to many that the food of Araby was not composed exclusively of sheep's eyeballs. But now we happily stuff our own vineleaves and aubergines, eat pitta with everything, fool around with *foul medames*, have *eggah* for supper, and understand the uses of burghul. *Baba ghanoush* holds no terrors for us; we can buy sheep's milk yoghurt at the late night grocer's; *tabbouleh* turns us on; and *we* swoon when presented with an essentially well-made *Imam bayildi*.

Oddly enough, this discovery of a new cuisine is not the result of travel or of the opening of a new restaurant, but is a domestic phenomenon. This must be one of the few times in history when a change in eating habits has been brought about by a book. (Of course, Elizabeth David's books had this sort of influence; but for the much more familiar cuisines of *our* part of the Mediterranean region.)

Mrs Roden, then, has no rival for the title of the world's foremost expert on the food of the Middle East. I once had a letter from a reader in Warsaw asking for a recipe for braised ox spleen, which he had once tasted in Palestine. Nothing dismayed, I sent his request along to Claudia Roden. A fortnight or so later, Mrs Roden sent me a copy of her letter to my reader in which she enclosed the recipe for this slightly arcane dish; she had had no difficulty in winkling it out of a Lebanese chef of her acquaintance.

Claudia Roden was born in Cairo, into an enormous, prosperous, and aristocratic family of Sephardic Jews. In her family photographic album, the man wearing the tarboosh is her grandfather; the other fellow in the splendid head-gear is *his* father, Haham Abraham Ha-Cohen Douek, Chief Rabbi of the Ottoman Empire, and a renowned Cabbalistic scholar. Her family were genuinely of the Middle East. They belonged there as much as the Turks, the Egyptians or the Arabs, a fact European Jews still find difficult to comprehend. But in 1951 Claudia was sent to school in France (French is the mother tongue of Cairo Jews, though Alexandrian Jews speak Italian). Not long after, she was studying art at St Martin's in London.

After 1956 Claudia Roden's family had lost its footing and its fortune in the Middle East in the aftermath of Suez. The entire Sephardic civilisation seemed to have collapsed – or at least to have stopped growing in its own soil. The nostalgia of the exile for the food of his native land was the spur to Claudia Roden's career as a food writer.

As a married woman with three children and a husband to feed, cooking took on a new importance in her life. She was encouraged in the belief that it was possible to recapture the tastes and culinary sensations of her childhood in Cairo by reading Elizabeth David's *Mediterranean Food*. Mrs David's books not only gave her heart, but the writing, and that of Jane Grigson, provided an example congenial to Mrs Roden's temperament and scholarly inclinations. She set about collecting recipes from the far-flung members of her own family. *A Book of Middle Eastern Food* resulted. Its initial publication in hard covers was not much of an event; but Jill Norman put it in paperback for Penguin, and the rest is history. It remains a best-seller here and in America and Israel, where a kosher version has been produced in Hebrew. Her latest fan is one of the richest merchants in Bahrain. 'He told me I'd changed his life,' Mrs Roden told me. 'After his cook died, he was distraught until a copy of my book fell into his hands. Now he tells me that he spends a lot of time in the kitchen himself.'

Once I met two members of her family at Claudia Roden's spacious and stylish north London house. There was a sister-in-law, a stunning archaeologist who is studying Egyptology, and whose eyes light up with equal interest at the mention of hieroglyphs or food. And her brother, a biochemist, who was thinking of leaving Southern California for the gastronomically lusher pastures of the Auvergne. Later, Mrs Roden prepared lunch for us – almost absentmindedly – as we talked with some intensity of her family's experience of exile and the cultural and psychological importance of food to people who are *déraciné*.

One of her funnier memories is of her parents' new neighbours in Golders Green coming to welcome the newcomers. Her mother, thrilled by the reception given her, invited quite a few of them back for coffee the next day. Of course, she stayed up all night preparing food. But when her new neighbours, all Ashkenazi Jews, saw the trays of sweetmeats and scented dainties she set out before them, they expressed alarm and serious doubts as to the Jewishness of their hostess. The Russian, Polish and German Jews of Golders Green still have difficulty understanding why their non-European neighbours eat hummus, lamb, phylo pastry pies and other dishes that they think of as 'Arab'. Claudia's parents remain a bit puzzled about Jews who eat smoked salmon and salt beef.

Our lunch was eggs poached in a garlicky fresh tomato sauce with a definite whiff of the *prochain-Orient*, warm leeks in a vinaigrette and soured cream (which might well have been yoghurt) dressing, fruit and Turkish coffee.

Claudia Roden's writing has the fascination of her conversation. Her books are treasure houses of information and mines of literary pleasures. *Picnic* has, as its epigraph, Milton's description in *Paradise Lost* of the first-ever picnic – 'A table richly spread in regal mode,/With dishes piled and meats of noblest sort/And savour' – in the Garden of Eden. It gives

Mrs Roden the chance to remind the reader that the passage ends with the Tempter's words: 'These are not fruits forbidden.'

Picnic, with its lovely illustrations by Linda Kitson, is not just a good read. It is also the most practical book I know on the subject of outdoor cooking and eating. The barbecue chart, printed as an appendix at the end of the book, gives the times and conditions for grilling food over wood or charcoal, and will save many a meal from disaster.

'A career founded on nostalgia' is how Claudia Roden describes her work. 'Even eating outside is nostalgia for the good weather of my childhood; and the entire institution of the picnic reflects the longing of sophisticated people for the simpler habits and customs of the past. The picnic is a Romantic idea.'

Mrs Roden has had huge success giving small courses in Middle Eastern cookery at her home. There is a demand for such instruction, she thinks, because 'Middle Eastern food is so easy to appreciate. It is not like Indian food, where you have to acquire a taste for hot and piquant food. It is subtle, certainly, but immediately palatable to most people.' Recipes have been garnered over the years from unusual, even unlikely sources. Mrs Roden has stood by the elbows of Turkish women as they stirred their pots, and noted down the details of what they were doing. Royal cooks have contributed some tips. Friends from all over the world have obliged with recipes or variants and, for the revised and enlarged edition of *A Book of Middle Eastern Food*, hundreds of readers have written Mrs Roden with new contributions.

This is one of those rare cookery books that is really a work of cultural anthropology, and Mrs Roden's standards of scholarship are so high as to ensure that it has permanent value. But the book also has merit as a work of literature, and is studded with quotations culled from Mrs Roden's wide reading – anecdotes, bits of verse and learned works of history all figure in her pages, and contribute to making the book one that can be read right through. The new volume has hundreds of recipes that were not in the old edition, and Mrs Roden has made a few concessions to modern ideas about healthy eating. Middle Eastern cooking divides into two camps: those who cook with butter and those who cook with oil. Naturally, those in the former category were lavish with the commodity they had, but their brothers to the east lacked. So in an effort to reduce coronary disease amongst users of her book, Mrs Roden has reduced the quantities of butter called for in her new edition.

It was to be expected that a book so original as *Middle Eastern Food* would be ripped off and, indeed, it has been widely imitated. Mrs Roden's sincerest flatterer is Arto der Haroutunian. She has stated publicly* that she is 'hurt and angry' that, in his books *Middle Eastern Cookery* (1982) and *Complete Arab Cookery* (also 1982), he has a great many of the same recipes as hers (some of which had never been in print before her 1968 book), similarly described and including some of the mistakes – even to leaving out an essential ingredient – that Mrs Roden corrected in the second edition of her book. Mr Haroutunian also included some of the same poems, background and historical observations that first appeared in Mrs Roden's book. She is the sort of cookery writer who does 'field work', gathering her recipes often at first hand. Because of this, she feels that in his borrowings, Haroutunian 'has stolen my shadow'. But it isn't just Haroutunian of whom she complains. 'It is tragic,' she says, 'when food writers add or take away an ingredient to make a lifted recipe "their own", and pass it off as authentic. They are falsifying tradition. This is how a culture ends up garbled and destroyed in the lap of another.'

Mrs Roden is happy to see her records of recipes that belong to a particular country, town, village or community passed around, and even changed to suit the taste of cooks who experiment with them. 'But,' she says, 'although there are no *standard* recipes in countries where they don't use cookery books and where dishes are passed down in the family – and although there are many versions of a dish – there are just so many and no more. When people from a different culture make up their own original version without bothering to find out the traditional one, it usually has nothing to do with reality. With so many recipes now lifted from one book to another, each with "one small change" to get around the law of copyright, nobody will know what the truth is any more.'

* In an interview used in *The Official Foodie Handbook* by Ann Barr and Paul Levy.

Elizabeth David

'It was mean,' said one London gastronome of the award of the CBE to Elizabeth David in the 1986 New Year's honours list. (She had already been given the OBE in 1976.) 'She should certainly have been made a dame.' Despite the best efforts of Mrs David herself, in her journalism and seven limpidly written books on food, the British still have a peculiar attitude to her subject. We may not be averse to eating well, but we are not about to reward anyone merely for writing well about it. (After all, it was not so long ago that it was taboo to talk about food while eating at a middle-class table.) This negative posture makes it difficult to analyse and understand the real contribution Mrs David has made to our national well-being.

Her first book, *Mediterranean Food*, was published in 1950, four years before food rationing actually ended. It wasn't just the dried egg, absence of lemons, the snoek and Namco or the Woolton pie to which the recipes in that book were the antidote. The ingredients called for by those recipes were not widely available anyway. What was important was the effect of the book on the morale of the middle classes, who were as starved of sunshine as they were of oranges and olive oil. Elizabeth David reminded them that the whole world was not as grey as post-war Britain, that only 18 miles away was the land where the lemon trees flower, and where there were also cream and butter, meat and cheese, real bread and wine – *and* that, one day soon, it would be possible to go there again. What she offered in her work was not just recipes, but a vision of civilisation, the civilisation that is now, owing to package tours, taken for granted by all classes of Britons. Then, though the numbers affected were not so large, what Elizabeth David did was to give heart to war-weary people. Her books achieved this because they were unlike any other books about food; they were full of history and anecdote, showed a strong sense of place, and were stunningly well written.

Mrs David has a love-hate relationship with America, where her books have never been as popular as they are here. Though America had a mild form of food rationing, the Americans lack the background of gastronomic suffering that endows the British with a proper appreciation of Elizabeth David's writing.

Mrs David's work has got increasingly specialised and scholarly – some would say her choices of topics are eccentric. After the French, Italian and Mediterranean books of the '50s and '60s she turned, in 1970, to England, and published *Spices, Salt and Aromatics in the English Kitchen*, whose subtitle called it volume one of 'English Cooking Ancient and Modern'. There hasn't been a volume two, but her next book, *English Bread and Yeast Cookery* (1977) was equally erudite; and her present researches are into the narrow subject of ice in cookery and food preparation. Not surprisingly, the honours she seems to value most are the quasi-academic ones, such as the Fellowship of the Royal Society of Literature she received in 1982 and her 1979 honorary doctorate from Essex University.

Born in 1913, Mrs David was brought up in Sussex, the second of four daughters of Rupert Sackville Gwynne, a Conservative MP, and the Hon. Stella Ridley. Her parents had no interest in or knowledge of food; but in one of her essays she writes, with tantalising brevity, about a childhood food experience: 'the real field mushrooms which, as children, we had so often brought home for breakfast after a dawn search in the fields round our home in the Sussex Downs. . . . We had had a Nannie who always used to cook our breakfast mushrooms over the nursery fire in cream, whisked away, no doubt, from the kitchen regions before the cook was up and about.' Following this perfectly conventional upper-class childhood, Mrs David left school at sixteen and went to France for eighteen months, where she studied at the Sorbonne and lived – and ate – with a Norman family who had a farmhouse near Caen as well as a Paris household. She returned to England, having learnt how to eat, determined to learn how to cook as well.

In her youth she was a very great beauty. She was an actress for a time, and though she says today that 'I had no talent in that sphere whatever, the brief experience was very, very interesting and I do not regret it'. Her looks made her suitable for employment as a *vendeuse* at Worth in London. In the late thirties she met the writer Norman Douglas. He was seventy-two to her twenty-four, and came to have a great influence upon her. She writes of 'an entanglement' that he advised her to break off: 'Had I listened to Norman's advice I should have been saved a deal of trouble. Also, I should not, perhaps, have seen Greece and the islands, not spent the war years working in Alexandria and Cairo [where she worked for the Ministry of Information as Librarian at Cairo], not have got married [in 1944 to Lt.-Colonel Ivor Anthony David] and gone to India, not returned to England, not become involved in the painful business of learning to write about food and cookery.'

It was John Lehmann, her first publisher, who encouraged her to write in a novel way about the pleasures of the table. 'He saw what was needed. It was that man who had the imagination to see that that was what would be interesting.' Its John Minton illustrations also hit the mark, and despite the fact that other publishers had rejected *Mediterranean Food*, it sold well and continues to sell. She has been mostly lucky in her publishers (though she is still cross with her most recent one, Robert Hale), especially with her paperback publisher, Penguin, who have been doing her books since 1955. It was there that she met Jill Norman, who has edited and encouraged her since joining Penguin in 1962, and continued to do so well after she set up on her own.

Mrs David became a journalist – a good one, too – in the mid-Fifties. She started in 1955 on *The Sunday Times* as cookery contributor. She did not enjoy the job – or rather, she did not enjoy working for her editor, the late Ernestine Carter, 'always appropriately ready with her cutting-out shears when it came to my cookery pieces', and she disliked Mrs Carter's punning headlines. She was much happier at *The Spectator*, where she did a fortnightly column during the golden reigns of Brian Inglis, Iain Hamilton and Ian McLeod, and, she says, benefited greatly from the editing of Katharine Whitehorn. Though she was not clubbable, and did not see a great deal of them socially, she remembers with fondness her colleagues Cyril Ray, Bernard Levin, Alan Brien and Jean Robertson.

Her journalism was fresh, as was her approach to writing her books. When she started, cookery writers customarily opened their articles 'with a short introductory piece relevant to the products of the season, or to one particular type of dish, let us say soufflés, omelettes, rice dishes . . . or perhaps it would be a little moan about the poor quality of our potatoes, or about not being able to buy courgettes. Whatever it was, once the opening piece was dutifully concluded, you filled the rest of your space with appropriate recipes and that was that.' Mrs David broke the mould of this kind of journalism, by seeming to enjoy invective and by realising that there is a difference between writing about cookery, a minority interest, and writing about food, a universal concern. Every journalist writing today who is aware of this crucial distinction (surprisingly, their number is not large), owes part of his living to Mrs David's example. She, however, was meagrely paid and received virtually no expenses to help her do her job. In the mid-Fifties, Elizabeth David suffered a mild stroke; for a time she feared it had damaged her tasting apparatus. She recovered fully from the stroke, but not from the car crash she was involved in in the late '70s, which had 'a much delayed and long-lasting effect' according to one of her friends, who thought it had shocked her badly.

In 1965 Elizabeth David opened the shop that bore her name near Sloane Square. Within months, there were other 'kitchen shops' up and down the country. She was a serious and dedicated shopkeeper, serving at the shop herself on the days she wasn't abroad buying the well-designed, functional goods that she wished the shop to offer. Indeed, she gave up her writing to run the shop, and it must have been heartbreaking for her when she severed her connection with the shop in 1973, because she disagreed with her partners' more commercial attitudes about the mechandise offered. Worse, she could not get her name back, and the ex-partners still have the use of her name, though she no longer has anything to do with the choice of the goods sold.

Mrs David is very old-fashioned in some ways. She says, for example, that she finds 'shopping quite different from what it used to be. There is no local greengrocer, no butcher. Luckily I have a good Italian delicatessen. That's at least something.' It would be easier to sympathise with this complaint if one were more certain that Mrs David was well acquainted with the relevant departments in the three showcase supermarkets that her area of Chelsea boasts. The contents of the greengrocery section of any one of them would make many northerners wish to migrate south.

Lots of things about the modern world seem to displease Mrs David. She loathes the current irreverent style of food writing, which often appears to cloak its erudition in humour, and displays its knowledge of foodstuffs in the creation of puns rather than new dishes. In her monthly column in the *Tatler*, she has written some very cross words about its practitioners, and heaps grumpy abuse upon younger heads (particularly my own, as she strongly disapproved of *The Official Foodie Handbook*).

Her choler is not reserved for the new generation of food writers, though. She also hates the kind of food she thinks they espouse. She regards their words as frivolous and flashy and the food – at least the debased British version of the *nouvelle cuisine* – as 'little mounds on the plate'. Her own taste is increasingly for simple, well-prepared food, chiefly vegetables and fish, or for 'ethnic' food, especially Indian and Middle Eastern. Her appetite is not large, she drinks wine almost exclusively, and she is bored by restaurants that emphasise the presentation of the food on the plate.

She is less reclusive than formerly, though, and has resumed going out occasionally in the evenings. When she entertains herself, it is almost always at the kitchen table in the basement of her house, and seldom for more than two other people. She is the best of dinner companions, say those lucky enough to have received an invitation.

Still, the same friends, when they talk about her at all, are always a bit defensive. It is as though there were something vulnerable, and in need of protection, about this great lady, this considerable scholar, to whom so many of us owe a very practical improvement in the quality of our everyday lives. It is touching, certainly; but it means that there will always be some mystery surrounding the life and character of one of the major benefactors of the British public.

Others are learned and others can write – though few so dazzlingly as she. Elizabeth David's hold over our culinary imagination and the loyalty and affection her readers feel for her spring from deeper sources. In part, I feel it is the appeal – and the natural authority – of a particular kind of good-humoured, slightly bossy upper-middle-class Englishwoman, the sort of woman whose speaking voice is instantly recognisable in her prose; the sort of woman who gets things right. Above all, a woman possessed of wit and taste.

When these are allied to the talents of a really good journalist, one who instinctively knows what will make a good story, and one, moreover, with an ear for words and phrases that makes it possible for her to describe the fugitive sensations of the nose and palate without ever landing up in Pseud's Corner, why, then you have some of the elements we cherish in Elizabeth David's writing. Added to this she has a capacious memory and a sense of place so strong that a good novelist would be grateful for it.

'Sometimes,' writes Mrs David, 'I meet people who ask me quite sincerely what is the point of taking so much trouble about cooking. Surely, they say, as long as your food is nourishing it'll do.' 'Well,' she says, comparing an unpleasant with a pleasant experience in a restaurant, 'there are people who take the heart out of you and there are people who put it back.'

That is an admirable summing-up of what Elizabeth David did for Britain. After a long and exhausting war was followed by a drab and tiring peace, with little relief from the everyday tediousness of rationing, Mrs David, in her books and in her journalism – such as the pieces collected in her recent *An Omelette and a Glass of Wine* – put Britain's heart back. What does the country owe her for this service? The Order of Merit has been given for smaller cause.

M. F. K. Fisher

Until five or six years ago I had not even heard of M. F. K. Fisher. This is like a general admitting ignorance of Clausewitz or Mrs Thatcher pretending never to have heard of Machiavelli. The magnitude of this confession can be assessed by the fact that her writing was admired by Auden and Updike, and that she was a regular contributor to the *New Yorker* magazine – perhaps the only writer on food who enjoyed that magazine's famous carte blanche commissioning policy. This terrible omission from a Foodie's library can only be explained by the fact that, like some delicate French wines and some dishes such as *bouillabaisse*, Mrs Fisher's work doesn't travel well. She is *very* American. Yet the appeal of her writing to her compatriots clearly has a good deal to do with her European sensibilities.

Mary Frances Kennedy Fisher (the three-initial by-line was originally used to conceal her sex, at a time when writing about food was an occupation for men) was born in 1908 in Mid-Western Albion, Michigan. But her small-town newspaperman father, Rex Kennedy, was an adventurous wordsmith, and took his family on a nomadic house- and job-hunting circuit, following the West Coast from Washington to Oregon and then south to California.

They settled in the Quaker-dominated town of Whittier, which has since been made infamous by being the birthplace of ex-President Nixon. Among provincial orange groves and vineyards, Mary Frances Kennedy's tastes were formed; negatively by her puritanical grandmother Holbrook, who had a nervous stomach and a frugal nature, and positively by her warm and generous mother, Edith.

Mrs Fisher owes a lot to her mother. Though it is evident from her writing that she is a jealously private person, the most obvious merit of her writing is the perspicuity with which she pins down the emotions connected with hunger and appetite, eating and drinking. 'It seems to me that our three basic needs, for food and security and love, are so entwined that we cannot straightly think of one without the other.' There are not many writers on food who have ever even stopped to consider the relationship of hunger to their subject.

But in two essays collected in her *As They Were* she explores, briefly but thoroughly, the varieties of hunger. 'Young hunger,' she reminds us, is a thing apart. 'It is very hard for people who have passed the age of, say, fifty to remember with any charity the hunger of their own puberty and adolescence.' She reminds us of the hostess discovering the cupboard or fridge stripped bare by youths 'who apparently could have eaten four times their planned share at the dinner table the night before.

'Such avidity is revolting, once past. But I can recall its intensity still; I am not yet too far from it to understand its ferocious demands when I see a fifteen-year-old boy wince and whiten at the prospect of waiting politely a few more hours for food.'

She wrote those words in 1946, when she was a sympathetic matron of thirty-eight. Nine years earlier, she had confronted head-on the issue of grown-up gastronomic greed, in the essay on a *bouffe* at a restaurant in northern Burgundy called 'I was really very hungry'. She details the meal's end: 'I remember feeling only amusement when a vast glass of *marc* appeared before me and then gradually disappeared, like the light in the warm room full of water-sounds. I felt surprised to be alive still, and suddenly very grateful to the wild-lipped waitress, as if her presence had sustained me through duress.'

Mrs Fisher's childhood is a reminder of a more genteel American past, a civilisation and a culinary tradition different from its European original, but not inferior to it. It disappeared finally and irrevocably with the Second World War, with the result that Americans began to yearn to experience – and to read about – their European roots.

Mrs Fisher was extremely well placed to satisfy this need. 'I first went to France in 1929, with my first husband, Al Fisher. We lived in Dijon, where he got his doctorate, and I studied for the *licence* and went to *Beaux Arts* at night. We stayed a third year, in Strasbourg and Cagnes-sur-Mer. (It was a fine time: Al had a lot of Princeton friends at Oxford, who came through Dijon often, and my younger sister, Norah, lived with us for the last year.)

'I started writing about food in 1935, I think. Al Fisher was instructor in the English Department at Occidental College in Southern California, and we were living on $650 a year, rather thin even in those comparatively inexpensive days, so I got a half-time job in Los Angeles.

'I did not realise it for some time, but in the small "art-store" I was the genteel façade for the heavy porn that was sold in the back room. I had to go to Los Angeles early each morning when Al went to College, so I had free mornings, which I spent in the reading rooms of the Public Library. I often sat next to an old man who left before I did and who always read very old, fine-smelling books. I began to read them, and found they were mostly Elizabethan-and-later cookery books; so I began to write about them to amuse my husband.

'(I had been writing since I was about five and had half a novel well under way by the time I was nine, but never thought of doing anything more about writing than that. Father was a fourth-generation journalist, and we were an articulate family.)

'My husband was pleased by the stuff, and showed it to a friend, who in turn showed it to his sister who was then a noted novelist, and it turned into *Serve It Forth*, my first published book, in 1937.'

A tantalising reticence is one of Mrs Fisher's most engaging literary traits. For several years I have wondered what became of Al, whose name recurs constantly in her mostly first-person narratives. In fact, she left him, in 1936, to marry Dillwyn Parrish, cousin of Maxfield Parrish and, by all accounts, a gifted painter himself.

She suffered a terrible wrench in leaving Fisher, of whom she remained fond; but Parrish was the great passion of her life. They returned to live in Europe, and stayed in Switzerland until war broke out. At their home near Vevey they had a garden and put up their own vegetables, which they served to their many visitors, in carefully prepared meals washed down by thin Swiss wines.

This passionate, intense interlude was terminated by the death of Parrish in 1941. Mrs Fisher bravely took herself off to Mexico, where her sister Norah lived with their brother David and his new wife. But only a few months later, David committed suicide. It was the time of America's entry into the War, and David 'told me he would never wear a uniform'.

In work she found solace, and some of her best-known books were published now: *Consider the Oyster* in 1941; the war-time work of gastronomy, *How to Cook a Wolf*, in 1942; and *The Gastronomical Me* the next year. (These have been reprinted by Pan in a paperback omnibus, *The Art of Eating*.) A few years later she brought out her celebrated annotated translation of Brillat-Savarin's *The Physiology of Taste*.

She was busy, and she married for the third time. With her publisher husband Donald Friede, she had two daughters. It was now, too, that she began writing for the *New Yorker*, and, somewhat surprisingly, went to Hollywood as a screenwriter for Paramount. In 1951 she divorced Friede, who 'was more trouble than the children'.

She had a brief resurgence of her career-changing habits in 1963, when she joined the civil rights movement and went to Mississippi as a volunteer teacher at a black school. 'Both my children were out of the nest and I was free. I wanted to see if the South was as rotten as I'd heard it was. Oh, it was worse!'

Now in her late 70s and somewhat infirm, Mrs Fisher lives in Sonoma County, northern California, in a house designed and built for her by the British architect, David Pleydell-Bouverie. The kitchen, with its black tile floor, is the centre of her house and her existence.

English colleagues whom she admires are Elizabeth David and Jane Grigson, 'who are important and good writers about the whole art of eating. I like what Alan Davidson is doing.' She also rates Sybille Bedford and Richard Olney, 'who is really American'. The only American names she mentions in this context are those of Julia Child and James Beard.

'I can't and don't put myself on the same level as E. David, Beard, Child and all the other fine people like them. For one thing, I have never "laboured". But I feel absolutely sure that they have done infinitely more good than harm to the tastes and indeed the basic hunger of current Western man. I think they would agree with me that there is no chance of stopping the increased use of fast food and "junk" food. It is here, and it will continue. But countless people are more aware that it can be fast and even junky and still help us to survive.'

What about her own favourite foods? 'Of course, they change with age as well as where one is; and right now they are, for me, almost any freshly picked vegetable or fruit, and fine unsalted butter and freshly caught fish. I love shellfish, but refuse to eat the ones caught in polluted waters and chemically washed before they are frozen. And I cannot afford fresh lobsters and oysters flown to California from New England. Now and then I can get oysters from Pacific commercial beds . . . excellent.

'I find wines as important as food. That is, I think wine provides its own nourishment and value, and eating anything without at least a few sips of it is like breathing without really inhaling. I am fortunate to live (as I have managed to do for some twenty-five years now) in a part of the world where wine is almost as good as water.'

———

Julia Child

Julia Child may be the most important person in the world of food. The American equivalent of Elizabeth David, she has taken on the unenviable task of civilising the cooking and eating habits of the Junk Food Continent by writing a small number of immensely influential cookery books. But she is also a television celebrity, and a superstar.

I well remember her first series of 'The French Chef' – the one she now refers to as 'the black and white' programmes. As a post-graduate student I used often to give up my Saturday nights to stay at home in front of the tube and watch her demonstrations on our local educational television station.

These performances had a double fascination. First, there was Mrs Child's excellence as a teacher, which ensured that any but the thickest beginner would learn how to make a soufflé or whatever. But, second, there was the thrill of the performance, for Julia Child was not intended by nature to be a television star.

She is physically large (over six feet tall) and not exactly gainly. In fact, she is disaster-prone. This is part of her appeal to her millions of viewers; for, over her stove, or knife in hand, she is scarcely less clumsy than the run of humanity, we her pupils. My favourite episode was the one when, demonstrating how to turn a whole poached salmon, she dropped it – splat – on the studio floor. 'I'm not sorry that happened,' said Julia Child, towering over the finny beast, 'as it gives me a chance to show you how to reconstruct a fish.'

And there was the programme on *crêpes* when she showed off her prowess as a pancake flipper: in an act of sheer hubris she was making a gigantic potato *crêpe*; she grasped the enormous pan in both hands, and with a twist of *both* wrists, sent the pancake flying – but it never returned.

The camera panned slowly upwards, to reveal the delicious object – stuck to the rafters of the studio set.

As her neighbour in Cambridge, Massachusetts, and like countless other Julia-worshipping cooks, I patronised the shops she was known to like, in the hope of some day running into her, at the fishmonger's, say, and receiving an impromptu invitation to lunch.

Years later, a life-time's ambition was realised. The Childs invited my wife and me to lunch at their second home. In 1960, in the hills above Grasse, they built a house on property belonging to 'Simca' Beck and her husband. Mme Beck was one of Julia Child's collaborators on her first and most important book, *Mastering the Art of French Cooking*. (That volume and its successor are available as Penguins.)

The directions she sent us were as explicit and complicated as any of the recipes in any of her books. (She prides herself on never leaving out a single step of any recipe, so that even a novice cook can follow it.)

Both Julia and Paul Child came out to greet us when we arrived at Bramafan-Pitchoune. They live in a part of the south of France I do not know well, and the first thing I remarked was their strange, unsettling garden, where, in early January, there were yellow roses and jonquils in bloom simultaneously, where mature pomegranates hung from a shrub, and olives were ripening on the tree.

The extraordinary hospitality of the Childs soon put me at my ease and, within minutes, I had grasped the secret of Julia Child's achievement: 'Julia Child', the television French chef, is actually a husband and wife team. Paul Child's contribution to the visual side of things is of large importance to the television series, and to the success of *Julia Child and Company* (half a million copies in print) and *Julia Child and More Company*. These are not available in this country.

But then, there is something about Julia Child, her New England drawl and her casual manner, that does not amuse the British. After the BBC was offered the television series, and viewed the pilot film, it was made plain to Paul that they had confused Julia's laid-back posture, her relaxed approach to failures as well as triumphs, with a tendency to use the brandy for more than making sauces. Deprived by this rejection of the best television cookery series ever made, the British now have an appallingly low standard – our television 'cooks' would not be tolerated by her more sophisticated American audience.

For lunch we had home-made *foie gras* – an entire liver from a specially fed goose, cooked in a delicious but fiddly way that involved removing nerves and other bits – served with toast fingers and 'Ivan's Apéritif': one measure dry white French vermouth, such as dry Martini or Noilly Prat; one measure sweet white vermouth or white Lillet or white Dubonnet; one tablespoon gin (which gives an unctuous quality to the cocktail and is therefore an essential ingredient) and a 2½-inch or 6-cm strip of fresh zest of orange. Pour the vermouths over several ice cubes in a clear, long-stemmed wine glass. Float the gin on the surface, but do not stir. Squeeze the zest over the glass, then rub it around the rim and pop it into the drink.

At table we were served duck cooked in two ways, the leg having been done as *confit*, preserved in its own fat, and the breast served rosy and pink. The garnishes were stewed lentils and roasted whole cloves of garlic. The sauce, we were told, was 'only the duck stock, much reduced, plus Armagnac, cream, green peppercorns, and things like that'. The salad, which was served with the cheese, was made of chicory, endive, sweet peppers, and dressed with a vinaigrette. Finally there was an apple tart, with completely regular slices of apple, glazed with apricot jam, topping the best puff pastry I have ever eaten – and that in a fortnight when I sampled the *feuilleté* of the *chefs pâtissiers* of MM Barrier, Pic, Bocuse, Charvet, Vergé and Haeberlin.

With this Lucullan lunch we drank Château Léoville Poyferré 1970 and a Châteauneuf du Pape 1976.

In *More Company* there is a long recipe for cassoulet, which is followed by a learned note on the history of the dish. (Julia Child – like Elizabeth David, Alan Davidson and Jane Grigson – is part of the international contingent of what I call the Scholar Cooks, those who are interested in the history and science of food and drink.) This discussion is in turn followed by 'A Note on Beans and Intestinal Mobility' – in short, flatulence. We spent a very entertaining ten minutes talking about, not only the solution to the problems of beans and wind, but how to avoid resorting to euphemism. We agreed, finally, to call a fart a fart.

Mrs Child cites scientists from California who say that 'beans contain the difficult-to-digest sugars, stachyose and raffinose. The human body does not have the enzymes to break them down, and when these culprits reach the lower intestine of some diners, their resident bacteria react violently, producing [wind], or, in a word, motility.'

The California solution to the Fart Problem is to boil beans for three minutes in ten times their own volume of water, 'soak them for ten hours or overnight in the same water, drain and rinse them, and set them to cook in fresh water', eliminating '80 per cent of the trouble'.

Nobody could fail to find Julia Child sympathetic as a person, but she is also to my taste as a cookery writer, when, for example, she explains to her hyper-cautious US readers that it is not necessary to cook pork until it is grey and rubbery, as '*trichinae* are eliminated when the meat is still almost rare', and recommends experiments (with the aid of a meat thermometer) at serving roast pork at various temperatures of more than 140°F/60°C.

Waverley Root

Waverley Root was one of the great writers in English on gastronomic subjects. I used to take the *International Herald Tribune* every day, because I was unable to work out which day it was his column appeared, and I wanted to be certain not to miss it. He shouldn't need any introduction to British readers, as his *The Food of France* sold out here immediately after the publication of Cyril Connolly's favourable review of it in 1958. But the publishers, Cassell, didn't reprint the book and though it has never been out of print in his native USA (it is now in its second paperback edition and is a Papermac here), Mr Root's name was not a household word here in Britain. This is understandable, because Waverley Root was very much a Yank; but it is a pity, as it is a very good book.

Born in Providence, Rhode Island, in 1903, and brought up in Fall River, Massachusetts, Root went to Paris in 1927, meaning to stay for two months. He was still there, living near the Boulevard Montparnasse, with his fourth French-speaking wife, and still working as a journalist, when I met him in the summer of 1982, shortly before he died. As you can tell from the dates, Waverley Root had to have known everybody. He was amused by this presumption, and teased that he had thought of calling a chapter of his memoirs 'I Never Knew Hemingway'. However, he did know Hemingway; he admits to having met Gertrude Stein at least once; and he knew Ezra Pound well enough to have lost 200 letters from him.

Actually, Root was bound to meet this sort of person: he single-handedly wrote the book page of his first paper, the Paris edition of the *Chicago Tribune*. It was one of three American newspapers then published in Paris, and other staffers included James Thurber, William Shirer and Henry Miller. Root stayed in Paris, writing for various papers and broadcasting for an American network, until, during the Second World War, he followed the government of France in its city by city retreat from Paris. At Bordeaux he made the last broadcast before the Occupation.

After the war his interest in food increased. He farmed in Vermont, growing nearly all his own food: 'Everything in the seed catalogues that would grow that far north, as well as goats, pigs, chickens and sheep; guinea fowl, rabbits and a calf that died before it could reach the table. But it never occurred to me to shoot the "partridges", which were so tame you could have hit them with a club.' At this point, Mr Root interrupted the narrative with a short but learned disquisition on the assimilation of the names of the game species of the New World to those of the Old.

Root came back to Paris in 1950, partly because he wanted to educate the daughter of his third marriage in France rather than America. (The marriage 'hadn't exactly broken up, it just petered out'.) He worked as a translator for Opera Mundi, and also ghosted books. 'There was a time when I couldn't go into a house in Europe without seeing a book I'd written – but not under my own name, as I'd ghosted about twenty.'

In 1957 he finally got 'into' food. 'I set out to do a restaurant guide to France, with 1500 places to be included. In the first place, it was rather dull – and there are a limited number of things you can say about a restaurant. In the second place, I had grouped the restaurants by regions, and written an introduction to each. The introductions were so much more interesting that I threw out the restaurant listings and published the introductions.' That was the genesis of *The Food of France. The Food of Italy*, which is, curiously, a much longer book than *France*, was published in 1971. It owed its birth partly to Time-Life's commission to do *The Cooking of Italy* in 1968, of which at least 500,000 copies were printed. But Root had been going to Italy regularly since he was sent to cover the Concordat in 1929.

Nearly 80 when I met him, Root suffered cheerfully from the bad back that had confined him to his flat for the previous four years. He was, thus, a little uncertain about his immediate surroundings, and warned me, when I proposed to call on him: 'There will be no one to give directions. There is a concièrge, but she is always out, and anyway she only speaks loud Spanish.' He seemed seldom even to leave his room, where he was very systematically surrounded by filing cabinets and bookshelves. He could answer almost any question about food without leaving that room. His own notes, his unfinished manuscripts, and thousands of letters from readers were filed and cross-indexed so efficiently that Root could find anything in a matter of minutes. It was this miraculous and meticulous filing system that allowed Root to compose a column chiding his *Trib* colleague, the humorist columnist Russell Baker, for calling Liederkranz a German cheese. (He was only testing Root, Baker replied. Everybody knows that Liederkranz is one of the only indigenous American cheeses, just as Rosencrantz is the only Danish one.)

His *Encyclopaedia of Food* ought to have been Root's *magnum opus*; published in the US in 1980, it sold 25,000 copies in two years. But it could have been a very great deal longer and more thorough, said Root, if anybody could have afforded to publish or buy it. And its amplifying chapters, or sequels, or companion volumes, depending on how you choose to regard these matters, were, he said, all in his files.

Waverley Root was a little worried about what would happen to his archive, and how it could be made to support his (fourth and present) wife Collette, after his death. He seemed to feel it belonged in a university library. As a matter of fact, it contains much that is not about food, but ought to be of historical significance. For, as a French journalist pointed out to me, Waverley Root was also the *doyen* of diplomatic correspondents in France. But that is another *histoire*.

Ken Hom

A new star was born overnight in the autumn of 1984. Relatively few people in Britain had heard of Ken Hom, but by the end of his first Chinese cookery programme on BBC 2 the face, features and voice of this handsome thirty-five-year-old Chinese-American were known to millions.

Sales of woks and soy sauce soared, over 300,000 copies of the book of the series were sold, Britons began serving each other Peking duck at dinner parties, and Ken Hom became (in Britain, at least) the best-known Chinese since Chairman Mao. Such is the power of television.

It couldn't have happened to a nicer guy. Like his Indian predecessor, Madhur Jaffrey, whose Indian cookery series was a television success story, Hom exudes charm, and, like Madhur Jaffrey, his sweet good nature instantly captivated the viewer. The BBC's casting was faultless.

But it wasn't easy. For the Indian series, the producers tested several potential presenters before concluding that the well-known actress was also the ideal cook. In the case of the Chinese series, the problem was more complicated, and the Beeb auditioned lots of Chinese cooks before deciding that Hom had the right combination of personality and accent – both strongly American.

The problem, bluntly, was language. Excellent though many of the cooks were, and expert as wokkers and wielders of cleavers, their English presented some of the problems familiar to clients of Chinese restaurants everywhere. The BBC producer Jenny Stevens insisted on a presenter who spoke English as though it was his native language.

English – or rather, American – *is* Ken Hom's native language. He was born in Tucson, Arizona, in 1949. His widowed mother then took him to Chicago, where, at the age of eleven, he found himself in the kitchen of his uncle's Chinese restaurant.

'My uncle,' Hom says, 'was a shrewd businessman,' and the restaurant was a good one. More importantly, the chefs sponsored by his uncle 'came from all over China: Shanghai, Peking, Canton, Sichuan and Hunan'. Thus, says Hom, 'these were some of the most educational years of my life'. It was then that he learnt the techniques of Chinese cooking; but also, and unusually, 'before I was twenty, I had been exposed to most of the regional cuisines of China'. This could not (and still does not) happen in China itself.

He says he hated the heat of the kitchen. But he was academically apt as well as culinarily clever, and he escaped to the University of California at Berkeley (where he still lives). There, during the era of the Free Speech Movement and Sixties radicalism, Hom studied art history, specialising in the mediaeval period. Like so many others at Berkeley in those days (Alice Waters, chef-owner of Chez Panisse, springs to mind), Hom's interests turned to France and food. He next fetched up in France, living with a family and learning the language and recipes of world Foodie culture. There was a hiatus while he made and studied films, before Hom returned to California and to his métier.

His modest, shuttered Berkeley bungalow conceals an extraordinarily well-equipped kitchen, in which Hom gives cooking lessons to other professional cooks – mostly Chinese, but he's also keen on an 'East meets West' mélange of ingredients and techniques. He is a genuinely brilliant, natural and intuitive cook, and the dishes that result from this combining of cuisines are unforced and appetising – such as the poached salmon with basil butter he cooked for me, with an orientally influenced mixture of fresh peas, baby courgettes with their flowers, tomato flesh, new garlic, spring onions, and fresh coriander, and a crusty dish of saffron-flavoured Basmati rice. This impromptu feast resulted from an inspiring visit to Oxford's covered market.

From Berkeley, where the BBC talent-spotters caught up with him, Hom emerges from time to time to take well-heeled groups of cookery students to Hong Kong, where they attend banquets and demonstrations arranged by him. In 1984 a group coincided with the BBC's location filming, and I was lucky enough to be in Hong Kong myself, to see Hom performing in his two different roles.

One day we slipped away from the camera crew to attend Ching Min, the Chinese day of the dead, with Hom's family, most of whom now live in Hong Kong, and his mother, who had come over from Chicago. At the Western Monastery, on the outskirts of the peninsula of Kowloon, we went to pay homage to Hom's ancestors, in a great, gaudy temple with burial chambers for ashes attached to the main building. The walls are completely enveloped in niches; they are priced according to their *feng shui*, i.e., the favourableness of their geomantic aspects.

Hom's grandparents' ashes were brought out from China in the 1980s, and installed here as expensively as he could afford at the time. His mother has an earthy humour, and when he asked her if the ashes should be moved to a more auspicious location, now that he is better off, she shrugged off the suggestion, saying 'it would be a waste of money now'.

It is traditional to take offerings for the dead at Ching Min, and our party had both a roast sucking pig and a roast goose with plum sauce, plus oranges and wine. But we took no flowers – Hom's mother thriftily insisted that 'we can't take them home, and they'll only wilt and die here'. We also burnt incense and a paper cone of paper 'money', after each family member kowtowed with it three times. Then we removed the goose and pig from the altar, and ate them ourselves.

Hom's mother had a cheerful bad word for everybody else's offerings. On seeing a roast pig so big that it had to be wheeled on a trolley, she remarked that it was bound to be tough, and 'anyway, you can see that ours is better cooked'. That night, there was a banquet for her sixtieth birthday, given by her son. It was a properly ostentatious affair for forty family members, and Mrs Hom was mightily pleased with her offspring.

In the first television programme, you could see a Peking duck banquet that was laid on by Hong Kong's Lee Gardens Hotel, whose chef has a justified reputation for this supreme dish of Chinese gastronomy. What you didn't see was me and a starving BBC camera crew, who had to show immense patience through the ten or twelve takes Jenny Stevens insisted on.

To gain a place at the banquet tale you had to be a Cantonese-speaking Foodie. If you don't speak Cantonese there is one joke you won't have got. The other diners are howling with laughter – at Hom's Cantonese. The dialect he and his mother speak is the Chinese equivalent of a particularly rural Mummerset-ish dialect, and the more linguistically urbane diners are creased with mirth every time he speaks.

You also didn't see the faces of the BBC camera crew – every one of them by now a connoisseur of Chinese food – as their chopsticks plied greedily over their rice bowls, when we who were not on camera were finally allowed to eat. Best of all was the last course – an unusual sweet soup (the Chinese are not big on puddings). How did they like it? I asked the cameraman, his assistant, the electrician and the soundman. They loved it: 'Something like tapioca in light custard,' opined Sparks. It is a pity the camera could not record their faces when they learnt that our hosts had prepared a rare Chinese delicacy to end our ten-course banquet, and that they had all just scoffed the last of the Snow Frog's Ovaries in Coconut Milk.

Christopher Driver

Christopher Driver is the personification of contradiction; in his own person a whole series of contraries is made flesh. He is the mildest-mannered man who ever made enemies, not only of dozens of restaurateurs who have been impaled on the sharp end of his pen, but of the odd fellow-journalist here and there. He is as assiduous a church-goer as he is a diner-out, and he is a Puritan who is deeply devoted to the pursuit of pleasure. He spent twelve years editing other people's words in the *Good Food Guide*, but he himself writes like an angel with a slightly poisoned pen. He is a famously fanatical anti-smoker, but he is so laid back about the world in general that it is hard to imagine him excited by anything, even by being made to dine in the company of a chain smoker. He always looks as if he ought to be wearing an anorak and sandals, with his nose buried in *The Guardian*. He actually edits the food and drink page of *The Guardian* – and he does sport the sort of beard one associates with anorak-wearers, but he is most often to be found wearing a business suit, and sometimes a positively elegant tie.

Following his retirement from the *Good Food Guide*, Driver wrote the book he was especially well-placed to do. Called *The British at Table* (Chatto & Windus), it is a history of British tastes and eating habits, and how they have changed, from 1940–1980. A scholar with a taste for the classics, he also enjoys the rough-and-tumble of polemic, and characterises his own style of verbal fighting as 'snide'.

Driver's cosy North London house has a surprisingly large, mature garden and a ground-floor room entirely given over to the making of chamber music: the two pianos seem almost as haphazardly placed as the cello and violin cases that litter the floor. The walls of this large room are lined with books about food, some of them acquired more easily because Driver inherited an antiquarian bookshop in Shaftesbury from his father.

Christopher Driver was born in 1932 in India, where his father was a medical missionary. The family returned to England in 1934, and Driver was brought up in Herefordshire and Birmingham. An only child, he was sent to board at the Dragon School in Oxford, before Rugby and Christ Church, where he read Greats, ending his career with 'a correct reflection of my interest, a 1st in Mods and a 3rd in Greats'. Impressed both by Hiroshima and by Duncan Sandys' famous hydrogen bomb Defence White Paper, Driver did alternative National Service from 1955–1957 in the Friends Ambulance Service. He worked first as a theatre orderly at Hackney Hospital and then in a Hungarian refugee camp in Austria, and then in Staffordshire, 'where I was greatly impressed by the ingenuity of Hungarians; they had no sooner arrived here than they were distilling liquor with no equipment but the camp fire extinguishers'.

'My basic ambition in life was to get on *The Guardian*, which I succeeded in doing after a two-year traineeship on the *Liverpool Daily Post*. It wasn't easy, as there was then a prejudice against graduates throughout the industry.' Nevertheless, promotion came quickly, and after four years of reporting by-elections, Driver became *The Guardian*'s Features Editor in 1964. His next career began during the economic crisis of 1967, when word went down that no freelances were to be employed, and that all copy was to be written by members of staff. 'As I'd been cooking all my life, I thought I might as well write the food and restaurant column, which I did under the pen name "Archestratus".'

Inspired by the events of 1968, Driver went freelance and wrote *The Exploding University*, which was a good subject in those heady days, though by 1971, when the book was actually published, the University revolution had become more a fizzle than the expected explosion. But something important happened to Driver then: Raymond Postgate became ill.

Postgate was the Christian Socialist founder and editor of the *Good Food Guide* (which was then a biennial publication). 'Raymond and I had the Classics in common, particularly a fondness for Greek and Latin verse; he too had been a pacifist – though in his case in the First World War – whereas my position was that of a premature CND member. Also, I am a Christian liberal, and have never been any kind of a socialist – the tradition of Old Dissent into which I was born is much too firmly liberal to produce socialists.

'When Postgate got ill the Consumers' Association, the publishers of the *Good Food Guide*, came to me because I knew about food – and because they knew I could put out a book in a hurry. Raymond – and I – saw absolutely no conflict between a concern for the quality of food and our respective political positions. After all, as Raymond always pointed out, the Rochdale Pioneers were damned careful about the selection of butter and cheese for the first co-operative shops.

'The CA itself had a Leftish political flavour attached to it – it was always regarded as an austere, number-crunching organisation. *Which?* once did a survey of cheese, which made no mention at all of the question of taste. There were never more than a minority in the CA who knew or cared what the *GFG* was about.

'There is an internal tension in the *Guide*, compiled as it is from readers' reports, which may in the end pull it apart. The idea of a *Guide* where the selection of restaurants is not homogeneous, but consists of recommendations of places in as many *genres* and on as many price levels as possible, doesn't make sense to much of the CA management. And they're right. Jolly few people are capable of eating both in the Diwana Bhel Poori House and at the Gavroche, with equal pleasure, and simply for the food.

'Because of the way the class system works in this country restaurants here are the property of a milieu of professional people who eat out regularly. The *GFG* – and my new book – are meshed into this class, and would be inconceivable without it.

'Egon Ronay's guides, for example, are nothing to do with this class, but are written *by* refugees from the catering trade *for* commercial travellers. Whatever the situation may be in France, these are not the sort of people who eat out here, or who are prepared to spend their own money on their meals.'

As for the other chief rival, Michelin: 'I don't think it can ever make a useful statement about eating out in this country, because everything depends on nuances that can only be expressed in words, and not by a uniform set of symbols.' In a country where the ethnic diversity of various immigrant communities, especially the Indians and the Chinese, is responsible for so much of the vigour of the restaurant industry, Driver thinks, the Michelin system, which is designed for uniformity, is hopeless. With respect to the new French challenger, 'I envy the freedom of the *Gault-Millau Guide* to be libellous in English – if I'd written some of the entries in their 1982 *London Guide*, which are both hilarious and true, I'd have been fired. In my entire twelve years on the *GFG*, we were only twice forced to apologise, and we were never sued.'

Christopher Driver feels that the political stance of the *GFG* in its Postgate period ensured that it 'never quite caught on with *Daily Telegraph* readers in Camberley and Cowes. The very refusal of the British to complain vigorously in restaurants which rob them of the quality of cooking they are entitled to expect for the price they pay does not derive only from native reserve (where is that reserve on sporting occasions?) but from bourgeois fear of being branded as hagglers by open-handed aristocrats. Restaurant criticism in the London glossies, in the style originally set by Quentin Crewe, is often instructive in this connection: it is not good form to question value for money too closely.'

Admitting that he has a 'sharp-to-snide way of expressing' himself, Driver has never been too surprised when he is attacked in his turn. 'Probably the most vicious personal attacks against me were made by Quentin Crewe and Bernard Levin. Crewe disliked the *Guide*'s mixture of moral sense and indulgence in lovely, costly meals. Both suspected me – perhaps rightly – of trying to have things both ways, of combining self-righteousness with snideness in my use of language. I suspected them of self-conscious aristocratic pretension and indifference to the lower orders. There was a whiff of the old distaste for trade clinging pretty closely to their words.'

Does this sound puritanical? 'I am always delighted to be accused of Puritanism. The idea of the Puritans as kill-joys is one that more properly belongs to the American Pilgrim Fathers,' says the scholarly Driver. 'Our Puritans here danced and ate well, they loved pleasure and they founded the Royal Society. It's all in Pepys' diaries.' And I wonder whether Christopher Driver might not have found the subject of his next book – an anthropological look at British eating habits, starting, of course, with those pleasure-loving Puritans.

Médecin Man

There are gastronome politicians everywhere – I know at least three in the House of Commons – but Jacques Médecin, the mayor of Nice, is probably the only important politician now holding office who has written a good cookery book.

In 1982 Médecin was in hot dispute with Graham Greene. There were those who thought that Nice's mayor was the real target of the novelist's book, *J'Accuse*, an exposé of alleged corruption in Nice, all copies of which in France have been seized following the success of a libel action against Greene. When he comments on Greene, even Médecin's abuse is couched in culinary metaphor: he accused Greene of 'spitting in the soup to get a bit of publicity for his latest novel'.

Jacques Médecin is almost the hereditary mayor of Nice. He was born as his father began his own first term as Nice's mayor, and there has been a Médecin ruling Nice for all his 53 years. His young second wife is an American heiress whose family owned Max Factor, and Médecin makes much of the American connection, speaking his ardent praise of President Reagan in faultless American English. Pugnaciously right-wing, he would like to think that Greene's outburst can be blamed on misinformation given the novelist by left-wingers.

His classic cookery book, *Cuisine Niçoise*, I have owned and used for years; it was at last published in 1983 in a translation (Penguin) by Peter Graham, who also wrote an interesting introduction.

Subtitled 'Recipes from a Mediterranean Kitchen', the book comes with a revealing – and sentimental – preface by the author, in which he gives his reasons for writing the book. The first is: 'because it seems to me that I belong to the last generation which has had traditional recipes handed down to it'. Love of Nice is another reason, as is the scarcity of genuine Niçois cooking, which 'simply cannot be found except in Niçois homes and a handful of restaurants in Nice'. 'All over the world,' Médecin complains, 'I have had the unpleasant experience of being served up leftovers masquerading as *salade Niçoise*.'

The recipes have come in part from Médecin's family collection: 'In the 1880s, my grandmother took down a multitude of centuries-old recipes dictated to her by an aged peasant woman, Tanta Mietta, who lived on the beautifull hill of Gairaut, behind Nice.' Surprisingly for such a self-consciously macho right-winger, Médecin says, 'In Nice and in my family, both men and women do the cooking, passing on their skills from father to daughter and from mother to son.'

Nice has only been part of France since 1860, and this is reflected in the independence of its cuisine from that of the rest of France. Naturally it has affinities with the cooking of Italy, especially of Genoa and Naples – and, of course, there are a lot of Provençal influences. But Nice's dishes also include some brought by seafarers, such as stockfish, wind-dried cod which originated in Scandinavia. (As Peter Graham points out in his introduction, cod is not a Mediterranean fish.) And the fact that Nice has been a winter resort for the English since the eighteenth century probably explains why Christmas Pudding is thought of as an indigenous dish by the Niçois.

In most other respects the Niçois diet is typically Mediterranean. Fish is more popular and plentiful than meat, olive oil is used in preference to butter, and many foods, such as olives and anchovies, are consumed pickled or salted. But Nice also has its special ingredients: globe artichokes, several varieties of courgettes – including the spherical *ronde de Nice* – mesclun salad, which is a mixture that includes red and white chicory, rocket, dandelion and chervil, and, above all, Swiss chard or *blette, bléa* in the Niçois dialect. 'The Niçois eat so much Swiss chard,' says Peter Graham, 'that they sometimes crudely refer to themselves as *caga-bléa* [*caga* means 'shit'].'

What about that genuine *salade Niçoise*? Médecin lists the canonical ingredients as tomatoes, hard-boiled eggs, anchovy fillets or tunny fish, cucumber, spring onions, small beans or tiny globe artichokes ('depending on the time of year, either one or the other, or neither, but not both'), garlic, black olives, olive oil and basil leaves. More important, of course, are the taboos: 'Never, I beg you, include boiled potato or any other boiled vegetable.'

Mars wars

Two of the most disgusting recipes I have ever read are Quentin Crisp's 'Tibetan Workhouse Soup', which is made by boiling water in a food-encrusted saucepan that has never been cleaned, and 'Soupe Mauvaise Femme', contributed by someone using the poison-pen name 'Lucrezia', and which uses dried onions, tinned carrots and a large packet of Smash.

These are contained in the funniest cookery book of 1980 – perhaps of all time – *Darling, You Shouldn't Have Gone to So Much Trouble* (Cape). Its black humour, its penchant for bizarre ingredients and macabre combinations, its mixed feelings of love and hate for food itself and its ironic distance from its subject all recall the other work of its compilers, Caroline Blackwood and Anna Haycraft.

Lady Caroline Blackwood is the author of four disturbingly exciting novels. *Great Granny Webster* had an immense critical success. Anna Haycraft is the author, as Alice Thomas Ellis, of *The Sin Eater* and *The Birds of the Air*. They are all published by Duckworth, and people who keep up with fiction will know in a flash how to characterise these novels.

Anna Haycraft *runs* the Duckworth fiction list. The cookery book *Darling, You Shouldn't Have Gone to So Much Trouble* was originally to be published by Duckworth, which is run by Anna Haycraft's husband, Colin. But, Caroline Blackwood suggests, Duckworth backed out because Colin Haycraft didn't like the feminist political slant of the book. While it may seem odd that a cookery book should be funny, and odder still that it should have political implications, Caroline Blackwood takes it all fairly seriously. When Duckworth wouldn't publish the cookery book, she took her novels as well to Cape. And Anna Haycraft half shares Caroline Blackwood's feelings. 'Food is a profound subject anyway,' she told me in a voice that had only a touch of self-mockery in it, 'the book is a political *gesture* – a work of absolute *philosophy*.'

What it boils down to is that both women, like the women they imagine will read and use their book, are 'in a state of mutiny. They recognise cookery to be an art, but they find it an art which becomes increasingly personally unfulfilling.' Like most modern women, especially those with both children and careers, though they want the food they serve to be good and to be praised, they have neither time nor servants to make it so.

It is not far-fetched to see them as writing about themselves when they say that 'They seem rather to enjoy praise which they can receive tongue-in-cheek, feeling that they deserve applause not because they have masochistically slogged and slaved, but because they have cleverly cheated.'

For Caroline Blackwood, who 'grew up as a cook' using Elizabeth David's books, the kind of labour-intensive cookery she advocates in this book is a reaction, a backlash to the Elizabeth David school of *soigné* cooking: 'I can't spend the whole day peeling spuds. And anyway, it's so unrewarding cooking for children.' She sees herself not as the vanguard, but as the last kick of Women's Lib. 'With the exception of Germaine Greer (who still believes in making your own pasta), Women's Libbers are only angry now about cooking. All the other issues of domestic work have been shelved. You can leave making beds for a day or two, but not the cooking. It's too basic.'

Was she ever a self-consciously good cook? 'Ask Lucien Freud,' Caroline Blackwood responded. The painter was her first husband. He contributes a joke recipe to the book, a very good one: having dealt very carefully with 'fresh tomatoes, country butter, and clotted cream' and simmered them slowly for hours, he tasted it and 'realised he had re-invented Heinz Tomato Soup'. Caroline Blackwood's last husband, the late Robert Lowell, 'was one of those American men who don't know how to work a kettle'. She no longer gives dinner parties, 'because I *have* to cook, every day' for her three children. Her favourite meal is perfectly cooked fish – 'in a restaurant such as Le Suquet or La Croisette'.

Anna Haycraft, despite her five children, still gives parties, 'luncheon mostly, though they last from one to seven o'clock'. She has been known to give lunch to 500 – in aid of Duckworth, of course – and for the launching of Michael Dummet's two books on the tarot pack, she gave a dinner for 250. Her recipe for successful party-giving is revealed in the book. Never apologise for any dish: 'Modesty is unbecoming in a cook and only stimulates the critical faculties of guests, the very faculties which should ideally be deadened by the plying of cocktails and good wine.'

The book proper then begins with a section of palate- and faculty-numbing cocktails, of which 'Colin's Killer' – '1 bottle of brandy to 6 bottles of sparkling white wine' – is the Haycrafts' self-explanatory favourite.

In all the recipes the emphasis is on speed – and deception: 'We have looked for recipes that are unusual and glamorous and taste and look as if they have taken hours.' Thus Caroline Blackwood suggested I quote the dessert given her by Angel Bacon, formerly of *Harper's & Queen* magazine: 'Melt Mars bars in bowl over hot water, add a dash of kirsch and pour over dairy ice cream. The effect is as of expensive fondue on freshly whipped cream!' (Will a Mars bar really melt in a bain-Marie, or is this a culinary disappearing hitch-hiker? I've read the recipe several times, but never actually encountered the dish.)

The book abounds with Household Hints: dry salad in a pillow-case in the spin-dryer – 'one very brief whirl' – and Barbara Cartland's advice on aphrodisiac foods. And there is a warning not to 'cook in front of an audience. Should things go amiss, for example – if the butter drops on the floor', you 'can pick it up and use it' so long as you are 'unobserved'. If the cook 'is cheating outrageously the cheating should take place before the arrival of her guests, i.e. the cans should be opened and hidden and their contents should be in a baking dish or saucepan, so that they retain prestige and mystery'.

The two women who have compiled this very funny, but, it has to be admitted, sometimes revolting selection of recipes, are both serious writers dedicated and devoted to their principal craft. And, at the bottom, they remain serious about the need for a book such as this. Caroline Blackwood said to me, 'A chef who's been cooking all day is not expected to go home in the evening and write a poem or three thousand words on the Constitution.'

Thus they rather invited a backlash. It came from an unexpected quarter – from Anita Brookner, Reader in Art History at the Courtauld Institute. Professor Brookner is generally better known for her work on Jacques-Louis David and for her Booker Prize-winning novel *Hotel du Lac* than for her soufflés.

The most notable aspect of the professor's sledgehammer attack on this nutcracker-worthy book is that it appeared in the staid, respectable pages of *The Times Literary Supplement*.

Professor Brookner not only loathed the book, she was *outraged* by it. For her own dinner parties, she rises 'at first light to see what the merchants of Fulham Road have to offer'. And she suggests a menu of fillet of beef, green bean and tomato salad, melon with port, rich chocolate cake and 'a mousse of egg yolks, orange juice, white wine and sugar . . . made the previous evening while you are listening to "The Archers", and then left to chill for twenty-four hours.'

Stung into replying from *her* address in SW10, Caroline Blackwood joined the literary-culinary ding-dong in the letters column of the *TLS*: 'I, too, live near the Fulham Road. Miss Brookner should know that anyone who is idiotic enough to "rise at first light" in order to go shopping in that area will find that almost nothing but the casualty ward of St Stephen's Hospital is open.'

Defending her own recipes ('simple but a little more interesting'), Caroline Blackwood finds Prof. Brookner's dinner party suggestions 'a little kinky'. And in a magisterial last paragraph, she rebukes the art historian: 'Finally she advises us how to make a mousse of egg yolks, orange juice, white wine and sugar. As a cook she has betrayed herself. The "mousse" she proposes is not a "mousse". It is mere custard.'

Humbled but not defeated, Professor Brookner replied in the *TLS* of 5 December: 'Living so near to the Fulham Road, Lady Caroline Blackwood must surely be aware that the excellent butcher next to St Stephen's Hospital is open for business at 7.30 a.m.' And, claims the writer, there is a good greengrocer who is open even earlier.

Reserving to herself the last word, Professor Brookner concludes, 'I am sorry about my mousse or custard. I think it tastes rather nice, whatever it is.'

This might have been the end of the matter. But readers will recall that I (like Professor Brookner) singled out for disapproval among the Blackwood–Haycraft recipes 'Soupe Mauvaise Femme', 'contributed by someone with the poison-pen name "Lucrezia" and which uses dried onions, tinned carrots and a large packet of Smash'.

In the same issue of the *TLS* that contains the Brookner defence, the Marketing and Sales Director of Cadbury Typhoo, the manufacturer of Smash, waxes wrathful. Writes Mr M. R. J. Newitt, 'I should like to point out that Cadbury's Smash is made from high-grade, fresh potatoes with the addition of milk solids and salt. Any vitamin C lost during the processing is replaced so that Smash has a consistently high level of this important vitamin. It is, therefore, a nourishing and convenient product used and appreciated by millions.'

Really, Mr Newitt! But now that the Smash has hit the fan, let's tell the whole truth. Mashed potato, whether real or instant, is an extremely poor dish nutritionally. Millions of people may be eating Smash – and other yucky things too – but that's no reason for sensible people to advocate that other people eat more of it.

Alain Senderens

Alain Senderens is one of only two *chef patrons* in Paris who enjoy the ultimate rating of four Gault-Millau toques and three Michelin stars. (The other is Joël Robuchon of Jamin.) For some reason it has always been more difficult for a chef-owner to achieve these distinctions in Paris than in the Provinces. Senderens, who was born in southwest France in 1939, has had his third Michelin star since 1978, so it is curious that he is not as well known in Britain as his provincial peers: Bocuse, Chapel, Troigros, Vergé and Guérard. He is much better known in America, where he has established and continues to supervise a New York restaurant, the Maurice at the Meridien Hotel. Very likely the reason is that his book of recipes, *La Cuisine Réussie* (or 'successful cooking'), has been published in the States (under the silly title *The Three-Star Recipes of Alain Senderens*), but is only now available in Britain.

This is a shame, as many of the recipes can be a real inspiration to the accomplished home cook, particularly the salads for which Senderens is celebrated. Moreover, Senderens himself has recently begun to explore new areas of cuisine, and to those who know what he's up to now, the recipes in the book seem slightly dated.

Senderens' cooking has already passed through several evolutions. After training at Lourdes, he came to Paris, aged twenty-one, and had the most orthodox cooking job in all France: he was *chef rôtisseur* at the Tour d'Argent, responsible for all the roasts served in that most old-fashioned of restaurants, including God alone knows how many roast ducks.

By good fortune his next move was to Lucas Carton, where he worked under the great Soustelle. His next two posts were at Paris hotels. Then in 1968, he opened the first L'Archestrate (named after the fourth century BC Greek gastronome – Senderens has always been hooked on antique cookery books) on the Rue de l'Exposition. Ten years later he had his four toques and third star, and in 1977 he moved to the hôtel particulier at 84 Rue de Varenne in the 7e, where he remained until May 1985.

Senderens then returned in glory to Lucas Carton, now as the owner of this ninety-seat *belle époque* establishment. The new restaurant accommodates nearly twice as many diners as L'Archestrate, and the decor is very different indeed. The orientally influenced lacquer of the previous restaurant is reflected only in the lacquer *cache-pots* of Lucas Carton. The sumptuous wood carvings have been left, but the famous rich red plush of Lucas Carton's banquettes is now a quiet beige. The single, huge flower arrangement on the ground floor provides the sole colourful focal point for the dining-room. Upstairs there are two more boldly decorated private dining-rooms and two 'club rooms' – places where friends of Monsieur Senderens can, presumably, always be certain of getting a table.

But the food's the thing. If you have been prudent enough to book several weeks in advance, and to reconfirm your reservation on the morning of the day you mean to dine, for about £100 for two people, you will have one of the gastronomic experiences of a lifetime. Senderens made his name as one of the most daring exponents of *nouvelle cuisine*: he successfully yoked together bizarre ingredients in combinations that would be sick-making in lesser cooks' hands. His most famous culinary miscegenation was lobster and vanilla (which, though it still features on the menu of Lucas Carton, was irritatingly not available either of the nights I dined there). Senderens says of this dish that it is only shocking because we associate vanilla exclusively with sweet foods and have not experimented with savoury foods flavoured with it.

Senderens' other strange dishes are mainly the results of his antiquarian researches. From the ancient Roman cookery book of Apicius, he took a recipe for pork, flavoured violently with raisins, honey, caraway, dill seed, mint, peppercorns, red wine and dried apricots. He has refined it and in the restaurant serves *canard Apicius*: duck encrusted with caraway and pepper, and two purées, one of dates, coriander, ginger and mint, the other a gasp-making combination of quince with apple and a great deal of saffron. Eventhia Senderens, a charming and handsome woman who acts as Lucas Carton's hostess and as her husband's domestic test cook, told me that 75 per cent of her clients choose duck Apicius, which is served with a glass of sweet red Banyuls, as it does no favours to more conventional wines.

For me, the homage to the ancient Latin was a mere curiosity which got in the way of the evening's serious eating. Starting with Middle Eastern and orientally inspired *amuse-gueules* of feta cheese in a miniature triangle of filo pastry, a tartlet of smoked crab, and a tiny rice pastry spring roll, we proceeded to a magical dish of langoustine barely cooked in a papillote of leek segments which was wondrously Eastern. Its garnish was a rice-flour yellow ravioli like a giant *jiao-tse* filled with oyster mushrooms and *girolles*.

We exulted, too, in the warm thickly sliced home-smoked salmon, meltingly uncooked inside, served on a puddle of *beurre blanc* with a *julienne* of cucumber and lime zest, scented with dill, and with a salty kick given by its dollops of black and red caviar. This was the only sauced dish we were given. At Lucas Carton Senderens has almost succeeded in banishing sauces altogether from the menu. The result is a huge gain in the diner's appetite. The last time I was there, everyone in my party of five was able to cope with the cheese course, and still eat dessert.

The grilled *foie gras* that came next had a crispy salted surface, and tasted, most impressively, only of itself. It sat upon a bed of wild sautéed mushrooms, seasoned only with a dusting of finely minced shallot and parsley. The only other garnish was dryly sautéed artichoke bottom. (On a later occasion, this course became *foie gras* steamed in a savoy cabbage leaf, served sauceless with little piles of coarse salt and cracked pepper.)

Before the *canard Apicius* made a nonsense of our inexpensive and very good bottle of Château Potensac 1980, we had veal sweetbreads in a carrot cream. Now this was exactly what it said it was: the sweetbreads roasted in the oven, creamy and pink inside, on a bed of blanched, still chewy spinach, surrounded by a ring of razor-thin carrot slices, in a pool, not of sauce, but of puréed carrot thinned to sauce consistency with stock.

Puddings included a chocolate sorbet served with orange segments and a tart of orange peel. Even more of a spectacle was the *gâteau de riz*: rice pudding sitting in *crème anglaise*, garnished with redcurrants, mint leaves and four tiny tarts of *pâté sucrée* filled with apple, pineapple, raspberry and passion fruit. The whole plate was surmounted by a fresh apricot, and there was an overriding flavour of vanilla.

Though he is (unfairly) identified as one who has stressed the exaggerated side of *nouvelle cuisine*, Alain Senderens is, in fact, one of the clearest *thinkers* in today's kitchens. All chefs love to 'philosophise', but Senderens is not woolly. In an interview with the Gault-Millau magazine in May 1984, Senderens said of the new, health-orientated cuisine he is developing (as is Anton Mosimann here): 'Fifty years ago, this would not have been even thinkable, for the pleasure of eating was still closely associated with the notion of the destruction of the body. You want to live well? It's your right, but at your own risk and at your peril. The *nouvelle cuisine* marked a turning-point. People suddenly understood that they could celebrate without ruining their health.'

His new recipes resemble Michel Guérard's *Cuisine Minceur* in their use of artificial sweeteners and paraffin oil, along with a small allowance of natural oils and butter and cream. They both differ in these respects from Mosimann's *cuisine naturelle*. But for Senderens, as for Mosimann, the goal of their new-style cooking is not slimming, but general good health.

Says Senderens: 'When, four years ago, I went to Japan, though I didn't much like Japanese cooking, I did find that it was the cleverest cuisine in the world, for it was capable of producing dishes, which, though they weren't sauced, had plenty of taste. That was what gave me the ideas, and

I must tell you that today, at Lucas Carton, it is the dishes without sauce that are the most popular.

'I am,' he says, 'obsessed by the relationship between cooking and health. When one goes to the opera, one does not expect to return having gone deaf; one does not expect to go blind as a result of going to the theatre. Why, then, must one do oneself a damage by going out to eat? For people who think this way there is, on the one hand, the *cuisine* for pleasure – but full of menace – and on the other, the diet – for the redemption of the body. This separation is odious, and we must find the means of reconciling pleasure and health. I dream of a cuisine that no longer does anyone harm.'

Foodiegate: Ritz and Escoffier at the Savoy

César Ritz was the best-known inn-keeper in history. He has given his name to hotels and to crackers; it figures in the titles of books and in the lyrics of popular songs, and, as 'Ritzy', can even be used as an adjective. For over twenty years he was associated with a chef, Auguste Escoffier, whose name is scarcely less celebrated than his own.

Together they presided over the first and greatest of the Edwardian dream hotels, the Savoy, in London. Their most important guest was the Prince of Wales himself. The ageing playboy actually carried on his affair with Lillie Langtry ('Jersey Lillie') under the roof of the Savoy; the smooth conduct and relative secrecy of the liaison owed much to the discretion of Ritz, the hotel's general manager.

Escoffier, meanwhile, made his name in the kitchen and restaurant, with his flamboyant culinary inventions such as peach Melba and *bombe* Nero. He is a hero to today's chefs, and he deserves to be. He preached the maxim of today's modern cooking, *faites simple*, which, despite Melba and Nero, he actually put into practice. He rediscovered the *fumets* and reductions of ancient French cookery, upon which the sauces of today's *nouvelle cuisine* are based. But above all, he improved working conditions and shaped the modern image of the chef. He replaced the standard, but dirty and dangerous coal ranges with gas ones, and he insisted that his chefs be proud of their white uniforms, seeing that they were always clean and worn only in the kitchen. He was the originator of Foodiebiz (though in 1917 he sold the factory that manufactured his famous Escoffier sauces, for a miserable pittance).

The directors of the Savoy were determined to have the most luxurious and modern hotel and the best restaurant in the world. And they were prepared to pay for them. In 1895 the joint salaries of Ritz and Escoffier came to £11,595 – about £100,000 in today's money. But suddenly, in 1898, after only nine years of the most successful hotel partnership in history, they were fired by the directors of the Savoy. Why?

The answer is that the pair was involved in the kind of kitchen larceny that is as old as the profession of chef (and which still goes on today). When the matter was finally settled in 1900, Ritz and his maître d'hôtel, Louis Echenard, though they denied 'that they have ever been guilty of appropriating or applying to their own use the monies of the Savoy Hotel Company, or taking monies by way of presents or commissions from the tradesmen of the Hotel', did pay the sum of £4,173, plus another £6,377 from Ritz, to make up for 'the astounding disappearance of over £3,400 of wine and spirits in the first six months of 1897' as well as 'the wine and spirits consumed in the same period by the Managers, staff and employees amounting to £3,000'.

They also admitted, in their 29 January 1900 confession, that they had known about, and not prevented, Escoffier from doing precisely what they denied having done themselves, accepting gifts and kickbacks ('commission') from the Savoy's suppliers amounting to over £16,000. Half this amount (£8,087) was actually recovered from the tradespeople, and Escoffier consented to a verdict against him for the other half, but being 'without means and unable to pay', he offered £500 in cash, which was accepted.

For eighty-five years the scandal lay undiscovered, sleeping at the Savoy. But Sir Hugh Wontner, until recently Chairman of the Savoy, gave me a statement: 'Regrettably,' said Sir Hugh, 'this story about Ritz and Escoffier is true. It was not the wish of the Savoy directors at the time to make public the facts, nor to disgrace either Ritz or Escoffier . . . They have never since disclosed anything about the scandal, but so many years have passed since it occurred that there is no reason to maintain the silence.'

I first learned about the matter two years ago, when a pile of papers appeared on my desk at *The Observer* in London. There were copies of transcripts of the confessions referred to above, plus some supporting affidavits. They were accompanied by an anonymous note saying that the writer thought these papers concerning the Savoy would interest me. That was the first anyone had ever heard of the Foodiegate scandal – I remain indebted to, but ignorant of, the identity of my benefactor, and call him or her Deep Palate.

I used the papers in the brief biographies of Ritz and Escoffier that appeared in my book (with Ann Barr) *The Official Foodie Handbook*. Few people noticed the charges made there against Ritz and Escoffier. One exception was Pierre Escoffier, the seventy-six-year-old retired oil industry executive, who is the great chef's grandson, and patron of the Foundation in the south of France dedicated to Escoffier's memory. Mr Escoffier was amiably cross with me for believing that Deep Palate's documents were genuine, and he remained unconvinced even after I let him read them.

I therefore gave a set of copies to the Savoy Hotel and asked them if they could confirm their accuracy. I was not surprised that, at first, no one at the Savoy knew anything at all about the papers, or about the allegations against Ritz and Escoffier. If the existence of either had been known generally, it was not likely that they could have remained secret for eighty-five years, and undiscovered by the writers of at least four books – histories of the Savoy by Stanley Jackson and Sir Compton Mackenzie, a novel based on the Savoy, *Imperial Palace* by Arnold Bennett, and the biography of Ritz by his widow, Marie.

When Sir Hugh Wontner, a sociable man who was once Lord Mayor of London, received me in the Savoy boardroom a week after receipt of my copies, he immediately confirmed the genuineness of Deep Palate's documents. He had been aware of rumours of the reason behind the sackings of Ritz and Escoffier: he couldn't say who had told him, and thought it was the sort of thing one learned 'from the walls' if one was around the Savoy for long enough. He had read 'Foodies', and wondered how I had come by such a lot of detail about the charges against the two men. But until I gave him a set of Deep Palate's papers to the Savoy, he had never looked into the secret file in the Savoy's professionally run archives. When he did, in the week of the 13th of May, he found that it contained the signed confessions of Ritz, Echenard and Escoffier, as well as the minutes of the many board meetings held over the years 1898–1900, at which these matters were discussed.

The man who had had the grand vision for building the Savoy was Richard D'Oyly Carte, the impresario of the Gilbert and Sullivan operas, which were performed in the Savoy Theatre adjoining the hotel. It was he who had the dream of a grand hotel on the sight of the mediaeval Savoy Palace, with every comfort: lifts, a high ratio of bathrooms to guests, electricity replacing gas, a kitchen close to the restaurant on the same floor, with all services provided in the cost of the room, and available all night. He opened his hotel in August 1889. But it was not a success until Ritz took over as manager in December, following a successful breach-of-contract suit by Ritz's predecessor, a Mr Hardwicke. D'Oyly Carte had met Ritz at Cannes, when the latter was thirty-eight. He had a difficult time persuading the Swiss hotelier to come to London; when Ritz finally agreed, he brought his forty-two-year-old chef, Escoffier, with him.

Ritz had an unusual contract. It allowed him to freelance, as it were, for six months a year. By 1896 he had set up the Ritz Hotel Syndicate Ltd, which, with backing from his satisfied former clients, was developing Ritz hotels all over the world. He also had Claridge's in his management portfolio, and had got far enough in setting up his deal that, when fired in 1898, he and Escoffier went directly to his new hotel, the Carlton (on the present-day site of New Zealand House in the Haymarket, London).

Ritz abused his position at the Savoy to solicit investors for his other ventures. The directors complained bitterly: 'They forgot they were servants and assumed the attitude of masters and proprietors. The Savoy, with its luxurious suites for the reception and entertainment of subscribers to schemes, formed an ideal machinery for company promoting . . . whilst the adjoining restaurant, full of rich and good-natured clients won over by the suave attentions which Messrs Ritz and Echenard from their positions could give them, formed a happy hunting ground for subscribers which left nothing to be desired.' By my count, Ritz and Echenard confessed to fifteen charges of wrongdoing.

Escoffier's much shorter confession is dated the same day – 3 January 1900 – as Ritz's, and admits to actual criminal acts, including fraud.

The directors of the Savoy had begun to get suspicious following the record year of 1895, for though overall receipts were increasing, including those from the kitchen, kitchen profits were declining, and in 1897, the kitchen actually showed a loss. This led to investigations, and, on 28 February 1898, after taking advice from the Rt Hon. Edward Carson, the most eminent lawyer of the day, the auditors informed the directors of the Savoy that they had a fiduciary duty to the shareholders 'to forthwith dismiss' Ritz and Escoffier, plus Echenard and another member of their staff called Darbilly.

With the arrogance born of success and the experience of Ritz's predecessor, they filed a counterclaim for wrongful dismissal. (In her book, Marie Ritz, who never knew the truth about her husband, said they had been sacked because of the malicious plotting of a housekeeper whom Ritz had displaced. Some people have identified the nameless housekeeper with Richard D'Oyly Carte's second wife Helen, who certainly had run the Savoy's business affairs before Ritz came, and who even lost her job as the hotel's interior decorator – to Mme Ritz.)

A 'Committee of Investigation' was set up by the Savoy and very heavy guns were trained upon the malefactors. D'Oyly Carte's son and successor, Rupert, was present when the investigations were discussed, and so, amusingly, was Sir Arthur Sullivan, the composer of the Savoy operas. It was in the light of evidence turned up by the committee that Escoffier and Ritz were obliged to confess.

Real dirt had been uncovered. Among Deep Palate's papers were sworn statements by Henry Mann and Robert Price, who were, respectively, shop assistant and manager of Hudson Brothers, grocers, on the Strand – just a few steps away from the Savoy Hotel. Mann said: 'During the whole of the time I was at the Strand branch, by the instructions of Mr Robert Price, the eggs supplied to the Savoy Hotel were always delivered short, for instance if seven hundred eggs were ordered, about four hundred and fifty to five hundred would be delivered.'

His evidence went on: 'I know from talk I heard in the shop that everything was delivered short to the Savoy Hotel. For instance, until Mr Escoffier left the Hotel, the hams were delivered under weight. I weighed them sometimes and weighed short . . . Mr Escoffier always had a regular 5 per cent commission from Messrs Hudson Brothers. Besides the 5 per cent paid to Mr Escoffier which was common knowledge in the shop, large presents consisting of packages of goods were sent every week addressed to Mr Boots, Southsea.'

The shop manager, Robert Price, testified that his predecessor had taken him to the various hotels with which Hudson did business, and told him who got kickbacks: 'When we got to the Savoy Hotel he introduced me to Escoffier. He said "he has Commission" or "he is a Commission man". I cannot remember the exact words.'

It is difficult to imagine the great Escoffier, who was certainly drawing a salary in his heyday equivalent to £40,000, going in person to collect his £30 or £40 backhanders. But this is just what happened, testified Robert Price: 'Mr Escoffier did not actually ask for the Commission but he came and hung about and talked in a way that I knew exactly what he had come for.' Faced with this evidence, Ritz, Echenard and Escoffier collapsed, withdrew their counterclaim, paid back some of the money and signed their confessions.

But it was precious little satisfaction for the Savoy. The Prince of Wales had followed Ritz, and taken his custom to the Carlton. At a blow, the Savoy had lost manager, chef and royal patron, while the guilty parties appeared to flourish in their new enterprise. The gossip of the day, and the verdict of history – until now – was that the directors of the Savoy were somehow in the wrong.

Escoffier died, leaving almost nothing, in Monte Carlo in 1935. He had used up his capital and the whole of his small income educating and looking after his own three children, his sister-in-law's two, and four grandchildren. Obviously, he was not good with money. But why did he need his 'commission'? What did he do with his enormous salary? Was he a gambler, perhaps?

Ritz was a manic-depressive. He fell ill in 1901 while preparing the Carlton to become the social headquarters for the coronation of Edward VII. He was to have been in charge of all the private events associated with the occasion, but it was postponed for a year, and then took place without him. He died, mad, in 1918 in a Swiss clinic.

In their confession, Ritz and Echenard had agreed that the directors might make what use they wished of it. Yet the Savoy kept its peace all these years. Indeed, the last D'Oyly Carte, Dame Bridget, the daughter of Rupert and granddaughter of Richard, only died on the 2nd of May, 1985. She took the secret to the grave with her.

Why the cover-up? I think the answer is simple. The Prince of Wales *had* to follow Ritz to the Carlton. He had used the Savoy as a place of assignation, and Ritz had played Pandar to him. The minutes of the directors' meetings are full of references to Ritz's 'tact' – i.e., the fact that, though placed to do so, he refrained from blackmailing the future king.

The gentlemen of the Savoy did not whinge when the Prince of Wales deserted them for the Carlton in 1898. They were certainly not, two years later, going to gloat over their victory or make public a scandal that touched so closely upon the soon-to-be-king, and which would certainly have upset the eighty-year-old queen. So they swallowed hard and kept their mouths shut. They'd do the same today.

Eating words

A new genre of fiction has sprung up recently – the novel with recipes. From America come reports of titles such as *The Baked Bean Murders*, a thriller with recipes. At least three such books have been published here.

The treatment of food (and drink) in imaginative literature divides into two distinct schools, recipe literature and menu literature. There are hundreds of examples of the latter, but the only instance of the former I can think of is *Macbeth*. 'Eye of the newt, and toe of frog, Wool of bat, and tongue of dog, . . . Nose of Turk, and Tartar's lips, Finger of birth-strangled babe / Ditch-deliver'd by a drab, Make the gruel thick and slab' may be a little imprecise as to quantities, but it's quite clear about the ingredients and the order in which they are to be added to the cauldron; the method of cooking is explicitly given. (P. G. Wodehouse wrote that Macbeth listened to these incantations and 'instantly recognising the recipe' greeted the speakers with the words, 'How now thou secret, black midnight Haggis'.)

One precursor of the current recipe fiction vogue was Elisabeth Ayrton's *The Cook's Tale*, in which the description of the chef's activities makes it clear, Katharine Whitehorn tells me, 'precisely how each delicious dish (and each *femme de chambre*, actually) is made'.

Menu literature is much more common. The first I can think of is the barbecue Achilles gave for Odysseus outside the walls of Ilium, when Patroclus roasted the backs of a sheep and a fat goat, as well as the chine of a wild boar. Aeschylus recorded a less appetising supper when Atreus dished up all but one of the children of his brother, Thyestes, and served them to their father in a concealing dish.

The best-known menu of antiquity was served at Trimalchio's feast and included: a hare done up with wings to look like Pegasus, a wild sow whose belly was stuffed with live thrushes, and roast pork got up variously to look like fish, songbirds and a goose. (We must remember, though, that this was noov food – Petronius was satirising the excesses of the *nouvelle cuisine* of Imperial Rome, and the menu should not be taken too literally.)

Other authors did not do so well by their gastronomically inclined readers. I have always been disappointed that we were not told the bill of fare for Belshazzar's feast. The Gospels are also uncharacteristically reticent about the menu for the Last Supper; only a few pages earlier,

Matthew (xxiii, 23) has castigated the lawyers, Pharisees and hypocrites with gastronomic precision for paying 'tithes of mint and dill and cumin'.

In English literature menus abound. A professorial friend reminded me of Chaucer's Clerk of Oxenford, who was 'Epicurus owene sone'. You might recall that 'it snewed in his hous of mete and drynke'. My informant thought there might be a full menu in *Troilus and Cressida*, but neither of us can find it.

We can forgive Keats for his gastronomic nasty, 'Isabella, or the Pot of Basil', because he also wrote the gastro-porn sequence in 'The Eve of St Agnes': while Madeline sleeps, young Porphyro 'from forth the closet brought a heap / of candied apple, quince, and plum, and gourd; With jellies *soother* than the creamy curd, And lucent syrops, tinct with cinnamon; Manna and dates, in argosy transferr'd / From Fez; and spicèd dainties, every one, From silken Samarcand to cedar'd Lebanon'. She didn't eat a thing, though the seduction appears to have succeeded.

I seem to remember lots of eats in Jane Austen, but Dr Chapman's index is not adequate to my purpose. Meals in Dickens there are aplenty, and his great-grandson Cedric has published an entire volume called *Drinking with Dickens* (Elvendon Press). My library has yielded a book that is a bit of a cheat called *Dining with Sherlock Holmes, A Baker Street cookbook*. Its authors admit that 'Sherlock Holmes does not enjoy a reputation as a gourmet', but try to place the blame on Dr Watson's failure to report Holmes' deep interest in food.

Indisputably the greatest writer of menu novels was Proust, as you can check by looking under 'Food' in Terence Kilmartin's splendid *A Guide to Proust* (Chatto & Windus). It starts with 'stewed beef at Combray' and ends with the Goncourts' description of the Verdurins' dinner party. And the recipes are given in Shirley King's *Dining with Marcel Proust* (Thames and Hudson).

Charles Arrowby, the hero of Iris Murdoch's *The Sea, The Sea*, is endearingly obsessed by food. A prime example of menu fiction, this book; though it presages the new genre to come, when the hero wonders if he'll ever get around to writing his *Charles Arrowby Four Minute Cookbook*.

The very first exemplum of the recipe novel seems to have been Kurt Vonnegut's *Deadeye Dick* (Cape), with its instructions for making 'Haitian Banana Soup', 'Mary Hoobler's Chitterlings' and *Linzer Torte*, among other dishes.

Next in time was Nora Ephron's *Heartburn* (Heinemann), which rightly attracted more interest as a *roman à clef* involving some well-known journalists, diplomats and telly people, than for its recipes. Some of them, such as 'Lillian Hellman's Pot Roast', with its 'low-rent ingredients like a package of onion soup mix and a can of cream of mushroom soup' are revolting, though others, such as the sorrel soup, look tolerable. The ostensible reason for introducing the recipes is that the narrator is a food journalist. I found the handling of the plot and the characters more accomplished than the recipes.

A recent exercise in the new genre is *The Antarctica Cookbook* (Duckworth) by Crispin Kitto, a first, un-slick and altogether amateurish effort by a young man who has worked as a chef. (It also looks like an amateurish effort by the publishers; the literals are at first charming – 'gardamom seeds' and 'muslim cloth' – but no page is without at least one.) Mid-way through the book, one of the heroes trains in a Los Angeles restaurant, and 'so William was exposed to the Nouvelle Cuisine', after which the recipes improve out of all recognition. I am looking forward to experimenting by putting a bit of grated unsweetened chocolate in my chilli con carne (there is chocolate in the classic Mexican *molé* sauce) and to making 'entrecôte of veal, with a soufflé of anchovies'.

I have come upon a short story in *The New Yorker* by Italo Calvino that almost combines recipe and menu fiction. 'The Jaguar Sun' is the tale of a love affair between two travellers in Mexico that is conducted entirely in terms of eating. The ingredients are given very fully – a sauce *mole* 'requires several different varieties of *chile*, as well as garlic, onion, cinnamon, cloves, pepper, cumin, coriander, and sesame, almonds, raisins, and peanuts, with a touch of chocolate.' Calvino's descriptions, though, stop just this side of the precision needed for recipes – which is just as well, as the story moves from an interest in modern Mexican cooking to an obsession with ancient Indian cannibal rituals. The heroine, Olivia, is endowed with too much culinary curiosity: 'But the priests . . . About the cooking of it – they didn't leave any instructions? . . . Perhaps that flavour emerged, all the same – even through the other flavours.' Her guide silences the morbid girl, saying, 'It was a sacred cuisine', and refuses to be drawn any further. Quite right, too. Imagine what life – and literature – would be like if Frazer had given recipes in *The Golden Bough*.

Index

Index

Index

dog eating 19, 39
  in China 82, 97–9
Dorje, Rinjing, *Food in Tibetan Life* 118–19
Douglas, Norman 196
D'Oyly Carte, Helen 229
D'Oyly Carte, Richard 227–8
D'Oyly Carte, Rupert 229
Driver, Christopher 212–15
  at Oxford Food Symposium 35
  The British at Table 212
  The Exploding University 213
duck 205
  canard Apicius 223
  foie de canard 17
  mousse de foie de canard 18
duck press 142
durian 19, 96
Dutournier, Alain 105, 141

eating habits 51–2, 191
  bulimia nervosa 63–9
  in China 86–7
  in Morocco 120–1
Echenard, Louis, scandal at the Savoy 226–30
Escoffier, Auguste 140, 143, 225–30
  confession 227, 228, 229, 230
  dismissal 226
  scandal at the Savoy 226–30
Escoffier, Pierre 227
Escudier, Jean Noel, *La Véritable Cuisine Provençale et Niçoise* 149
Eugénie-les-Bains, Les Prés d'Eugénie restaurant 57

Ferretti, Fred 89
fish 96–7
  cooked in red wine 176
  Giant Catfish of the Mekong 19, 189–90
  in Hungary 131
  in Japan 103–4
  menu of fish dishes 184
  opah 184–5
  ray 185
Fisher, M. F. K. 200–3
  favourite foods 203
  marriages 202
  on varieties of hunger 200–1
  publications 202
  Serve It Forth 202
flatulence 206
food and hunger 200–1

food and romance 181–3
food as art *see nouvelle cuisine*
food as nostalgia 191–2
food habits
  in China 81–9
  in Japan 101–5
food in literature 231
food in space 171–3
Forest Mere health farm 48, 68
freezer clearance 26–8
freezer disasters 24–5

Gail, Ada, and pickled cucumbers 154
garlic 38, 40
  anti-allium stew 38
gastronomic conferences 37
  see also Oxford Food Symposium
Gault, Henri, *nouvelle cuisine* 139
Gault-Millau 18, 20, 105, 142, 175, 215, 221
  magazine 224
gherkins 153–5
Giant Catfish of the Mekong 19, 189–90
Gill, Nick 18
Giovannetti, Prof. Giusto 164
Girardet, Freddy 12
Giugiaro, Giorgetto 164, 165–6
Glasse, Hannah, *The Art of Cookery* 41
globe artichokes as baby food 46
Greene, Gael 11, 105, 109, 115
Greene, Graham, *J'Accuse* 216
Grigson, Jane 19, 187, 191, 203
  at Oxford Food Symposium 37
  English Food 170
  frozen fruits recipe 28
  learns about truffles 162
grits 34
grouse 168–70
Guérard, Christine 57, 58, 61, 62
Guérard, Michel 12, 62, 222
  and *Cuisine Minceur* 36, 57, 144, 224
  and *nouvelle cuisine* 140
  Cuisine Gourmand 36
  diet meals 57–63
Gundel, Károly, *Hungarian Cookery Book* 131

Haeberlin, the brothers 206
Hamilton, Iain 197
Haycroft, Anna 219
  Darling, You Shouldn't Have Gone To So Much Trouble 218
health farms 48

Index

Index

Sokolov, Raymond, at Oxford Food
    Symposium 33–4, 35–6
  nouvelle cuisine 139
Soulé, Henri 7
Sri Lanka 115–17
Stevenson, Sonia 19
Stobart, Tom, *The Cook's Encyclopaedia*
  165
Strang, Jillian, at Oxford Food Symposium
  36
Sullivan, Sir Arthur 229

tagine 120, 121
Tagliaferro, Francisco 164
Taillac, Alain de 175
Taroudant
  Hotel Palais Salam 122
  market 123
Tazaki, Tadayoshi 103, 104
Terrail, Claude 142
Thailand
  River Restaurant, Nongkhai 189–90
Thuiller, Raymond 139
Tibet 118–19
Tokay 131–2
Tokyo
  Narita Prince Hotel 102
tomatoes 182
Toomre, Joyce, at Oxford Food Symposium
  36
Tours
  Barrier restaurant 17
Troisgros, Olympe 105
and *nouvelle cuisine* 139
Troisgros, Pierre 11, 12, 222
  and *nouvelle cuisine* 36, 139
  danced cancan 109
  in India 105, 106, 108
truffles 161–4
Tsuji, Shizuo 90

Vatel, Henri, 24
vegetarianism in Japan 104

Vergé, Roger 206, 222
Veronelli, Luigi 89, 92
vodka 127

Waters, Alice 18, 210
Whitehorn, Katharine 26, 197, 231
Willan, Anne 151
  Great Cooks and Their Recipes 41
wine 155–6
  and cheese 161
  Banyuls 223
  Burgundy 161
  Chablis 1983 110
  Chambertin 1952 17
  Ch. Léoville Poyferré 1970 206
  Ch. Potensac 1980 224
  Chateauneuf du Pape 1976 206
  claret 161
  for cooking with 175–7
  Hungarian 131–2
  Kosher 43, 44
  Mateus rosé 19, 99
  Mondavi Fumé Blanc 1982 91
  Port 161
  price in Hong Kong 74
  Rhône 161
  Russian 130
  Sauternes 161
  see also champagne
Witzigmann, Eckart 105, 114
Wolfert, Paula, *Couscous and Other Good
  Food from Morocco* 121, 123
women as cooks 19–21
Wontner, Sir Hugh 226–7

yoghurt 38
  Greek 148

Zagora 124–6
Zeldin, Theodore, at Oxford Food
  Symposium 31, 34
Zubaida, Sami, at Oxford Food Symposium
  38